William Thomas Stead

Satan's Invisible World Displayed

Or, Despairing Democracy. A study of greater New York

William Thomas Stead

Satan's Invisible World Displayed
Or, Despairing Democracy. A study of greater New York

ISBN/EAN: 9783744722001

Printed in Europe, USA, Canada, Australia, Japan

Cover: Foto ©Suzi / pixelio.de

More available books at **www.hansebooks.com**

THE CITY HALL, NEW YORK.

SATAN'S INVISIBLE WORLD DISPLAYED

OR,

Despairing Democracy.

TUDY OF GREATER NEW YORK.

MOWBRAY

LONDON :

PRINTED BY WILLIAM CLOWES AND SONS, LIMITED,
STAMFORD STREET AND CHARING CROSS.

PREFACE.

For the past four years I have devoted the ANNUAL of the REVIEW OF REVIEWS to a romance based upon the leading social or political event of the year. This year I intermit the publication of the Series of Contemporary History in Fiction in order to publish a study of the most interesting and significant of all the political and municipal problems of our time. To those who may object to the substitution of a companion volume to my Chicago book for their usual annual quantum of political romance, I reply, first, that "changes are lightsome" and a novelty is attractive, and, secondly, that nothing that the wildest imagination of the romance-writer could conceive exceeds in startling and sensational horror the grim outline of the facts which are set forth in this survey of that section of "Satan's Invisible World" which was brought to light by the Lexow Committee.

The trite old saying that "Truth is stranger than Fiction" has seldom been better exemplified than in the story of the way in which the Second City in the World has been governed, unless it be in the consequences of the resulting despair. For if the revelations made before the Lexow Committee are almost incredible, the deliberate decision of the ablest and most public-spirited Americans that there is no way of escape save by the hamstrung·Cæsarism of the Charter of Greater New York is still more ·marvellous as a confession of the shipwreck of faith. Sin, when it has conceived, bringeth forth Death, and the corruption that rotted the administration previous to 1894 has only brought forth its natural fruit in the adoption of a bastard Bonapartism of the Second Empire as the best government for the First City in the American Republic.

The election of the first Mayor for Greater New York, which is progressing while these pages are being written, gives a special actuality and interest to this study. But its permanent value does not depend upon the issue of the *plébiscite* which has decided who will sway the destinies of the Second City of the World at the eve and on the dawn of the Twentieth Century.

It will, I hope, render available to the whole English-speaking world the gist and essence of the evidence taken before the Committee appointed by the Senate of the State of New York to inquire into the Police Department of the City. This Committee, presided over by Senator Lexow, held seventy sittings in the year 1894, and ultimately published the Report of their inquiry in five stout octavo volumes of 1100 pages each. All their proceedings were public, and the New York papers published ample reports from day to day. Outside New York nothing but brief telegrams or occasional letters informed the world of what was taking place, and the final Report was never published in the British or Colonial press. Yet the lesson of the state of things revealed by the Lexow Committee was one which every great city would do well to take to heart. What New York was, London, Glasgow, or Melbourne may —nay, will certainly—become, if the citizens lose interest in the good government of their city.

When I was in New York in September, I tried in vain to purchase a copy of the Lexow Report. As for exhuming the files of the daily papers, one might as well try to resurrect Cheops. Fortunately, just as I was stepping on board the *Teutonic*, the five bulky volumes were handed over to me as a loan. Dr. Shaw had at the last moment succeeded in borrowing the office copy of the Report from the Society for the Prevention of Crime. It was apparently the only available set in the whole city. I deemed it well therefore to master the voluminous evidence in order to construct a readable and authentic narrative which would make this great object-lesson accessible to the world.

W. T. STEAD.

Mowbray House,
Norfolk Street, London, W.C.
November, 1897.

CONTENTS.

THE JANITRESS OF THE LAND OF LIBERTY.

"SATAN'S INVISIBLE WORLD DISPLAYED";

or,

DESPAIRING DEMOCRACY.

PART I

THE GATEWAY OF THE NEW WORLD.

CHAPTER I.

LIBERTY ENLIGHTENING THE WORLD.

THE entrance to the harbour of New York is not unworthy its position as the gateway—the ever open gateway—of the New World.

And the colossal monument raised by the genius of Bartholdi at the threshold of the gateway is no inapt emblem of the sentiments with which millions have hailed the sight of the American continent.

The harbour, though guarded by great guns against hostile intruder, and infested by the myrmidons of the Customs, is nevertheless an appropriate antechamber of the Republic, from whose never-dying torch stream the rays of Liberty enlightening the world.

Over the great lagoon-like waters flit the white-winged yachts—the butterflies of the sea—dancing in the rays of the rising sun. On shore the luxuriant foliage of the trees betrays but here and there the hectic flush that portends the glories of the Indian summer. The islands, as emeralds in the setting of the sea, are a doubly welcome sight to eyes which for days past have seen nothing but the heaving billows of the broad Atlantic. Here and there, flecking with colour the sunlit scene, flutter the Stars and Stripes. Far away in the West, faintly audible in the distance, come the multitudinous sounds of the awakening seaport. The great Liner, which shuddered and throbbed for three thousand miles as it forged five hundred miles a day across the sea, is gliding smoothly and softly as a gondola towards the Venice of the Western World. Except when approaching the Golden Horn, no more beautiful scene greets the traveller on approaching a great capital than that presented by the entrance to the harbour of New York. And right in the centre of the fair vision stands the Bartholdi monument, with its gigantic figure hailing the pilgrims from the Older World with the glad welcome of the New. What more appropriate janitress of the Land of Liberty ?

The cynic may sneer that the analogy between the City of the Great Assassin and the City of the Boss extends further than the sea-gate to the city. But to the millions whose eyes have rested hungrily upon the nearing land such reflections are unknown. To them the New World, of which New York holds the keys, has ever been arrayed in the rainbow garment of Hope. New York, merely as the portal of the continent, had long been to them as a kind of New Jerusalem, let down from Heaven in mercy to hard-driven, hopeless men. From their earliest childhood they had heard of the great Commonwealth beyond the sea, where the blood-tax of the conscription was unknown, where all men were free and all men were equal, and where, in solid, unmistakable reality, the dreams of the poets were found embodied in a Constitution that was at once the envy and despair of the world :—

> There's freedom at thy gates and rest
> For earth's downtrodden and oppressed;
> A shelter for the hunted head,
> For the starved labourer toil and bread;
> Power at thy bounds
> Stops, and calls back his baffled hounds. ·

What wonder that the storm-tossed emigrant, as he first saw the city of New York glimmering through the haze, felt the magic charm with which the tribes of Israel first gazed upon the confines of the Promised Land.

To the great mass of the English, Scottish, and Irish people—as distinguished from the travelled and more or less cultured minority—the United States has for a hundred years been the land of their ideal, often dearer to them than their own. A very large section, possibly a majority, of our race has ever been more in sympathy with the people that was believed to have sprung from the loins of the men of the *Mayflower* than with the nation which recalled Charles the Second and still tolerates the ascendency of the Establishment and the dominance of the landed aristocracy. It is quite recently that this enthusiastic devotion to the American Commonwealth has been somewhat dashed in Great Britain. It still exists in full force across the Irish Channel. To the Irishman the United States is much more of a fatherland than the British Empire. We are, indeed, but a step-motherland to the Irishman, whereas in the United States he is not merely at home, but in most of the cities he is at the head of the household. But forty, thirty, and even twenty years ago it was practically the accepted creed of the English Radical that America led the van, and whenever he was downcast and dispirited by the temporary triumph of the Tories, he found consolation in the reflection that in the great Republic beyond the Atlantic a new and vigorous race was carrying out his ideals, free from the hateful clog of the hidebound Conservatism of the Old Country. No one can read the speeches of Bright and Cobden without feeling that it was on the Hudson and the Mississippi they found their spiritual fatherland, and the generation that sat at their feet learned from them to regard America much as Walt Whitman painted it in his swinging dithyrambs in praise of "Liberty's Nation." We all more or less were brought up to exult in the belief that—

America is the continent of the Glories, and of the triumph of Freedom,
And of the Democracies, and of the fruits of Society, and of all that is begun.

Hence nothing more extravagant can be said in praise of New York Harbour than that even to those nurtured on such pabulum it is no unworthy approach to the sea-gate of a new and better world.

Nor is it only the outside of the harbour that is most impressive. The Hudson—that stately river compared with which the Rhine is but a muddy creek, and the Thames a sluggish rivulet—is not less worthy of its *rôle* as the throne of the great city. It is impossible to exaggerate the impression which the Hudson at night must produce on the peasant from the Carpathians or the labourer from Connemara. Even to those who have more travelled eyes, and are not unfamiliar with seagirt citadels, the spectacle is superb. Never shall I forget my first impression of the mighty river.

It seemed as if I had strayed to the entrance of faerie-land, or that, unawares, I had been transported to the sea-gate of some enchanted city. Midnight was near. In the sky overhead the stars gleamed, but they were faint and speck-like, for the moon was shining unveiled by cloud. But it was neither the lapping of the rippling water nor the silver sheen of the moonlight on the wave that gave the scene its fascination of wonder. These things are the universal poetry of Nature—the music of the waves and the magic of the moon. And there is no speech or language where their voice is not heard. But here there was something more. For on either side of the expanse of water rose high banks of irregular outline, from whose rugged shadows gleamed the lights as of a myriad eyes :—

Behold the enchanted towers of Carbonek,
A castle like a rock upon a rock,
With chasm-like portals open to the sea,
And steps that met the breaker.

Up and down either side, as far as you could see, until the dark outlines merged in the distant horizon, these innumerable eyes

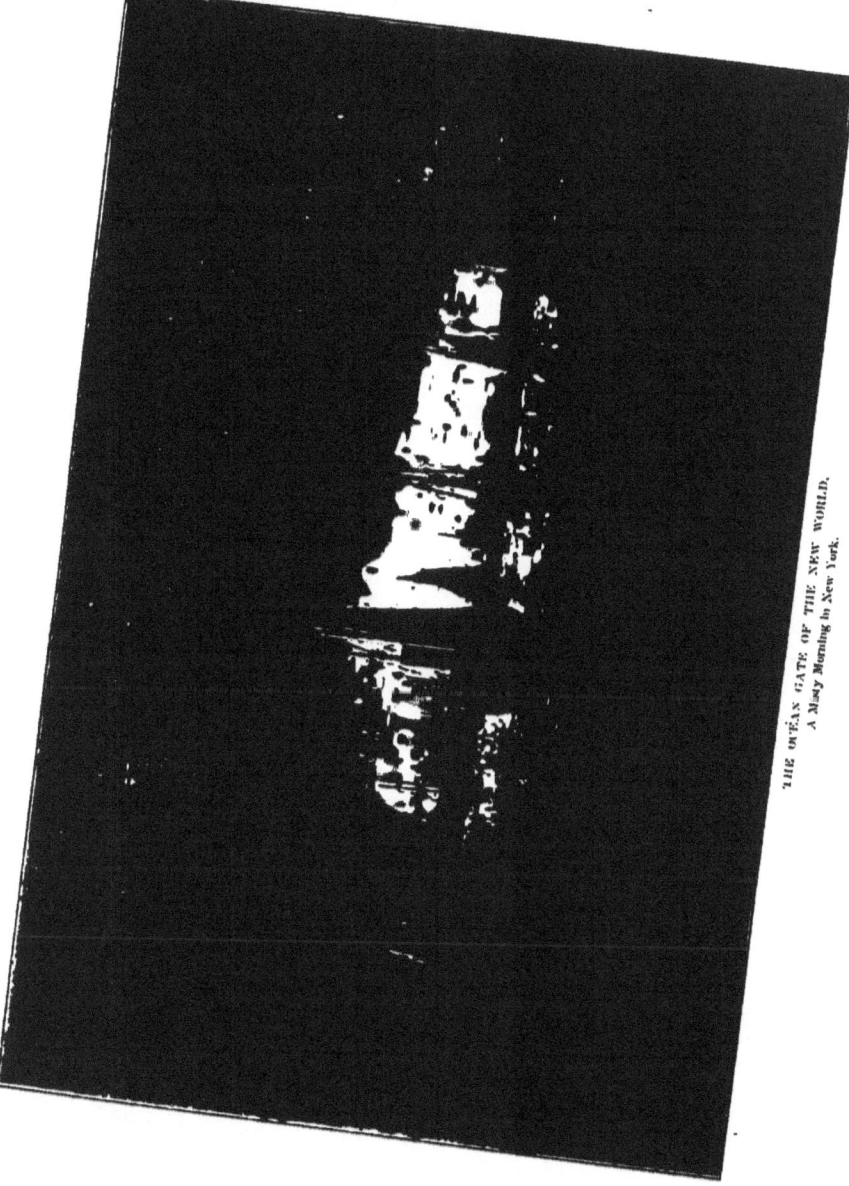

THE OCEAN GATE OF THE NEW WORLD.
A Misty Morning in New York.

looked out over the water. Sometimes they winked, and now and then one or another would close. It was as if each bank were guarded by some vast monster with a thousand times the eyes of him who watched the treasure of the Golden Fleece.

And behind the basilisk of the shore there rose, tier upon tier, the buildings of the city, in which dwelt millions and millions of the children of men. Palaces and temples, brightly outlined in light or towering dark against the luminous haze behind, pierced the sky-line. Amidst the vast confusion two lofty eminences stood out conspicuous, dominating the whole. One was a crown-like dome, poised in mid-air, shining resplendent with jewels of electric light; the other a lofty tower girdled with a blazing zone of fire. Stars of flame shone on its summit, while ever and anon a beam of white light, quick and piercing as a two-edged sword, flashed like the brand of an archangel over the shadowy city. And it was as it was written of old time, when our first parents, after being cast out of Eden, looked back and saw "a flaming sword turning every way to keep the way of the tree of life." The sword was not of fire, but of pure white light. Above and below it made darkness visibly black, but revealed with startling distinctness everything on which it fell.

That was but the background, the framework of the picture. For the great scene was on the water. Never until at Spithead this midsummer, when six square miles of the Solent crowded with the warships of the world burst at a signal into a glittering wilderness of lights, had I ever seen anything to compare to the Hudson at midnight. In Paris on the night of the fête of the Republic in Exhibition year, when the Seine was crowded with steamers, all illuminated and decorated from stem to stern, there was something like this. But the Seine was but a skein of silk stretched across the city; the water was hidden by the craft. Here the whole expanse of waterway exceeded even that of the Neva at St. Petersburg; and, although full of life and colour and sound, was nowhere crowded.

Imagine a great arm of the sea across which, between the two shores, were swiftly, ceaselessly gliding like silent faerie shuttles in some enchanter's loom huge floating palaces, radiant from end to end with innumerable lights. They moved with such strenuous rapidity that the waters foamed beneath their keel, and the anchored vessels seemed to fly past as we left them behind. No great galleon of Spain illuminated in honour of her patron saint ever shone more resplendent, and none ever moved with half the fierce, resistless rush of these monsters of the river. No sails had they or visible means of propulsion, they sped as if thought-impelled. Seldom had I seen anything more weirdly beautiful, or more calculated to impress the imagination.

Now and then a smaller palace would float down the stream, reviving, I know not how, strange reminiscences of the great State barges in which the Rinaldos of mediæval romance would be rowed to some high festival in Armida's garden. Two starry lights overhead, as at the masthead—though masts there were none—dimly revealed the contour below, where the light streaming from serried windows produced a curious effect, as if banks of illuminated oars were speeding the galley on her way. And then again, silent and slow, with but one light burning at her prow, a sombre melancholy scow would drift across the moonlit waters—like

> the barge
> Whereon the lily maid of Astolat
> Lay smiling like a star on darkest night.

On sea and on shore it was one perpetual feast of lanterns. Mingled with the golden and silver rays of the electric lights there shone everywhere lamps of ruby and of amethyst and of emerald, glowing like jewels of intense colour, set in a tiara of diamonds and pearls.

And to add to the weirdness and mystery of the scene, ever and again there would rise from the waters a strange melodious murmur, increasing in intensity to a wail, which would continue a minute and then die away as it arose. It was like the plaintive lowing of sea-monsters for their lost or wandering calves. Otherwise all was still, save the lapping of the waves on the shore.

"And behold I saw," said the seer of the Apocalypse, "as if it were a sea of glass mingled with fire. And lo——"

It was New York seen from a New Jersey ferry-boat on the Hudson, plying between 23rd Street and the Pennsylvania railway. Could there be a more sudden descent from the poetry of faerie-land to the vulgar prose of a work-a-day world? The light-crowned dome was the office of the *World* newspaper, the flashing beam from the tower the advertisement of a dry goods store from Chicago. Yet, nevertheless, the effect of the reality, as it may be seen every fine night, far exceeds my poor description. To those who have eyes to see it is one of the most wonderful and beautiful and suggestive of scenes.

Such then is the outward and visible aspect of the Empire City, a city which from its situation is beautiful exceedingly, and which until quite recently was regarded as the joy of the whole earth, and which still does honour to the statue of such a martyr of Liberty as Nathan Hale. How it has come to pass that the mighty has fallen, and the city which was once a name at the sound of which men renewed their hope and faith in the progress of the world, has become a byword, a hissing and reproach, it will be the object of this volume to explain. It is a subject in which we of the Old World

have weighty reason to be interested. For we have suffered a severe
blow and a grievous discouragement in the betrayal of the cause of
Liberty in the very vestibule and entrance chamber of the Republic.
For all round the world the shame of New York darkens the
sombre shade which encompasses the oppressed and gladdens with
evil joy the heart of the oppressor.

STATUE OF NATHAN HALE.
City Hall Park, New York.

THE GRIDIRON STREETS OF THE NOISY CITY.

New York Post Office, Broadway.

CHAPTER II.

A PANDEMONIUM of type-writing machines—of gigantic type-writing machines driven by demons who never tire—in some vast hall of Eblis. The clank of the type, the swish of the machine, the quick nervous ring of the bell, all indefinitely multiplied and magnified, fill the vast space with a reverberating clangour. This clangour continuously increases until its very vibrations seem to become clotted and fill the air with a sound that can be felt in every pore. It is like the pressure of an atmosphere so dense you can almost cut it with a knife, an atmosphere that is never still, but perpetually frets, and moans, and snarls with feverish unrest.

How many machines there must be to crowd the air with this million times multiplied misery of click and clang—ring-ring—ring-ring—and clang and click, that never stops, but rises and falls, rhythmless and rude, like the waves of a choppy sea on a rocky beach! Now and again through the infernal hubbub there pierces a dreadful wail,

> As it were, one voice in agony
> Of lamentation, like a wind that shrills
> All night in a waste land, where no one comes
> Or hath come since the making of the world.

How hot the air is! a temperature of the antechamber of Tophet. As the perspiration bursts in great beads of moisture from your brow, you hear the faint hum of circling wings, faint at first, but ever growing shriller and more acute—hiss, zip—as the invisible fiend circles round his prostrate victim. Hiss, zip, nearer, louder than before, audible clearly even above the metallic storm of the type-writing machines. And as the mosquito settles on your ear, you awake with a start and suddenly realise where you are.

You are not in even the outermost circles of Dante's "Inferno." You are trying to sleep in the heart of Central New York, in the midst of all the thunder and the rush and the roar of her million-crowded streets, along which surges as a restless tide the turbid and foaming flood of city life. The bells of the tramcars continually sounding, the weariless trampling of the ironshod hoofs over granite roadway, the whirling rumble of the wheels, the roar of the trains which on the elevated railways radiate uproar from a kind of infernal firmament on high, all suffused and submerged in the murmurous

B

hum that rises unceasing from the hurrying footsteps in the crowded
street, that inarticulate voice of New York—

> Sad as the wail that from the populous earth
> All day and night to high Olympus soars.

And that dreadful shriek is the farewell of an Ocean liner sounding
a sonorous note with stentorian lungs as it quits the wharf.

There is nothing like it in London. Chicago, with all its bustle,
has nothing to compare to this harsh metallic clangour of struggle
and strife—although there the mournful death-tolling bell on the
locomotives which thread the streets supplies a note of pathos and of
awe that is missing in the racket and roar of New York.

One grows used to it in time, just as after a few days you become
used to the thrust and swirl of the screw which drives the liner
across the sea. The great ship vibrates in every nerve of steel, and
the state-room throbs with the thud of the engines. So the great city
pulses with strenuous power, and in the multitudinous uproar of its
streets we hear the sound of the friction of the two-million man-
power engine which has made even Lesser New York one of the
greatest driving forces of the American Republic.

It is a dynamo of the first order. And like the dynamo it is
instinct with magnetic power. All great cities are great magnets,
and New York is the greatest—but one—in the world.

The figures of the portentous growth of cities in our epoch recall
the familiar story in the "Arabian Nights Entertainments" of the
vessel which, sailing too near the Loadstone Mountain, was whelmed
into sudden destruction. For the attraction of the loadstone was
such that all the iron nails in the vessel were drawn out of their
fastenings, and the timbers that were once a ship became mere
flotsam and jetsam on the water. It is a wild and romantic fable in
the mouth of the Princess Scheherazade; but it is grim reality in the
world to-day. For the great city is to the rural population exactly
what the Arabian loadstone mountain was to the heedless sailor
who came within the range of its fascination. All the iron in the
rural ship of State is attracted to the mighty Babylon. The men with
iron in their blood, the girls whose pulses leap and tingle with the
eager flush of adventure and ambition, desert the village and the
farm to crowd the roaring mart and glaring street. The country is
denuded of its most vigorous children. The city engulfs into its
insatiate maw all those the brightest, the bravest, and the best.

The process goes on at an ever accelerating ratio. As Mr. Godkin
has well observed :—

Parks and gardens, cheap concerts, free museums and art galleries, cheap means
of conveyance, model lodging-houses, rich charities, such as every city is now
offering in abundance to all comers, are so many inducements to country poor to
try their luck in the streets. They are the exact equivalents, as an invitation to
the lazy and the pleasure-loving, of the Roman circus and free flour which we all

use in explanation of the decline and fall of the Empire. They are luxuries which seem to be within every man's reach gratis, and they act with tremendous force on the rural imagination.—*North American Review,* June, 1890.

The percentage of urban to the total population of the United States, defining as urban all dwellers in cities of more than 8,000 population, was 3·35 in 1790. Forty years later it had doubled. But in 1860 it was 16·13, and in 1890, 29·12. But the growth of the cities which alone deserve the name of great has been still more phenomenal. In 1840—not sixty years ago—the ten greatest cities of America contained a total population of 711,652. To-day Brooklyn alone, which has been merged as a kind of suburb in Greater New York, has a population of a million, while the ten great cities, to be hereafter known as the Great Ten—New York, Chicago, Philadelphia, Brooklyn, St. Louis, Boston, Baltimore, San Francisco, Cincinnati, and Cleveland—had in 1890 a population of 6,660,402, and will have in 1900 a population of eight millions. In fifty years the population of the United States did not quadruple itself, for it only expanded in round numbers from 17 millions to 62½ millions. But the great cities increased themselves nearly ten-fold in the same period, and to-day they contain 11 per cent. of the whole population of the Union. The latest estimate of the present population of the country gives the cities 25 millions out of the 72 million citizens of the United States.

If one-third of the inhabitants of the American Commonwealth dwell in cities, these urban centres possess even more than one-third of the wealth of the nation, and far more than one-third of its actual power. A writer in one of the recent American magazines points out that the wealth of the Great Ten in 1890 exceeded the wealth of the whole country, cities included, in 1850. The revenue of the same Great Ten amounted in 1890 to £25,000,000 per annum, a greater sum than was raised for State purposes in all the federated States and Territories. The annual Budget of New York and Brooklyn in 1890 dealt with ten millions sterling, a sum almost exactly equalling the Budget of the United States forty years ago.

It is now half a century since De Tocqueville wrote:—" I look upon the size of certain American cities, and especially upon the nature of their population, as a real danger which threatens the security of the Republic." Since then this " real danger " has gone on increasing at an ever accelerating ratio. When De Tocqueville wrote, there were only three or four cities with a population over 100,000. To-day there are thirty. And most remarkable fact of all, the population of Greater New York is now equal in number to the total population of the United States at the time of the Declaration of Independence. Her 3,200,000 inhabitants exceed nearly four-fold the total number of the inhabitants in all the cities in the States at the time De Tocqueville visited America.

In the State of New York, sixty per cent. of the inhabitants live in cities; in Massachusetts, seventy per cent.

This tendency townwards, which is one of the most striking characteristics of the English-speaking race all round the world, is nowhere more conspicuous than in the United States; and New York, of all American cities, is that where this centripetal law is just now seen to be operating most powerfully. In the amalgamation by which the Greater New York has come into being we have the latest manifestation of the craving on the part of all modern men to come together in ever-increasing agglomerations of humanity. The fissiparous tendency so perceptible in politics is not visible in cities. There are numerous instances of two cities fusing into one; but no city having once achieved its unity splits it up. Amalgamation, not separation, is the order of the day. Where a river does not divide—as for instance, in the case of Gateshead, that " long, narrow, dirty lane leading into Newcastle-on-Tyne," or in the case of Salford—the larger town invariably swallows up its minor neighbours, as a large raindrop on the window-pane attracts the smaller drops in its immediate vicinity. In the case of Greater New York, not even the dividing river has been able to prevent the law of gravitation doing its will.

The City of New York is indeed seated upon rivers, and if State boundaries had not stood in the way, there is little doubt that Jersey City would have shared the fate of Brooklyn and Long Island. But even without Jersey City, the new urban conglomerate will be the second city of the world in populousness and greater even than London in area.

The City of New York has an area of 39 square miles, while the area of Greater New York is over 300 square miles. Brooklyn contains 29 square miles, Staten Island comprises nearly 60 square miles, Westchester County annex has an area of about 20 square miles, and the Long Island townships included in the scheme have an aggregate extent of perhaps 170 miles.

At the first election for the Greater New York, held this year, no fewer than 567,000 citizens were registered as electors in this colossal constituency. The Greater New York charter divides the city into five boroughs. (1) Manhattan, consisting of the island of Manhattan, and the outlying islands naturally related to it. (2) The Bronx, including all that part of the present City of New York lying north of the Harlem, a territory which comprises two-thirds of the area of the present City of New York. (3) Brooklyn. (4) Queen's, consisting of that portion of Queen's County which is incorporated into the Greater New York. (5) Richmond; that is, Staten Island. The population of the City of New York which before the amalgamation was close on 2,000,000, is now swollen to 3,200,000, of whom nearly 2,000,000 live in tenement houses.

The size of New York is by no means its most notable distinction. Chicago some day may, by right of its more central position, win the prize of being recognised as the real if not the political capital of the United States. But the position to which Chicago aspires has, for nearly a century, been held by New York. For New York is one of the few cities in the States which are not of yesterday. Of course, compared with London, which dates back to the Cæsars, New York is but a mushroom upstart. But as in the realm of the

blind the one-eyed man is king, so in the New World a city which can count its history by centuries may be regarded as possessing quite a respectable antiquity.

To us in the Old World it is the window through which we look into America. Peter the Great built his capital on the Neva in order to have a window from which he could look into Europe. New York serves much the same purpose. It is through the window-pane of New York that the Old World sees what little it does see that is going on in the American Republic. All the newspaper correspondents of the European press without a single exception, so far as I know, cable from New York. Not a single British newspaper has a correspondent at Boston, Philadelphia, Chicago, or

Washington. As for the suggestion of publishing telegrams from New Orleans or San Francisco, it would be more reasonable to expect to see despatches from Mars. This leads, no doubt, to much misconception. The New York window is by no means of transparent crystal. Those who consent to see the United States solely through their New York window-pane will often be egregiously misled. Nevertheless, the fact remains that New York is the only window through which the Old World peeps into the New.

Nor is that the only special reason why New York is better known to us of the older branch of the race than any other part of the American Continent. New York is not more the only window than it is the only door of the New World. The Atlantic is furrowed by a thousand keels, but all the liners steer for New York. Steamers no doubt ply to Boston and to Philadelphia, but the great trade route—the only passenger route—lies past Sandy Hook. New York is the front gate of the Western hemisphere. Even Canada finds it more convenient to use the New York entrance than the ice-blocked mouth of the St. Lawrence. Hence, whatever else the Old World man may see or fail to see in the New World, the one place he is certain to see, the one place which he cannot avoid seeing, is the Queen of the Hudson.

And as New York is the first American city which every traveller sees, and the last which he leaves, so New York has attracted a greater number of European residents than any other city, with the doubtful exception of Chicago. In 1888, thirty-six per cent. of the citizens were either Irish or of Irish descent. The German element was in 1891 estimated at twenty-five per cent. In the City of New York the indigenous American only numbers twenty per cent.

But it is not its imported population which makes it so peculiarly European. Chicago is at least as cosmopolitan, but the city on Lake Michigan counts herself much more American than her sister on the Hudson. During the last Presidential Campaign New York was constantly singled out for attack by the Bryanite orators of the West and South as if it were a foreign and hostile colony encamped on American soil. Wall Street, the centre of the financial system of the United States, was as sound on the currency question as the Old Lady of Threadneedle Street, and the advocates of Free Silver confounded New York and London alike beneath their savage anathema. Community of interest begets community of ideas, and the Western men angrily declare that New York is no more a typical American city than London or Liverpool. This is an exaggeration, no doubt. But neighbourhood counts for something, and New York is a thousand miles nearer to London than to Chicago.

New York is only six days' steaming from Europe. It is the centre from whence the mighty shuttles ply back and forth across

ONE OF THE WINDOW-PANES OF THE WINDOW OF THE NEW WORLD.
Printing-House Square, New York.

the Atlantic, weaving the ocean-sundered sections of our race into one. Of the threads, some end at Southampton and others at Liverpool. But they all start from New York.

There is another distinctive element about New York. It is the great literary producing-centre of the American people. Boston has long since been dethroned. No other city has even ventured to contest the primacy of New York. There is not a single magazine printed in America that has any circulation outside the United States which is not edited, printed, and published in New York. The advantages of a more central position enjoyed by Chicago are as nought compared with those which New York enjoys in other ways. When I proposed to publish the American *Review of Reviews* in Chicago, I was promptly silenced by the statement that with the exception of the *Ladies' Home Journal* there was not a single periodical published outside New York which could claim to have achieved a success. New York, from the publishing point of view, is the hub of the American universe. Her magazines, admirably edited and marvellously illustrated, circulate in every nook and corner of the English-speaking world. The magazines of the other cities are virtually unknown outside the Republic, and often, it may be said, outside the city that gives them birth. New York, then, as the window and front door of the United States, with an unchallenged financial, commercial, shipping and literary ascendency, has the pull over all her rivals. To nine-tenths of mankind New York is America. All the rest of the country is but the pedestal upon which New York stands.

This pre-eminent position carries with it a grave responsibility. If the world at large judges the American Commonwealth by New York, then New York owes a double duty both to the American Commonwealth and to the world at large. Hence the extreme interest which the latest evolution in the civic development of New York naturally arouses. This Greater New York—what does it mean? How did it come into being? What were the issues at stake at the late Election? All these questions every one is asking. I propose to attempt to supply some answer.

It is a task of some difficulty and no little importance; for not merely is New York—rightly or wrongly—regarded as the most typical and best known American city, but the United States tends more and more to become not a federation of States and territories, but an association of huge cities. The Great Ten not merely include within their boundaries nearly eight million persons, or more than ten per cent. of the whole population; they do the thinking and the guiding and the managing of a very large proportion of the remaining nine-tenths. Draw a circle with a three-hundred-mile radius round the Great Ten, and you inclose an area which is practically dominated by the Ten and educated by their newspapers. The Newspaper Area

THE FRONT DOOR OF THE NEW WORLD.

is a phrase not yet naturalised in geographies, but it is the most real and living area of all those into which the social organism is divided. For the newspaper collects its news every day, and sells its news every morning and evening, thereby creating a living, ever-renewed bond between the dwellers within the radius of its circulation infinitely superior to the nexus supplied by the tax-collector and the policeman. It is not difficult to define the length of the range within which a newspaper can create a constituency. It is rigidly limited by the distance from the printing-office in which a newspaper can be delivered before breakfast. After breakfast the influence of the newspaper dwindles every minute. Any one living so far off as not to be able to obtain his newspaper before dinner is practically outside the pale—unless, of course, he lives remote from any local centre of news distribution. In that case the range of influence is almost indefinite, as is shown to this day in the hold which the weekly *New York Tribune* exercises over farmers scattered everywhere between the Atlantic and the Rocky Mountains. But speaking generally, the range of the Newspaper Area is limited by breakfast-time.

Greater New York has come into being in order to increase, not to diminish, the influence of New York in the Republic and in the world at large. This influence may be for evil. " Under the new charter," says Mr. W. C. De Witt, Chairman of the Committee which drafted that document, " the City of New York at one bound becomes the mistress of the Western hemisphere and the second city of the world. It should be to its people what Athens was to the Greek, Rome to the Romans, Florence to the Florentine—an object of constant solicitude and of civic pride."

The question whether they intend to obey the voice of their friendly mentor is one on which the future fortune of the American Commonwealth will largely depend. For, as Mr. J. C. Adams pointed out in a thoughtful article on " The Municipal Threat in National Politics," which he contributed to the *New England Magazine* in July, 1891 :—

> The misgovernment of the cities is the prophecy of misgovernment of the nation ; just as the paralysis of the great nerve-centres means the palsy of the whole body. There is graver danger to the republic in the failure of good government in our cities than arises from the moral corruption which accompanies that failure. The misgovernment of our cities means the break-down of one of the two fundamental principles upon which our political fabric rests. It is the failure of local self-government in a most vital part. It is as great a peril to the republic as the revolt against the Union. For the republic is organised upon two great political ideas, both essential to its existence. The first is the principle of federation, which is embodied in the Union ; the second is the principle of local self-government, which places the business of the states and the towns in the hands of the people who live in them. Both of these are vital principles. The republic has survived the attempt to subvert one of them. It has just entered on its real struggle with a serious attack upon the other.

The fate, therefore, of the American Republic may be bound up with the fortunes of Greater New York.

CHAPTER III.

HITHERTO, the city government of New York has not been a credit to the Republic; otherwise I should not be publishing a survey of the way in which New York has been governed as "Satan's Invisible World Displayed." The title, of course, is an adaptation, not an invention. The original holder of the copyright was one Hopkins, of the seventeenth century, who, having had much experience in the discovery of witches, deemed himself an expert qualified to describe the inner history and secret mystery of the infernal regions under that picturesque title. I have adopted it as being on the whole the most appropriate description of the state of abysmal abomination into which the government of New York had sunk before the great revolt of 1894 broke the power of Tammany—for a season—and placed in office a Reform Government charged to cleanse the Augean stable. The old witchfinder had no story to tell so horrible or so incredible as that which I have drawn up from the sworn evidence of witnesses exposed to public cross-examination before a State Commission in the City of New York. In the reports of the infernal Sabbats, for attending which thousands of old women were burnt or hanged in the seventeenth century, there always figures in the background, as the central figure in the horrid drama, a form but half-revealed, concerning whose identity even the witchfinders speak with awe. The weird women, with their incantations and their broomsticks, their magic spells and their diabolical trysts, are but the slaves of the Demon, who, whether as their lover or their torturer, is ever their master, whose name they whisper with fear, and whose commands they obey with instant alacrity. For the Master of Ceremonies in the Infernal revels, the Lord of the Witches' Sabbat, is none other than Satan himself, the incarnate principle of Evil, the Boss of Hell!

In the modern world, sceptical and superstitious, these tales of witches and warlocks seem childish nonsense, unworthy of the attention of grown-up men. But although the *dramatis personæ* have changed, and the *mise-en-scène*, the same phenomena reappear eternally. Here in the history of New York we have the whole infernal phantasmagoria once again, with heelers for witches, policemen as wizards, and secret sessions in Tammany Hall as the Witches'

Sabbat of the new era. And behind them all, always present but dimly seen—the omnipresent central force, whose name is muttered with awe, and whose mandate is obeyed with speed—is the same sombre figure whom his devotees regard with passionate worship, and whom his enemies dread even as they curse his name. And this modern Sathanas—this man who to every good Republican is the most authentic incarnation of the principle of Evil, the veritable archfiend of the political world—is the Boss of Tammany Hall.

Among the many legends which have clustered round the beginning of the great association which has played so conspicuous a part in the history of New York, there is one which appeals specially to the sense of humour. Tammany, according to tradition, was the name of a Delaware Indian who in ancient days belonged to a Redskin confederacy that inhabited the regions now known as New Jersey and Pennsylvania. His name has been variously spelled as Temane, Tamanend, Taminent, Tameny, and Tammany.

Curiously enough, by a kind of metamorphosis by no means without precedent among more historical saints, his name has been attached to a locality which he probably never visited, and with the inhabitants of which he and his people lived in hereditary feud. This was not, however, due to any of his conflicts with the Mohicans, who in those days pitched their wigwams on the island of Manhattan. He owes it to a battle which he fought with no less a personage than the great enemy of mankind. In the days when St. Tammany passed his legendary existence, there were no white men on the American Continent; but although the Pale-Face was absent, the Black man was in full force, and one fine day St. Tammany was exposed to the fell onslaught of the foul fiend. At first, as is his wont, the bad spirit, with honeyed words, sought to be admitted to a share in the government of Tammany's realm.

"Get thee behind me, Satan!" rendered in the choicest Delaware dialect, was the Saint's response to the offers of the tempter. But as a more illustrious case attests, the Devil is not a person who will accept a first refusal. Changing his tactics, he brought upon St. Tammany and his Delawares many grievous afflictions of body and of estate, and while the good Chief's limbs were sore and his heart was heavy, the cunning deceiver attempted to slink into the country unawares.

St. Tammany, however, although sick and sore, slept with one eye open, and the Devil was promptly ordered to "get out of that," with an emphasis which left him no option but to obey. Again and again the Devil, renewing his attacks, tried his best to circumvent St. Tammany, but finding that all was in vain, he at last flung patience and strategy to the winds, and boldly attacked the great Sagamore in order to overwhelm him by his infernal might.

UNION SQUARE, NEW YORK, WITH THE WASHINGTON MONUMENT.

Then, says the legend, ensued the most tremendous battle that has ever been waged between man and his great enemy. For many months the great fight went on, and as Tammany and the Devil wrestled to and fro in mortal combat, whole forests were broken down, and the ground was so effectually trampled under foot that it has remained prairie land to this day. At last, after the forests had been destroyed, and the country trodden flat, St. Tammany, catching his adversary unawares, tripped him up, and hurled him to the ground. It was in the nick of time, for Tammany was so exhausted with the prolonged struggle that when he drew his scalping-knife to make a final end of the Evil One, the fiend, to the eternal regret of all the children of men, succeeded in slipping from Tammany's clutches. He escaped across the river to New York, where—so runs the legend, as it is recorded by a writer in *Harper*—" he was hospitably received by the natives, and has ever since continued to make his home."

Such, in the quaint but suggestive narrative of the ancient myth, is the way in which the Devil first came to New York, where, as if in revenge for his defeat, he seems to have christened the political organisation which has been his headquarters after the name of Tammany.

The Tammany organisation did not in the beginning take its rise in New York. It first sprang into being in the ranks of the revolutionary army of Pennsylvania. Tammany, or Tamanend, as he was then called, was adopted by the Pennsylvanian troops under General Washington as their patron saint. There were two reasons for this. In the first place, it was Hobson's choice, for St. Tammany was the only native American who had ever been canonised ; and, in the second place, nothing seemed more appropriate to the revolutionary heroes than to adopt as their patron saint a brave who had " whipped the Devil." St. Tammany, therefore, came to be adopted by the American army as a kind of counterpart to our own St. George. St. Tammany and the Devil seemed to be a good counterpoise to the legendary tale of St. George and the Dragon. The 12th of May was Tammany's Saint's Day, and was celebrated with wigwams, liberty poles, tomahawks, and all the regular paraphernalia of the Redskin. A soldier attired in Indian costume represented the great Sachem, " and, after delivering a talk full of eloquence for law and liberty and courage in battle to the members of the order, they danced with feathers in their caps and buck tails dangling on behind." The practice spread from the Pennsylvania troops to the rest of the army, and so popular did Tammany become that May 12th bid fair to be much more a popular national festival than July 4th.

It was not until this century had begun that the Tammany Society was domiciled in New York. It was introduced there by an upholsterer of Irish descent, named William Mooney. He did not take much stock in St. Tammany, but preferred to call his Society the Columbian Order, in honour of Columbus. The transactions of the Society dated from the discovery of America. Besides the European head, who was to be known as the Great Father, there were to be twelve Sachems, or counsellors—"Old Men" being the Indian signification of the word; a Sagamore, or master of ceremonies; a Wiskinkie, or doorkeeper of the sacred wigwam; and a Secretary.

The Society from its outset appears to have been political, but in its early days it combined charity with politics. In the second year of its existence it undertook the establishment of a Museum of Natural History, and got together the exhibits which formed the nucleus of Barnum's famous museum. It was a social and convivial club, which met first in a hotel of Broadway, then in a public-house in Broad Street, and finally in the Pig-pen, a long room attached to a saloon kept by one Martling. In 1811 it erected a hall of its own. Its present address is "Tammany Hall, Fourteenth Street."

There is no necessity to do more than glance at the curious beginnings of a society which is perhaps the most distinctively American of all the associations that have ever been founded in the New World. A writer of "The Story of Tammany," which appeared in *Harper's Magazine* many years ago, from which most of these facts are taken, says:—

The Tammany Society, or Columbian Order, is doubtless the oldest purely self-constituted political association in the world, and has certainly been by far the most influential. Beginning with the government, for it was organised within a fortnight of the inauguration of the first President, and at a spot within the sound of his voice as he spoke his first official words to his countrymen, it has not only continued down to the present time—through nearly three generations of men—but has controlled the choice of at least one President, fixed the character of several national as well as State administrations, given pseudonyms to half a dozen well-known organisations, and, in fact, has shaped the destiny of the country in several turning-points of its history.

Few suspect, much less comprehend, the extent of the influence this purely local association has exerted. To its agency more than any other is due the fact that for the last three-quarters of a century New York city has been the most potent political centre in the world, not even Paris excepted. Greater than a party, inasmuch as it has been the master of parties, it has seen political organisation after organisation, in whose conflicts it has fearlessly participated, arise, flourish, and go down, and yet has stood ready, with powers unimpaired, to engage in the struggles of the next crop of contestants. In this experience it has been solitary and peculiar. Imitators it has had in abundance, but not one of them has succeeded in catching that secret of political management which has endowed Tammany with its wonderful permanency.

What is that secret? It is unquestionably to be traced, in part, to the sagacity which Tammany's leaders have at all times shown in forecasting the changes of political issues, or availing themselves of the opportunities afforded by current events as they have arisen. Tammany has not only furnished the most capable politicians the country has possessed, but has managed to ally itself with the shrewdest ones to be found outside of its own organisation. It has always shown a willingness to trade in the gifts at its command, and rarely indeed has it got the worst of a bargain.

The writer in *Harper*, however, while attempting to explain the secret of Tammany, only raises a still more difficult question. How is it that Tammany should have been able to discern the signs of the times better than its rivals? How is it that Tammany has been able to furnish the most capable politicians the country has ever possessed, and how is it that it has displayed so much wisdom? There is one explanation, which, no doubt, commends itself to many of those who have spent their life in fighting Tammany Hall. Tammany has little regard for the innocence of the dove, but it has always displayed the wisdom of the serpent. Considering the place where the Author of all Evil found refuge after his discomfiture by St. Tammany, a Republican may be pardoned for suggesting that the wisdom of

FIRST TAMMANY HALL, ERECTED 1811.

Tammany is due to the wisdom of the Old Serpent. Certainly, many innocent persons have been accused of dalliance with the foul fiend on much worse *primâ facie* evidence than that which is furnished by the universal admission that Tammany, out of the most uncompromising materials, has succeeded in achieving exploits which antecedently would have been absolutely impossible. For Tammany, although preserving and maintaining from first to last a discipline which is the despair of all the other political machines in the country, has never been without fierce internecine fights. It has cast out leader after leader, and the ferocity of the feuds within Tammany has exceeded that of any of the combats which have been waged against the common enemy. Nevertheless, notwithstanding all schisms, all reverses, all exposures, Tammany remains to this day the strongest, the best disciplined, and the most feared political organisation in the world.

Mr. Croker, in the series of interviews which I reported in the October number of the REVIEW OF REVIEWS, argued with much force and plausibility that it was contrary to the law of human nature that an organisation could live and last so long if it were composed of Thugs and desperados, and that witness no doubt is true. Even so stout and stalwart an opponent of Tammany as Dr. Albert Shaw has frequently felt himself constrained to admit that the

TAMMANY HALL, OPENED 1860.

insane fashion in which New York has been governed rendered even the rule of Tammany preferable to the constitutional and legal chaos which was the only substitute. Dr. Shaw, speaking of the system under which New York has hitherto been governed, said :-

To know its ins and outs is not so much like knowing the parts and the workings of a finely adjusted machine as it is like knowing the obscure topography of the great Dismal Swamp considered as a place of refuge for criminals.

Again he wrote :—

In New York, the absurdly disjointed and hopelessly complex array of separate boards, functions, and administrative powers, first makes it impossible for the community to focalise responsibility anywhere in the formal mechanism of municipal government, and then makes it possible for an irresponsible self-centred political and mercenary society like Tammany to gain for itself the real control, and thus to assume a domination that ought to be centred in some body or functionary directly accountable to the people. Government by a secret society like Tammany is better than the chaos of a disjointed government for which there can be no possible location of central responsibility.

It is not for me to dogmatise where experts, native to New York, hopelessly disagree, But viewed from the outside the secret of Tammany's success seems to lie chiefly in the fact that Tammany has from the first been really a democratic organisation. No one was too poor, too wicked, or too ignorant to be treated by Tammany as a man and a brother if he would stand in with the machine and join the brotherhood.

This secret of Tammany—the open secret—was explained to me in Chicago by a saloon-keeper of more than dubious morals who had been a Tammany captain in New York. I saw him the night after Dr. Parkhurst had scored his first great success over the politicians of New York. The ex-Tammany Captain shook his head when I asked him what he thought of Dr. Parkhurst's campaign. He had no use for Dr. Parkhurst. For a time, he thought, he might advertise himself, which was no doubt his object, but after that everything would go on as before. The one permanent institution in New York was Tammany.

I asked him to explain his secret. " Suppose," said I, " that I am a newly arrived citizen in your precinct, and come to you and wish to join Tammany, what would be required of me ? "

" Sir," said he, " before anything would be required of you we would find out all about you. I would size you up myself, and then after I had formed my own judgment I would send two or three trusty men to find out all about you. Find out, for instance, whether you really meant to work and serve Tammany, or whether you were only getting in to find out all about it. If the inquiries were satisfactory then you would be admitted to the ranks of Tammany, and you would stand in with the rest."

" What should I have to do ? "

" Your first duty," said he, " would be to vote the Tammany ticket whenever an election was on, and then to hustle around and make every other person whom you could get hold of vote the same ticket."

' And what would I get for my trouble ? " I asked.

" Nothing," said he, " unless you needed it. I was twenty years captain and I never got anything for myself, but if you needed anything you would get whatever was going. It might be a job that would give you employment under the city, it might be a pull that you might have with the alderman in case you got into trouble, whatever it was you would be entitled to your share. If you get into trouble, Tammany will help you out. If you are out of a job Tammany will see that you have the first chance of whatever is going. It is a great power, is Tammany. Whether it is with the police, or in the court, or in the City Hall, you will find Tammany men everywhere, and they all stick together. There is nothing sticks so tight as Tammany."

Therein, no doubt, this worthy ex-captain revealed the great secret of Tammany's success. Tammany is a brotherhood. Tammany men stick together, and help each other.

The record of Tammany, however, hardly bears out the claim made for it by Mr. Croker as to the honesty and purity of its administration. From its very early days Tammany has had a bad record for dishonesty and utter lack of scruple. As early as 1837, two Tammany leaders, who had held the federal offices of Collector of the Port of New York, and of United States District Attorney for the Southern district of New York, skipped to Europe after embezzling, the one £250,000, the other £15,000. About twenty years later, another Tammany leader, who was appointed Postmaster for New York, advanced £50,000 of post-office money in order to carry Pennsylvania for Buchanan. These, however, were but bagatelles compared with the carnival of plunder which was established when Tweed was Tammany Boss.

It was not until about the middle of the century that Tammany laid the hand upon the agency which for nearly fifty years has been the sceptre of its power. A certain Southerner, rejoicing in the name of Rynders, who was a leading man in Tammany in the Forties, organised as a kind of affiliated institution the Empire Club, whose members were too disreputable even for Tammany. These men, largely composed of roughs and rowdies, who rejoiced in the expressive title of the Bowery Plug Uglies, were the first to lay their hand upon the immigrant and utilise him for the purpose of carrying elections. Mr. Edwards, writing in *McClure's Magazine*, says :—

It was the Empire Club, indeed, which taught the political value of the newly arrived foreigner. Its members approached the immigrants at the piers on the arrival of every steamship or packet; conducted them into congenial districts; found them employment in the city works, or perhaps helped them to set up in business as keepers of grog-shops.

"Politics in Louisiana," General Grant is reported to have said on one occasion, "are Hell." They seem to have been very much like hell in the days when the Plug Uglies with Rynders at their head ruled the roast at Tammany. Mr. Edwards tells a story which sheds a lurid ray of light on the man and manners of that time. Mr. Godwin, who preceded Mr. Godkin in the incessant warfare which the *Evening Post* has waged against Tammany, had given more than usual offence to Rynders. That worthy, therefore, decided to assassinate the editor as he was taking his lunch at the hotel. Mike Walsh, however, a plucky Irishman, interfered,

c 2

and enabled Godwin to make his escape   When the intended victim had gone out—

Rynders stepped up to Walsh and said: "What do you mean by interfering in this matter? It is none of your affair."

"Well, Godwin did me a good turn once, and I don't propose to see him stabbed in the back. You were going to do a sneaking thing; you were going to assassinate him, and any man who will do that is a coward."

"No man ever called me a coward, Mike Walsh, and you can't."

"But I do, and I will prove that you are a coward. If you are not one, come upstairs with me now. We will lock ourselves into a room; I will take a knife and you take one: and the man who is alive after we have got through, will unlock the door and go out."

Rynders accepted the challenge. They went to an upper room. Walsh locked the door, gave Rynders a large bowie-knife, took one himself, and said: "You stand in that corner, and I'll stand in this. Then we will walk towards the centre of the room, and we won't stop until one or the other of us is finished."

Each took his corner. Then Walsh turned and approached the centre of the room. But Rynders did not stir. "Why don't you come out?" said Walsh. Rynders, turning in his corner, faced his antagonist, and said: "Mike, you and I have always been friends; what is the use of our fighting now? If we get at it, we shall both be killed, and there is no good in that." Walsh for a moment said not a word: but his lip curled, and he looked upon Rynders with an expression of utter contempt. Then he said: "I told you you were a coward, and now I prove it. Never speak to me again."

Mike Walsh, the hero of this episode of the bowie-knife, is notable as having been the first man to publicly accuse Tammany of tampering with the ballot-box. He was not the last by any means; but Tammany seems to have begun well, for, says Mr. Edwards:—

Roscoe Conkling once said, chatting with a group of friends, that Governor Seward had told him that the Tammany frauds committed by the Empire Club in New York City in 1844 unquestionably gave Polk the meagre majority of five thousand which he obtained in New York State, and by which he was brought to the Presidency.

FERNANDO WOOD.

It is not surprising that with this beginning things went on from bad to worse until Mike Walsh, a few years before the War, publicly declared in a great Democratic meeting in the city :—

"I tell you now, and I say it boldly, that in this body politic of New York there is not political or personal honesty enough left to drive a nail into to hang a hat upon."

There is a fine picturesqueness about this phrase which enables it to stick like a burr to the memory. It was not, however, until the Irish emigration began in good earnest that Tammany found its vocation. Fernando Wood was first elected to the Mayoralty in 1854. Fernando Wood was a ward politician who first became known to the public by a prosecution in which it was proved that he had cheated his partner by altering the figures in accounts. He did not deny the charge, but pleaded statutory limitation. Having thus succeeded in avoiding gaol, he promptly ran for the Mayoralty, and was duly elected. With him came what Mr. Godkin calls "the organisation of New York politics on a criminal basis." The exploits of Fernando Wood, however, were thrown entirely into the shade by the lurid splendour of his successor.

This was William M. Tweed, the famous "Boss" Tweed, who began his life as a journeyman, and ended it in Ludley Street Gaol, after having ruled New York for years, as if he were a Turkish Pasha. After serving apprenticeship as a Member of the New York Senate, Deputy Street Commissioner, and President of the Board of Supervisors, he gradually made his way upwards until he was recognised as Boss of Tammany. It was not, however, until the year 1868 that he succeeded in giving the public a true taste of his quality. Even hardened Tammany politicians were aghast at the colossal frauds which he practised at the polls—frauds not only unique in their dimensions, but in the exceeding variety and multiplicity of their methods. On January 1st, 1869, Tweed and his allies began to plunder the city in a fashion which might have made the mouth of a Roman proconsul water. His ally, Connolly, was made Comptroller, while Tweed himself found ample scope for his fraudulent genius in the posts of Deputy Street Commissioner and Supervisor. In the first year he issued fraudulent warrants for £750,000. The money was spent fast and furiously. Tweed was a fellow of infinite variety, and he seemed almost to revel in the diversity of methods by which he could plunder the public. One very ingenious and simple fraud was his securing an Act of the Legislature, making a little paper which he owned the official organ of the City Government. In that capacity he drew £200,000 a year from the rates and taxes, as compensation for printing the report of the proceedings of the Common Council. Mr. Edwards says :—

He established a printing company, whose main business was the printing of blank forms and vouchers, for which in one year two million eight hundred thousand dollars was charged. Another item was a stationer's company, which furnished all the stationery used in the public institutions and departments, and this company alone received some three millions a year. On an order for six reams of cap paper, the same amount of letter paper, two reams of notepaper, two dozen pen-holders, four small ink-bottles, and a few other articles, all worth not more than fifty dollars, a bill of ten thousand dollars was rendered and paid.

The frauds upon which the conviction of Tweed was obtained consisted in the payment of enormously-increased bills to mechanics, architects, furniture-makers, and, in some instances, to unknown persons, for supplies and services. It was the expectation that an honest bill would be raised all the way from sixty to ninety per cent. In the first months of the ring's stealing the increase was about sixty per cent. Some of the bills were increased by as much as ninety per cent., but the average increase was such as to make it possible to give sixty-seven per cent. to the ring, the confederates being allowed to keep thirty-three per cent.; and of that thirty-three per cent. probably at least one-half was a fraudulent increase.

After a time the outrageous nature of his stealings provoked a revolt in Tammany itself. It is to this which Mr. Croker looks back with such proud complacency as marking the advent of reformed Tammany. Tweed was beaten at the elections, and his opponents secured a majority on the Board of Aldermen. Thereupon the resourceful rascal promptly went down to Albany, bought up a sufficient number of Congressmen and senators to give him control of the Legislature, and so secured a new Charter for New York, which legislated his opponents out of office. By this Charter a board of audit was created which consisted of Tweed, Connolly and Mayor Hall. What followed is thus described by the *Nation* :—

> The " Board ", met once for but ten minutes, and turned the whole " auditing " business over to Tweed. This sounds like a joke, but is true. Tweed then went to work, and " audited " as hard as he could, Garvey and other scamps bringing in the raw material in the shape of " claims," and he never stopped till he had " audited " about 6,000,000 dols. worth. Connolly's part in the little game then came in, and that worthy citizen drew his warrants for the money, which that simple-minded " scholar and gentleman " the Mayor endorsed, without having the least idea what was going on. Tweed's share of the plunder amounted to about 1,000,000 dols. in all. The Joint Committee, reporting on the condition of the city's finances, declared that the discoverable stealings of three years are 19,000,000 dols., which is probably only half the real total.

Never was a more unblushing rascal, as Mr. Tilden said in his account of Tweed's sovereignty. The Tammany Ring

> controlled the State Legislature, the police, and every department or functionary of the law ; several of the judges on the bench were its servile instruments, and issued decrees at its command ; it secured the management of the election " machine," and " ran " it at its own free will and pleasure ; a large part of the press was absolutely at its disposal. In the course of three years it had paid to eleven newspapers the sum of 2,329,482 dols. (about £466,000) nominally for advertisements, most of which were never even published, or never seen. Not only the City government, but the lion's share of the State government also had fallen into the hands of " Boss " Tweed and his confederates. Millions of dollars were stolen by the conspirators by means of " street openings," " improvements," new pavements, and other frauds. The Ring took from the public treasury a sum amounting to over £1,500,000 for furnishing and " repairing " a new Court-house. The charges for plastering alone came to about £366,000. For carpets, warrants were drawn for £120,000, although there were scarcely any carpets in the building. The floors were either bare, or covered with oil-cloth. Nearly £100,000 was alleged to have been paid for iron safes, and over £8,200 for " articles " not defined and never found. The total sum stolen was over £4,000,000.

Tweed's brief but dazzling career—for he was indeed a hero clad in Hell-fire—is said by President Andrews to have cost the City of New York 160,000,000 dols. The fine levied by Germany on the City of Paris after the War of 1870-1 was only one-fourth that amount. Fraud may be more costly than War. The total direct

WILLIAM M. TWEED.

MR. TILDEN.

property loss occasioned by the great fire at Chicago in 1871, when three square miles of buildings were burned down, and 98,500 persons rendered homeless, was only 30,000,000 dols. above the plunder of Tweed and his gang. Thus Fraud can be almost as ruinous as Fire.

Tweed was a fellow, if not of infinite jest like poor Yorick, at least of infinite insolent humour. In 1871 he boasted that he had amassed a fortune of 20,000,000 dols. Nor did he in the least scruple to avow the means by which he acquired it. President Andrews, of Brown University, in telling the history of the last quarter century, says, " He used gleefully to show his friends the safe where he kept money for bribing legislators, finding those of the Tammany-Republican stripe easiest game. Of the contractor who was decorating his country place at Greenwich he inquired, pointing to a statue, 'Who the hell is that?' 'That is Mercury, the god of merchants and thieves,' was the reply. 'That's bully,' said Tweed; 'put him over the front door.'"

Tweed was to the last popular with the masses of the people. Even when the whole town was ringing with proofs of his guilt, he stood as candidate for the Senate of New York State, and was elected. He had distributed in the poorer districts some £10,000 worth of coal and flour, and one of his champions brought down the house by declaring that "Tweed's heart has always been in the right place, and, even if he is a thief, there is more blood in his little finger and more marrow in his big toe than the men who are abusing him have in their whole bodies."

This man, with this excessive development of marrow in his big toe, was ultimately run down by Mr. Tilden and the Committee of Seventy. Connolly, the Comptroller, weakened and made terms with his opponents by appointing Mr. Green as Deputy-Comptroller. Mr. Green had little difficulty in laying hands upon all that was necessary in order to secure the prosecution and conviction of Tweed. Tweed's two infamous judges were driven from the bench, and he himself was clapped into gaol. He made his escape, and sought refuge in Spain. He was, however, delivered up to the American authorities, and reconducted to prison, where he died. To the last Tweed retained possession of much of his ill-gotten wealth. An offer which was made to surrender the residue of his millions in return for his liberty was rejected.

Tweed thought himself on the whole an ill-used man. The judge who tried Tweed declared that he had perverted the "power with which he was clothed in a manner more infamous, more outrageous, than any instance of a like character which the history of the civilised world afforded.". But Tweed himself declared that he believed he had done right, and was willing to "submit himself to the just criticism of any and all honest men:" From this it would seem that Mr. Croker is not alone in his imperturbable consciousness of public rectitude. Tweed on one occasion admitted that he had perhaps erred, but he explained he was not to blame. The fault lay with human nature in the first place, and with the system under which New York was governed in the second. Therein, no doubt, he was right. "Human nature," he said, "could not resist such temptations as were offered to men who were in power in New York, so long as the disposition of the offices of the city was at their command."

The most outrageous thing that Tweed ever did was to pass a bill through the State Legislature at Albany, giving the judges unlimited power to punish summarily whatever they chose to consider to be contempt. By this law, which was fortunately vetoed by the Governor, every newspaper in New York would have been gagged as effectually as the press of Constantinople.

After Tweed fell, Tammany was reorganised under Honest John Kelly and Richard Croker. Mr. Godkin declares that Honest John Kelly was only honest in name. He says :—

John Kelly practised the great Greek maxim "not too much of anything," simply made every candidate pay handsomely for his nomination, pocketed the money himself, and, whether he rendered any account of it or not, died in possession of a handsome fortune. His policy was the very safe one of making the city money go as far as possible among the workers by compelling every office-holder to divide his salary and perquisites with a number of other persons.

The same system had prevailed down to the year 1894, when Tammany, for the first time in many years, was driven from power. Just before the upset, the New York *Evening Post* published the records of the twenty-eight men who now or recently composed the Executive Committee of Tammany. It showed that they were all professional politicians, and that among them were one convicted murderer, three men who had been indicted for murder, felonious assault, and bribery, respectively, four professional gamblers, five ex-keepers of gambling houses, nine who either now or formerly sold liquor, three whose fathers did, three former pugilists, four former rowdies, and six members of the famous Tweed gang.

Seventeen of these held office, seven formerly did, and two were favoured contractors.

By these men New York was governed down to the year 1894. All the efforts of the reformers seemed in vain.   Mr. Godkin reluctantly confessed :—

The power of the semi-criminal organisation known as Tammany Hall not only remains unshaken, but grows stronger from year to year.   Every year its management descends, with perfect impunity, into the hands of a more and more degraded class.

But it is ever the darkest hour before the dawn.   Although on the very eve of the November election of 1894 it was declared that "Mr. Croker held almost as despotic a sway over New York as an Oriental potentate over his kingdom," one month after that statement had been made he was hurled from power by a great outburst of popular indignation.   How that was brought about I will now proceed to tell.

MR. E. L. GODKIN, EDITOR OF THE "EVENING POST," NEW YORK

The sworn foe of Tammany.

CHAPTER IV.

MR. LOWELL good-humouredly chaffed John Bull when he declared that

> He detests the same faults in himself he neglected,
> When he sees them again in his child's glass reflected,

and we only need to glance at current English criticisms upon American affairs to justify the poet's remark. Especially is this the case with a vice which of all others is regarded as distinctively English. John Bull has plenty of faults, but of those which render him odious to his neighbours there is none which is quite so loathsome as his "unctuous rectitude." That phrase, coined by Mr. Rhodes to express the contempt which he and every one who knew the facts felt on contemplating the hypocrisy and Pharisaism displayed in connection with the Jameson Raid, is likely to live long after Mr. Rhodes has vanished from this mortal scene. This tendency to Pharisaism and self-righteous complacency, which thanks God that it is not as other men are, is one of those vices which John Bull's children seem to have inherited in full measure. We are pretty good at Pharisaism in the Old Country, but we are "not a circumstance," to use the familiar slang, when we compare ourselves to some of the Pharisees reared across the Atlantic. This has nowhere been brought into such strong relief as when on the very eve of the exposure and discomfiture of Tammany their spokesmen took the stump and talked like very Pecksniffs concerning the immaculate purity of Tammany Hall.

The same characteristic is observable in all of them. Whether it is Boss Tweed, appealing confidently to the verdict of honest men upon a career of colossal theft and almost inconceivable fraud; or Mr. Croker, who, after surveying his whole life, declares that he has not discovered a single action which he has reason to regret, for he has not done anything but good all his life; or Bourke Cochran, who was at one time the Apollo and the Demosthenes of Tammany, the same unctuous rectitude oozes out of every pore. When Tammany was at its heyday of prosperity and power in 1889, it assembled in its thousands to cheer enthusiastically the impassioned oratory of Mr. Cochran, who declared, as among the self-evident truths which found an echo in every breast, that "if corruption prevails among the people, liberty will become a blighting curse, subversive of order. Corruption once begun, decay is inevitable and irresistible; the destruction of the Republic is immediate, immeasurable, irredeemable; since history does not record a case of a popular government which has been arrested in its downward course." Tammany listened to this with ecstatic admiration, cheered to the echo their eloquent oracle, and then went on using the proceeds of a system of blackmail for the perfecting of an engine of corruption to which it is difficult to discover a parallel in the annals of mankind.

In Mr. Croker's case, his calm consciousness of incorruptible virtue seems to be based upon a curious inversion of a belief in a Divine Providence. Tammany is not strong in theology, but Mr. Croker, in talking to me, based his argument in favour of the excellence of Tammany on the postulate that the government of the universe was founded on the law of righteousness. . This being the case, it was only possible to reconcile the continued existence of Tammany on one of two hypotheses. Either the domination of evil was permitted for a season for some sufficient cause hidden in the inscrutable mysteries of the Divine councils, or we must boldly assert that, all evidence to the contrary notwithstanding, Tammany rule was in accordance with the eternal law, *Credo quia impossibile*, rather than admit that so great an anomaly as a terrestrial Inferno could be permitted to exist by the good government of God. Mr. Croker, of course, adopted the latter hypothesis. There is much in it, no doubt, especially to those in Mr. Croker's position. It is, however, open to the fatal objection that the same process of logic would *à fortiori* secure a certificate of good conduct for the Great Assassin of Stamboul himself. The Ottoman Empire has lasted even longer than Tammany Hall, but even Mr. Croker would shrink from maintaining that Abdul Hamid was on that account the exemplary vicegerent of the Almighty.

This Pharisaic panoply in which Tammany was clad, as in a coat of mail, was no small element of its strength. The consciousness of wrong-doing is always an element of weakness. Not until a man can do evil and persuade himself that he is doing good can he silence that conscience which makes cowards of us all. Probably this unctuous rectitude on the part of Tammany and its Boss should be estimated as one of the chief obstacles in the way of the scattered and despairing band of reformers who, five or six years ago, confronted the stronghold of iniquity entrenched in their midst.

Its position, indeed, appeared almost impregnable. Tammany Hall commanded an annual revenue large enough to equip and maintain a small army. It had under its orders the whole of the executive force in its police—a body of men practically above the law, armed with powers hardly inferior to those of the police of St. Petersburg. Besides the police, all the persons on the pay-rolls

RICHARD CROKER IN HIS GARDEN AT WANTAGE, BERKSHIRE.

of the City and County were under the thumb of the Boss. There was hardly a city official, from the highest to the lowest, who did not hold office by the sovereign will and pleasure of Tammany. As there are 27,000 names on those pay-rolls, all of whom were voters and were taxable to an almost unlimited extent whenever the Tammany exchequer needed to be replenished, it is obvious how enormous were the odds against the assailants of Tammany.

But the unctuous rectitude of its leaders, the prompt obedience of the police Janissaries, and the discipline of the standing army of the twenty-seven thousand Pretorians on the city pay-rolls, were by no means the only difficulties which had to be overcome. Tammany Hall itself might be compared to a central citadel or keep of a Norman fortress. The outworks consisted of all the saloons, gaming hells, and houses of ill-fame in the City of New York. Some of these, no doubt, were by no means enthusiastic in support of the powers-that be, but they resembled tribes which, having been subdued by force of arms, are compelled to pay tribute and use their weapons in support of their conquerors. In New York, just before the revolt against Tammany, the number of licences for the sale of intoxicants in New York City was over 6,000. The number of unlicensed drinking places was estimated at from 2,000 to 3,000. Each of these saloons might be regarded as a detached outwork, holding a position in advance of the main citadel, and covering it from the attack of its foes.

In those days it used to be said that licences were granted by the Excise Board to anybody who had not served a term in a penitentiary. One indignant divine declared that it was perfectly safe to say that, if the Devil himself should apply to the Excise Board for a licence to set up a branch establishment on the children's playground in the Central Park, it would be granted. As to the other establishments of even worse fame than the saloon, there was an unwritten contract by which, in return for tribute paid directly or indirectly, they were shielded by the strong arm of Tammany from the enforcement of the law. It was calculated that if all the saloons in New York were placed side by side, averaging them at only twenty feet frontage each, they would form a line of circumvallation twenty miles long. To put it in another way, there was on an average one saloon for every thirty voters.

In addition to its control of the saloon, Tammany had two extremely important financial resources which have not yet been mentioned. The first was the control of the city contracts. A great city like New York, with an expenditure that exceeded that of the whole Federal Government of the United States fifty years ago, had an enormous means of influence at its disposal in the mere granting of contracts. But even this was a comparatively trivial element in the financial strength of Tammany. There existed in New York, as

in almost every city, great corporations representing enormous capital, and dividing gigantic dividends, which, in the Tammany scheme of the universe, might have been created for the express purpose of furnishing an unfailing supply of revenue to the party chest. The corporations which enjoyed franchises from the city, giving them control of the streets, whether for the purpose of traction, of lighting, or of electrical communication, were Tammany's milch cows. They all possess monopolies, granted to them in the first instance either by corruption or by negligence, which enable them to plunder the public. These monopolies can only be terminated or modified by the Legislature, and the Legislature can only act in obedience to the party machine. All that needs to be done when the campaign fund runs low is for the Boss to intimate to the various corporations that milking time has come, and that if they do not contribute liberally of their substance to the party treasury, Tammany will no longer be able to give them protection when the usual attack is made next session upon their monopoly or their franchise. Money is the sinews of war, and as the Tammany war chest was always full, Tammany snapped its fingers at all its enemies, and contemptuously declared that the reformers did not amount to a row of pins.

The outlook undoubtedly was very gloomy. From the point of view of practical politics it was simply hopeless; nevertheless, in a couple of years the fortress was stormed, and the government of New York placed in the hands of the Reformers. The story of the way in which this was brought about should never be forgotten by all those who are called upon to lead forlorn hopes against immense odds. As long as the world lasts, such narratives are among the most precious cordials which in times of danger and distress restore the courage and revive the faith of man. Dr. Parkhurst's attack on Tammany is one of the latest of a long series of victories achieved by the leader of an outnumbered handful. When Gideon went forth against the hosts of Midian with only three hundred followers, he left a leading case on record for the encouragement of all who should come after. How many reformers and revolutionists who have helped the world forward in the path of progress have been cheered by the dream in which the Midianitish soldier saw a cake of barley bread smite and overturn the multitudinous camp of the conqueror, history does not record! But if ever a man needed the inspiration of that barley cake it was Dr. Parkhurst, when in 1892 he set himself to the desperate task of wresting New York City from the grasp of Tammany.

Dr. Parkhurst was a Massachusetts minister of Puritan ancestry, who, in 1880, at the age of thirty-eight, had been called to Madison Square Church, in New York. For ten years he went in and out among the people, quietly building up his church, ministering to his congregation, and learning at first-hand the real difficulties which offered almost insuperable obstacles to right living in New York. In 1890, on the eve of the November election, he preached a sermon on municipal politics, which, although it failed in influencing the polls, nevertheless marked Dr. Parkhurst out as the man to succeed Dr. Howard Crosby as President of the Society for the Prevention of Crime. He took office in 1891. In less than twelve months he began the campaign from which he never withdrew his hand until the government of the city was wrested from the control of Tammany.

Nothing is more characteristic, both of the state of things in New York and the uncompromising directness of Dr. Parkhurst, than the fact that he had no sooner assumed the control of the Society for the Prevention of Crime than he adopted as his motto the significant watchword, " Down with the Police ! " That fact alone speaks volumes as to how utterly New York City had fallen under the control of the Evil One. For a society for the prevention of crime to adopt " Down with the Police ! " as its watchword, seems to us of the Old World absolutely inconceivable. The police exist for the prevention of crime, yet here was a society of leading citizens, presided over by a doctor of divinity, putting in the forefront of its programme the formula " Down with the Police ! "

Strange though it may seem to us, the best people of New York understood and appreciated what Dr. Parkhurst was after. But it was not till the 14th of February, 1892, that he put the trumpet to his lips and blew a blast the echoes of which are still sounding through the world. His sermon was an impeachment of the Government of New York, the like of which had seldom been heard before in a Christian pulpit. If any one questions the justice of the title of this volume, let him read what Dr. Parkhurst said ' in the sermon, of which the following sentence is a fair sample :—

There is not a form under which the Devil disguises himself that so perplexes us in our efforts, or so bewilders us in the devising of our schemes, as the polluted harpies that, under the pretext of governing this city, are feeding day and night on its quivering vitals. They are a lying, perjured, rum-soaked and libidinous lot.

That was plain speaking in honest, ringing Saxon, for Dr. Parkhurst knew that there was no better way of spoiling the trump card of the Devil's game than to refuse to let him keep things mixed. He maintained that the district attorney, or, as we should say, the public prosecutor, was guilty of complicity with vice and crime : that " every effort to make men respectable, honest, temperate, and sexually clean was a direct blow between the eyes of the mayor and his whole gang of drunken and lecherous subordinates, who shielded and patronised iniquity." Criminals and officials, he declared, were hand-and-glove, and he summed up the whole matter in the following concise exposition of the *status quo* in " Satan's Invisible World " in New York, 1892 : —" It is simply one solid gang of rascals, half of the gang in office

D

From *Frank Leslie's Weekly.*]

REV. C. H. PARKHURST, D.D., DENOUNCING TAMMANY'S GOVERNMENT OF NEW YORK.

and the other half out, and the two halves steadily catering to each other across the official line."

Of course there was a great outcry. Some good people were scandalised, while as for the bad ones, they were simply outraged at such "violent and intemperate utterances in the pulpit." One of the police captains declared "it was a shame for a minister of the Gospel to disgrace the pulpit by such utterances." Dr. Parkhurst was summoned before the Grand Jury, and solemnly reproved for making statements which he could not for the moment substantiate with chapter and verse. When the Grand Jury condemned him and the judge rebuked him, Tammany was in high glee; but Dr. Parkhurst bided his time. He was not a man to be "downed" by censure. Finding that his general statements were scouted because he could not produce first hand evidence as to the literal accuracy of each particular instance on which he built up his general finding, he took the bold and courageous step of going himself through the houses of ill-fame, gaming hells, and other resorts which were running open under the protection of the police. He was accompanied in his pilgrimage by a detective and a lawyer, and for three weeks every night Dr. Parkhurst, to use his own phrase, "traversed the avenues of our municipal hell." They entered into no houses not easy of access, went into no places which were not recognised as notorious, and were perfectly well known by the constable on the beat. In one case they succeeded in proving police collusion by getting the policeman on beat to stand guard while they visited the house, ostensibly for an immoral purpose, in order to warn them against any signs of a possible raid.

Having thus mastered his facts and obtained incontrovertible evidence at first hand as to the fact of police complicity in the wholesale violation of the law, Dr. Parkhurst stood up in his pulpit on the morning of March 13th, 1892, and once more arraigned the city authorities. This time, however, he was armed with a mass of facts ascertained at first hand, and supported by unimpeachable, independent testimony. He brought forward no fewer than two hundred and eighty-four cases in which the law was flagrantly violated under the noses of the police, who, he maintained, were guilty of corrupt complicity in the violation of the law they were appointed to enforce.

It was a great sermon, and one that shook the city to its centre. Some idea of its drift and spirit may be gained from this extract:—

There is little advantage in preaching the Gospel to a young fellow on Sunday, if he is going to be sitting on the edge of a Tammany-maintained hell the rest of the week. Don't tell me that I don't know what I am talking about. Many a long, dismal, heart-sickening night, in company with two trusted friends, have I spent since I spoke on this matter before, going down into the disgusting depths of this Tammany-debauched town ; and it is rotten with a rottenness that is unspeakable and indescribable, and a rottenness that would be absolutely impossible except by the connivance, not to say the purchased sympathy, of the men whose one obligation before God, men, their own consciences, is to shield virtue and make vice difficult.

Now, that I stand by, because before Almighty God I know it, and I will stand by it though buried beneath presentments as thick as autumn leaves in Vallombrosa, or snowflakes in a March blizzard.

And stand by it Dr. Parkhurst did. He was promptly summoned again before the Grand Jury, and this time he had his facts at command. Instead of being rebuked, the Grand Jury reported emphatically that it was impossible to reconcile the facts presented by Dr. Parkhurst with any other theory than that of wholesale police corruption.

The following month various keepers of disreputable houses were prosecuted upon Dr. Parkhurst's evidence, when every effort was made to damage Dr. Parkhurst by representing him as the vicious criminal who was responsible for the very evils which he had brought to light. It is the old, old story. As long as you sit still and say nothing you are all right, but the moment you call attention to a hideous wrong or a shameful crime, all those whose iniquities you have disclosed combine with your enemies in order to make a busy public believe that it is you who have exposed the crime who is the real criminal, while they, poor innocents, are the injured parties, for whom a respectable public should have nothing but sympathy and commiseration.

The ferocity of the attacks upon Dr. Parkhurst provoked a reaction in his favour. The City Vigilance Society was formed by the association of forty religious and secular societies of the city. The work of sapping and mining went steadily on. In order to bring odium upon Dr. Parkhurst, the police suddenly decided to close up several houses of ill-fame, so as to turn their unfortunate occupants into the streets on one of the coldest nights of the winter of 1892. Dr. Parkhurst met this by promptly providing homes for all the dispossessed women. Foiled in this cruel manœuvre, the police prosecuted Dr. Parkhurst's detective for an alleged attempt to levy blackmail. This was Satan reproving sin with a vengeance, and for the moment it had a temporary success. The detective was convicted, in the first instance, but on appeal the verdict was set aside. Undaunted, however, by this reverse, Dr. Parkhurst began to carry the war into the enemy's camp. He got up cases against forty-five of the sixty-four gambling and disorderly houses which were allowed to run by the police captain of a single precinct. The trials followed with varying results. It was evident that the difficulties in the way of obtaining a full disclosure of police corruption could only be overcome by special measures. Public opinion was now deeply stirred, and the Chamber of Commerce memorialised the Senate of New York City to hold an inquiry into the Police Department of New York.

The Senate appointed a Committee of Investigation, and passed a bill providing for the payment of its expenses. This bill was vetoed by Governor Flower, himself a Democrat, whose veto elicited another illustration, if it were wanted, of the marvellous Pharisaism of Tammany and its friends.

Where party feeling runs high, anything that one party proposes the other one opposes, and Governor Flower, finding the Republican majority of the Senate in favour of the investigation into the misdeeds of the New York police, could only see in it

GOVERNOR FLOWER.

a Republican plot for the manufacture of political capital in the division of political patronage. So he took special objection to any investigation of the Police Department of New York. The following passage from the veto message deserves to stand on record as one of the most extraordinary eulogies ever pronounced upon a rotten system on the very eve of its exposure. Speaking of New York, Governor Flower said:—

> Except for political objects, there is no good reason why that city should be singled out for legislative scrutiny. The same men who do the investigating in public will admit in private what every well-informed person knows is true—that no city in the State is so well governed as New York. No city in the State has a lower tax rate; no city has a better police regulation; no city has a lower ratio of crime; no city has better streets; no city has a better fire department; no city has better parks; no city has better schools; no city has a better health department; no city has a better credit; no city is so comfortable a place to live in. That bad men sometimes get in office there is true. That frauds upon the city treasury sometimes occur is true; that mal-administration sometimes happens is true; that ideal municipal government has not yet been attained there is true; but these things are as equally true of every city in the world, they are truer of other cities of our State than they are of New York.—Lexow Commission, vol. i., p. 10.

In order to get round the Governor's veto, prominent members of the Chamber of Commerce guaranteed to the Committee counsel's fees to an amount necessary to enable them to prosecute the investigation. Thereupon the Committee was appointed and set to work. All its members were Senators of the State of New York. It was presided over by Mr. Clarence Lexow. The names of the other members were Edmund O'Connor, George W. Robertson,

JOHN W. GOFF.

Cuthbert W. Pound, Charles T. Saxton, Jacob A. Cantor, Daniel Bradley, with William A. Sutherland and John W. Goff as counsel. The only member of the Committee representing New York City was Mr. Cantor, who presented the minority Report, which maintained that the Republicans were as bad as the Democrats, and that most of the officials in the Police Department implicated in blackmail, fraud and corruption were Republicans.

The Committee held its first meeting on the 9th of March, 1894. At the earlier sittings the Police Department was represented by counsel, but after a while he was withdrawn, and the Committee was left to conduct its inquiries as best it could. It was fortunate in securing the services of a famous lawyer, Mr. John W. Goff, who is now Recorder of New York, "succeeding a man who fined him for contempt because he insisted upon his rights as counsel in protecting one of Dr. Parkhurst's agents." As even the one dissentient member of the Committee reported, "No more tireless, industrious or effective counsel was ever employed by a Committee charged with the responsibility of its character." As I read over the voluminous reports of the evidence taken by the Lexow Committee, I could not repress a sigh : would that we had enjoyed the privilege of having such an examiner as John W. Goff on the South Africa Committee ! But, of course, there was one great difference : the Lexow Committee was appointed for the purpose of finding out the facts and exposing scandal, whereas the South Africa Committee seems to have accepted the theory that it was appointed for exactly the opposite purpose of hushing them up, and of screening Mr. Chamberlain at any cost.

The members of the Lexow Committee when they undertook their duties had no idea as to how far it would lead them. They thought that two days a week for three weeks would complete the investigation. No sooner, however, had they begun to apply the probe than they came upon evidence of such rottenness that even the laziest of them felt they had no option but to go on. Go on they did day after day, taking evidence from morning till night, but it was not until the end of the year that they were able to finish their Provisional Report. This was dated January 16th, 1895. In the Report they thus summarise the evidence which they took :—

The record shows a total of 10,576 pages of proceedings. This does not include a mass of documentary exhibits which were read and considered in evidence, for the purpose of information. Of this testimony, 1,077 pages embrace the subject-matter of police interference at the polls, and the balance, or almost 9,500 pages, refer to the subject-matter of blackmail, extortion and corruption. In all, 678 witnesses were examined, of whom 81 were examined on the first and 597 on the second branch of the inquiry. In all, about 3,000 subpœnas were served, of which upwards of 2,750 were with reference to the second branch of the inquiry.—*Ib.*, vol. i., p. 4.

It is upon this immense body of evidence taken on oath, under cross-examination in public audiences, that I have based this volume. " Satan's Invisible World " is thus displayed, not by a stranger or a casual observer, or an amateur investigator. The revelation has been made by American subjects testifying on oath before an American tribunal as to the state of things that actually existed in the City of New York. As the result of the investigation the old system of Tammany rule was overthrown, and the police thoroughly reorganised. They have now as Chief Commissioner Mr. Moss, who, after Mr. Goff, was the chief instrument in exposing the corruption of the old system. If any one doubts the accuracy of the picture of what actually existed down to 1894, which is set forth in this and the following pages, I can only refer him to the volumes of evidence to which reference is made throughout in the passages quoted.

It is not surprising that men who have lived in the midst of such a city should sometimes burst out like Dr. Parkhurst with the despairing cry :—

You can love your country and work for it, pray and plead for it, but there is a stage of rotteuness which once reached, the country is damned beyond the power of the Holy Ghost to do anything for it.

That such a state of rottenness has been reached in any part of the English-speaking world we must all be loath to admit. The great popular uprising which swept Tammany from power in 1894 was a healthy sign that the rottenness had not eaten to the vitals of the community. But the Charter of Greater New York proves only too well how deeply distrust has sapped the faith of the citizens in the possibility of governing their city by the ordinary democratic machinery of an elective assembly.

SENATOR LEXOW.

PART II.

SATAN'S INVISIBLE WORLD.

CHAPTER I.

THE POLICE BANDITS OF NEW YORK.

THE Lexow Committee experienced great difficulty in procuring evidence owing to the Reign of Terror which was established in New York by the police. The story reads more like a description of an Indian province terrorized by a band of Thugs than a statement of how New York was governed. When unwilling witnesses—and the vast majority of witnesses were most unwilling —were placed on the stand, they were thus addressed by the Chairman :—

Any testimony you give now, under oath, before this Committee with reference to bribery or corruption, cannot be used against you in any form, shape, or way. The fact of your confession here before this Committee will be a complete bar against any prosecution against you for that offence. In other words, if you sit here and tell the truth, and confess that you have committed any crime of that description, you will be absolutely relieved from any punishment for the commission of that crime. On the other hand, if you swear to anything that is false, then, not only could you be punished for the crime that you committed, if you did commit the crime of bribery, but for the crime of false swearing, or perjury, besides ; you understand that ?—Vol. iv., p. 3,615.

Notwithstanding this, the amount of perjury committed, especially by policemen, was appalling. One of them, of the name of Interman, admitted frankly that it was the common understanding among the members of the force that it was their duty to swear falsely to conceal the facts about bribery and corruption. If they spoke the truth they would be bounced or persecuted, whereas if they came forward and perjured themselves they would stand high with their superiors. The wrath of a captain who can make it hot for you next day evidently weighed much more with the police than the wrath of an offended God, whose mills grind so slowly that retribution may not begin till the day of judgment.

The answers to questions put to brothel-keepers and others as to their belief in the binding character of an oath and the reality of a future state were hardly edifying. One woman, Julia Mahoney, broke the record for the unhesitating candour with which she answered counsel's questions.

"Do you not know," said Mr. Goff, "that you would meet your punishment in the world hereafter?"

"I hope not," Julia replied simply.

"And you know that you would be liable to go to the State's prison?" persisted Mr. Goff. But Mrs. Mahoney was proof against that threat.

"If I was in prison I would be out in twenty-four hours," she remarked. "She has got a pull," sagely observed Senator Bradley.

It must be admitted that it was a task of uncommon difficulty to extract the truth from witnesses such as these, who fear not God neither regard man. Why should they? They have got a pull, and the pull ends all things.

Two competent American observers have recently told us what a policeman is in an American city. Both confirm to the letter what was stated by a leading citizen of Chicago five years ago. "Never mind what is said about this or that system of city government. In Chicago and all the West the police govern the city, and that is all there is to it." In New York it would appear to have been much the same. Mr. Theodore Roosevelt, who was head of the New York police in the first two years of the Reform Administration, writing in the *Century Magazine* for October, says:—

> The police occupy positions of great importance. They not merely preserve order, the first essential of both liberty and civilisation, but to a large portion of our population they stand as the embodiment as well as the representative of the law of the land. To the average dweller in a tenement-house district, especially if born abroad, the policeman is in his own person all that there is of government: he is judge, executive and legislature, constitution and town meeting.

The other witness is Mr. Godkin, the editor of the *Evening Post*, who, writing in the *North American Review* seven years back, says of the newly landed immigrant:—

> No sooner has he established himself in a tenement-house or a boarding-house than he finds himself face to face with three functionaries who represent to him the government of his new country—the police justice of the district, the police captain of his precinct, and the political "district leader." These are, to him, the Federal, State and municipal governments rolled into one . . . . These three men are to him America. Everything else in the national institutions in which Americans pride themselves he only sees through a glass darkly, if he sees it at all.

These dwellers in tenement-houses in New York, to whom the police—of whom there were then 4,000—are judge, executive, and legislature, constitution and town meeting, comprise two-thirds of the population of the city. To the foreign denizen of these districts—say one-half of the whole—the policeman and his masters of the political machine are all of America that he can see or understand.

Now let us see what kind of an America the New York police presented to the eyes of the majority of the population of the city.

The Lexow Committee in its final Report, after commenting on the difficulty of obtaining evidence owing to the terrorism practised by the police, said of a typical case:—

> This situation was characteristic. A consuming desire to put an end to an outrageous servitude on the one hand, and a dread lest failure might result in a still more galling thraldom on the other! It seemed, in fact, as though every interest, every occupation, almost every citizen, was dominated by an all-controlling and overshadowing dread of the police department.
> Those in the humbler walks of life were subjected to appalling outrages which to some extent continued, even to the end of the investigation. They were abused, clubbed and imprisoned, and even convicted of crimes on false testimony by police-men and their accomplices. Men of business were harassed and annoyed in their affairs, so that they too were compelled to bend their necks to the police yoke, in order that they might share that so-called protection which seemed indispensable to the profitable conduct of their affairs. People of all degrees seemed to feel that to antagonize the police was to call down upon themselves the swift judgment and persecution of an invulnerable force, strong in itself, banded together by self-interest and the community of unlawful gain, and so thoroughly entrenched in the muni-cipal government as to defy ordinary assault. Strong men hesitated when required to give evidence of their oppression, and whispered stories; tricks, subterfuges and schemes of all kinds were resorted to to withhold from this committee and its counsel the fact that they had knowledge of acts of corruption or oppression by the police. The uniform belief was that if they spoke against the police, or if the police discovered that they had been instrumental in aiding your Committee, or had given information, their business would be ruined, they would be hounded from the city, and their lives even jeopardised.—Vol. i., pp. 25, 26.

For wrongs inflicted by the police there was no redress. Mr. Goff in the concluding stages of the investigation referred to this phase of the question in the following significant terms:—

> A great many innocent people who have been clubbed by the police in our city have thought that the city was responsible for the actions of its employés; but the courts have held time and time again that the city is not responsible; and then from the further fact that nearly every policeman in the city has his property in his wife's name, it has become a notorious thing that it is useless to bring an action for assault against a policeman .... Mr. Jerome reminds me now of the celebrated case of Mr. Fleming; I think it was a Decoration Day parade. Captain Williams clubbed him in Madison Square, and he got a judgment of $2,500; but the judgment was never collected. We have never been able to get it on the record that a judgment against a police official has been paid.—Vol. v., p. 4,661.

It is not surprising after this to read the answer of a witness, a journalist of standing, who had been nearly murdered by a police captain in the cells of the police-station. He was asked if he had taken proceedings against his assailant. He replied:—

> "I never did, sir. It is no use going to law with the Devil, and Court, and Hell!"

To quote the more formal but not less emphatic finding of the Lexow Committee:—

> It appears, therefore, that the police formed a separate and highly privileged class, armed with the authority and the machinery for oppression and punish-ment, but practically free themselves from the operation of the criminal law.—Vol. i., p. 30.

A VIEW IN ST. PETERSBURG.

CHAPTER II.

ONE of the most pathetic of human fallacies is the assumption that you have only to pass a law in order to extirpate an evil. The touching faith of English-speaking men in the efficacy of statute-made law is nowhere more strikingly illustrated than in the great cities of the United States. The fact that a statute is only so much good paper inked by a printing-press does not seem to occur to the citizens, even after the repeated demonstrations of its impotence. Nowhere can severer laws be found for the suppression of all manner of vice and crime than in those cities where vice and crime hold high carnival under the patronage of the police. It has been frequently observed that this habit of finding relief for moral indignation by placing a stringent law upon the statute-book is exactly the instinct which leads the private citizen to say "Damn!" There is a great deal of this swearing at large in the passing of rigorous statutes, which are no sooner passed than they appear to be forgotten. Take, for instance, the laws which were passed from time to time to secure the extirpation of vice and crime in the City of New York. They certainly did not err in the direction of leniency. The usual complaint of the police elsewhere is that they are not vested with sufficient power in order to deal with the vicious and criminal classes. This cannot be said with truth of the New York police, as will be seen from the following extract from the proceedings before the Lexow Committee :—

Mr. Moss: We have got a situation here as autocratic as anything than can be found in St. Petersburg; a law was passed in 1873 for the purpose of giving the police abundant opportunity to enter such places for any purpose that they might see fit to enter.

Mr. Goff: Judicial functions have been vested in the Superintendent of Police, in a policeman of this city, who, on his own motion, can under Section 285 of the Consolidation Act issue a warrant, and on the execution of that warrant the doors of any house in the City of New York may be broken in. If we had time to introduce evidence of cases, we could do so where from spleen and malice on the part of some common policeman, the respectable houses have been invaded without colour or authority of right, except this arbitrary power given to the police by law.

Senator O'Connor : That is simply a horrible condition of affairs; better submit to a thousand disorderly houses than that one decent house should be treated in such a manner.

Mr. Goff: Under the law as it exists to-day in the City of New York, a policeman who is the Superintendent of Police—that is all he is, a policeman—has the power to issue his warrant fully equal to that exercised by the Prefect of Police in St. Petersburg. . . .

, Counsel then read as follows :—

"If any member of the police force, or if any two or more householders, shall report in writing under his or their signature, to the Superintendent of Police that there are good grounds, and state them, for believing any house, room or premises within the said city to be kept or used as a common gaming-house or common gaming premises or room for playing for wagers, or for money at any game of chance, or to be kept or used for lewd and obscene purposes or amusements, or the deposit or sale of lottery tickets or lottery policies, it shall be lawful for the Superintendent of Police to authorise in writing any member or members of the police force to enter the same, who may forthwith arrest all persons there found offending against the law, but none other, and seize all implements of game or lottery tickets or lottery policies and convey any person so arrested before a magistrate and bring the article so seized to the office of the clerk ; it shall be the duty of the said Superintendent of Police to cause such arrested person to be rigorously prosecuted and such articles seized to be destroyed as the orders, rules and regulations of the Board of Police shall direct."

There has been no law in our country under our system of a more complete, sweeping and comprehensive measure placed within the powers of a simple executive office, as the Superintendent of Police is, as this law. It exceeds that of the Common Law, where the power is vested in a judicial officer to issue a warrant ; but here a policeman may authorise in writing any members of his police force to enter any place complained of by either a member of the police force or by two householders, and arrest all such persons found therein.—Vol. iv., 4,493–7.

Notwithstanding this right of domiciliary visitation, which equals or exceeds that possessed by the Prefect of St. Petersburg, we have it admitted on all hands that it utterly failed in attaining its end. The police machine, Mr. Goff declared, was by no means inefficient. Regarded as a machine it was indeed, in his opinion, the most perfect machine ever invented in New York. Notwithstanding all its mechanical perfection the result was nothing but organised impotence.

Witness after witness appeared on the stand to attest the extraordinary inability of the police authorities to cope with the flagrant evils in the city or in the force under their command. On one occasion it was proved that the agents of the Society for the Prevention of Crime had been hunted by a mob of bullies and crooks for half a mile through Bowery. It was a regular riot, in which the agents for the Society were struck and stoned through the whole of Captain Devery's precinct; the police officers looking on as amused spectators. They were appealed to for assistance, and took no notice. At last, the hunted men jumped on a car, and escaped with their lives. But although this riot had taken place in the heart of the city, and created a scandal through the whole of New York, Superintendent Byrnes reported that he could not find any evidence that there had been a riot (p. 4,834.) The extraordinary inability of the police to see what was going on under their noses, although apparently phenomenal, was so habitual that it ceased to excite any surprise. Saloons ran open all Sunday under the eyes of the patrolmen. The Superintendent of the Society for the Prevention of Crime gave evidence on this subject as follows :—

I pointed out an open saloon to a patrolman, whose name I do not know, and inquired why he did not close it ; he said that if I insisted upon it, he supposed he must do so; but it would do no good, and only get him in trouble with the department and cause his removal to some undesirable precinct.—Vol. v., p. 4,835.

But it is only when the Police Commissioners, who stand at the head of the whole force, are under examination that we discover the extent of their utter inability to find out anything. There was, for instance, Mr. Sheehan, who at that time was Police Commissioner,

JOHN C. SHEEHAN.
Ex-Police Commissioner. Boss of Tammany.

and who now is the titular Boss of Tammany Hall. The question of pool-rooms was under consideration when he admitted that they existed, and that he knew they were corrupting the police. Then the Chairman put the following question :—

And, notwithstanding the fact that you knew or had heard that those pool-rooms were corrupting the police, you thought it was not necessary to take any action upon it?.

Mr. Sheehan replied :—

I did start an inquiry to find out if those pool-rooms were paying, what they were paying, and who they were paying it to. I did that within a few months after I became a Police Commissioner, but I couldn't get any authoritative information of any kind on the subject ; but I got it from all sides that they were paying, and it was believed that they were, but no person would substantiate or stand for it.—Vol. iv., p. 3,765.

So he abandoned the subject as one which it was no use discussing any further.

It was just the same with Mr. Commissioner Martin. He was asked concerning the existence of corruption in the police force. I quote the following from the Record :—

Examined by Mr. Sutherland : What did you do to restore the tone and efficiency of the police ?
A. The Board of Police was waiting for any evidence of that character to be brought to it.—Vol. i., p. 483.
Q. What investigation has the Police Commissioners ever instituted to discover the falsity of those charges ?
A. No special investigation.—Vol. i., p. 484.

It was the same thing with disorderly houses.

Examined by Mr. Nicoll : And, during all the years you have been Police Commissioner, you never have examined the record to see how many there are or where they are located ?
A. No, sir ; I have not.
Q. And hasn't that led you to go to these records to see what houses were put down as disorderly in this category ?
A. No, sir ; I have not.
Q. Has the subject of suppression or diminution of these disorderly houses been a matter of discussion before the Board of Police ?
A. No, sir.—Vol. i., p. 528.

Even when crime was discovered, when the criminal was, as it were, taken red-handed, there seemed to be a strange paralysis that prevented his appearance in court. This affected other Boards besides that of the Police. When the action of the Excise Board was under consideration, it was admitted by Mr. Andrews, a Commissioner of the Board, that in one notorious case the licence had been obtained by false swearing. Mr. Goff asked :—

Q. Did you ever, when you discovered these false papers, as you say, and of perjuries having been committed before the Board—did you ever take any steps to have the perpetrators called to answer for the crime ?
A. No steps were ever taken for indictment ; no.—Vol. iv., p. 4,386.

It was not for want of painstaking on the part of the Legislature that the police force was not more efficient. Every constable before being appointed had to comply with the provisions of the Civil Service law, which were thus explained by Commissioner Martin :—

The candidate is required to have the names of a certain number of citizens, usually five, to vouch for him as to his character—their acquaintance with him ; and all those papers having been finally completed, the papers are sent to the Civil Service Board, where examinations are held from time to time of batches of such applicants. Application is made to the captain for examination of his character and as to the persons who signed the paper, and a report is made in writing by the captain. There are three Civil Service Commissioners appointed by the Mayor ; I do not recollect the names just at this time. Once a year the Civil Service Board made an examination of all applicants for patrolmen, and they usually examine in batches of from 400 to 600.—Vol. i., p. 567.

The Commissioners themselves, when asked about the subject, were at a loss to explain how it was vice and crime flourished under their very eyes. Mr. John McClave, the Republican Police Commissioner, told the Committee that he had always voted with his Tammany Commissioners on the Board, because "he had never known them to do anything wrong." There was a very touching little scene described by Mr. McClave's son-in-law, as to the grief which the appointment of the Lexow Committee occasioned Mr. McClave. Mr. and Mrs. McClave were going to a reception one night, and, said Mr. Gideon Granger, the son-in-law—

Mr. McClave was quite nervous, and Mrs. McClave turned to him and said, "Why, Johnnie, what is the matter with you?" And he says, "Oh, nothing, nothing." And she says, "Oh yes, there is; it is that police investigation business. I would not worry over that." And he said, "I don't see why it is those hayseed politicians up in Albany want to come down here and bother us honest men."— Vol. i., p. 1,162.

Notwithstanding Mr. McClave's pathetic lament, the Lexow Committee went on with its work, and the conduct of these "honest men" was brought forth to the light of day. With results.

SUPERINTENDENT BYRNES.

E

CHAPTER III.

THE New York Police Department as it existed in 1894 was like the Scribes and Pharisees in the Gospel. It was like unto whited sepulchres, which indeed appear beautiful outward, but are within full of dead men's bones and of all uncleanness. Hardly a single thing that was proved to exist could have existed if the laws, rules and regulations had been faithfully enforced. Therefore until the searchlight of the Lexow inquiry was turned on, it was the correct thing to deny that the abuses, the corruption, the blackmail had any existence. On paper the New York police was the finest in the world. It was the most perfectly equipped, and it was armed with authority as great as that of any autocrat. What then could possibly be wrong ?

The answer of the Lexow Committee, after hearing the evidence, was short and succinct. Their answer to the question, What is wrong in the Police Department? might be summed up in one word—Everything. From the crown of the head down to the sole of the feet, the department was proved to be one mass of putrefying sores. There was no health in it, and it was worst of all at the top. The Lexow Report says:—

The conclusion which has impressed itself upon your Committee is that the disorganising elements at work in the Police Department are such that operate from the higher officials down, rather than from the patrolmen up.—Vol. i., p. 29.

But the origin of the mischief was found to exist not in the department at all; but outside the department. The first thing that was wrong was that the police were practically run by Tammany Hall politicians in the interest of their party, and that the real governing power in the force lay outside of it. Two of the Police Commissioners in whose hands the control of the force was nominally lodged were leaders in their own districts for Tammany Hall, and their sense of their obligations to their party far outweighed their obligations to the law or to the city. As one of the witnesses put it bluntly :—

So long as our municipal departments are run by Boss Croker, they will be regarded as adjuncts of a political organisation, and will be used to perpetuate its power. A police commission controlled by such influence is incapable of rendering justice.—Vol. i., p. 114.

E 2

From an English point of view what New York needed most was a City Council, with some effective control over the affairs of the city. The shadowy unreality known as the Board of Aldermen cuts no figure in the inquiry into the forces which actually governed New York. Tammany Hall, the executive committee of Tammany Hall, came much nearer to the ideal of a Municipal Assembly than the Board of Aldermen. It was to Tammany Hall, and not to the Board of Aldermen, that the Police Commissioners appealed when they wanted to enforce their authority over the men under their own orders. This came out very plainly in Commissioner Martin's evidence. He found that his subordinates were taking so active a hand in politics, joining political clubs and the like, that he wished to check it. He went, not to the Board of Aldermen, but to Tammany Hall. He was asked :—

Q. Why did you go there?
A. I took occasion to speak in Tammany Hall about it, because there I could reach people from different assembly districts; I have spoken to representatives of the different districts about it in my office.
Q. And you went to Tammany Hall to engage their co-operation in securing greater efficiency of the police force in New York city?
A. To aid in making it efficient; yes, sir.
Q. Was that because there was no other place to go to?
A. There was no other place to go to that would be as effective as that.—Vol. i., p. 443.

No wonder the Committee reports :—

No stronger illustration is necessary to show how under the then existing conditions a political faction had impressed itself so strongly upon the police force that its authority was more potent than that of the nominal chiefs of the department.— Vol. i., p. 19.

It was to Tammany Hall also that the liquor dealers appealed for protection from the intolerable exactions of the police. "There was no other place to go to." The legal authorities were paralysed by the extreme distrust felt by Americans in all elective assemblies. Tammany Hall naturally and inevitably became the one living centre of popular authority in the city. Its moral authority in New York was something like that of the Land League over Ireland under Mr. Parnell. The Lexow Committee report with a certain jealous awe concerning the "supreme head of authority," Mr. Richard Croker, who, although a private citizen, unconnected with the Police Department, but leader of Tammany Hall, "was able to do what all the other legally constituted authorities failed to accomplish." They say :—

The same private citizen whose authority was so potent to accomplish all this, was able, by a word of command, at once to shut up all the pool-rooms then in full operation, and which, according to the testimony up to that time, neither the whole force of police, of detectives, of superintendent, or of the Commissioners themselves could effectively close.—Vol. i., pp. 18-19.

" Taken as a whole," says the Lexow Report, " the records disclose the fact that the Police Department, from the highest down to the lowest, was thoroughly impregnated with the political influence of Tammany Hall " ; and they add, what naturally follows, " that the suppression and repression of crime depended not so much upon the ability of the police to enforce the law, but rather upon the will of that organisation or faction to have the law enforced " (vol. i., p. 19).

The leaders of Tammany, no doubt, were not " agin the law " in the abstract. But they owed their first allegiance to their party, and their first thought was not of the duty they owed to the city, but of the duty they owed to Tammany. The claims of that great brotherhood had precedence over such trifles as the laws of the State, which after all were passed by " Hayseed " legislators, or, in plain English, by the rustic vote of the rural districts of the State of New York. One redoubtable worthy, Judge and ex-Senator Roesch, who figures conspicuously in this American Tartarus as one of the minor Plutonian deities, gave very interesting evidence on this point. He was a Judge, an ex-Senator, and a leader of Tammany Hall. His aid in the latter capacity seems to have been generally invoked by the various law-breakers of the neighbourhood. He was asked by Senator O'Connor whether it was not one of the duties of the district leader, " if the members of his party were labouring under any kind of difficulty at all, for the purpose of conducting his organisation and making that solid with the parties, to do what he could to give them aid ? "

The Senator answered unhesitatingly, " In every case." When he was proved to have received money from keepers of disorderly houses, whose girls were run in by the police, he said that he received it entirely as a lawyer for giving legal advice. But he admitted that when he went to the station-house to bail out the girls, he acted as a political leader. So the Chairman observed, " You advised as a lawyer and acted as a political leader in carrying out your advice." Mr. Senator Roesch is in many ways a more typical representative of Tammany than Mr. Croker himself. Both, however, agree on one principle. They always stick by their friends, and when anything is going they see that their supporters are not left out in the cold. This, which would be denounced as scandalous nepotism on the part of a less democratic Government, was unblushingly proclaimed as the sole saving principle of appointing officials under Tammany. . Senator Roesch had used his influence or political pull in order to induce the Police Commissioner Martin to transfer one Sergeant Schryer to another precinct. Questioned by Mr. Goff before the Committee as to the grounds for this intervention on his part in the promotion of the police, he made the following answer :—

A. I will tell you; when a man comes to me and wants to get an appointment or transfer, or anything like that, I never stop to consider who is in the place he wants to go to, but my object is to get him there; necessarily, somebody has got to get out of the way, and here it happened to be Sergeant Schryer. . . .

If I can get a friend of mine on the force, or get him a promotion or position on the force, I always try to do it.

Q. And without inquiring, whether or not the man who is going to suffer by the removal, who was to suffer?

A. That was none of my business; it was sufficient for me to know the man they appointed to that place was competent and worthy of it, was a friend or party organisation.

By Senator O'Connor: A political leader or a man holding a high position here in the city, regardless entirely of the merits of the man whom he seeks to remove, when requested by one of his friends—political friends—to secure his position, that leader does everything in his power to bring about that result?

A. For his friend.

By Mr. Goff: Now, we have it that both parties do it?

A. Certainly.

Q. Only that the Republican leaders do not have a pull?

A. Well, Republican leaders are not in the majority; New York city is more a Democratic city.—Vol. ii., pp. 1,283–4.

Mr. Roesch confessed with frank brutality the principle upon which all the politicians acted in relation to the patronage to which they believed they were entitled. To make room for their friend, to secure a place on the city pay-rolls for a political comrade, was ample justification for insisting upon the removal of any officer who might happen to be in the way. Let no one imagine that this was an exceptional case. Commissioner Martin admitted frankly that from eighty-five to ninety per cent. of all the appointments which he had made when he was chairman of the Police Board were endorsed, in the first instance, by the district leader of Tammany Hall for the district in which the applicant resided.

Under such a system promotion by merit was practically non-existent. On this point Commissioner Martin was equally frank. He was questioned very closely as to whether he had ever promoted an officer simply for merit. After thinking a bit, he said he thought he could name one or two cases. Then said Mr. Goff:—

So far as your recollection goes, with the exception of two instances, so long as you have been police commissioner, you have not recommended for appointment, promotion or transfer a single man, except one, who was backed by political influence?

A. I do not recollect of any others. I think there are others of them.— Vol. vi., p. 448.

But if a district leader of the type of Roesch was able to nominate officers to the police, what becomes of the law by which all officers were to be appointed by open competition in an examination conducted according to Civil Service rules? The answer to this question is twofold. In the first case, a certain margin was allowed to the Commissioners. They were not bound always to appoint the candidates who came out on top. If they were tolerably near the top, it was held to be sufficient. The second answer is much more extraordinary. It was proved before the Committee that by connivance with a police clerk it was quite possible for candidates to be returned as having passed their examinations who had never been

CITY HALL PARK, BROADWAY.

in the examination-hall, and who never had written a single answer to any of the questions! This was done by personation. A competent person entered himself in the name of the candidate, filled in his examination papers, and passed in his name. By this means there was no difficulty in driving a coach and four through the Civil Service rules. The persons who obtained a position on the force by this means were known as the pupils of those who passed their examinations in their study, and were blackmailed accordingly.

John Schlie, examined by Mr. Moss, described how one of the personators went gathering in his fees :—

> I went down one day with Dave Brant to the police headquarters. We met an officer; the next thing I know I saw two 10-dollar bills slipped in his hand : he said, "That is good;" I said, "How did you get that?" He said, "That is one of my students;" I said, "What do you mean?" he said, "I passed for them people;" he said, "That is good;" so we went and had a drink and walked a couple of blocks; he commenced scratching his head, and he said, "I guess I have another student;" he goes down there and gets 15 dollars more."— Vol. ii., p. 1,474.

Of course, it was impossible thus to cheat the Civil Service examinations without the connivance of some of the officials, and this connivance had to be paid for at a price. Thus the natural process, promotion by pull, led up to promotion by purchase. The evidence on this point was overwhelming. It appeared that in a very great number of cases—so many indeed as practically to establish the rule—candidates who wished to be appointed to the force had to pay 300 dollars to a go-between, who negotiated the matter with the police authorities. How much money stuck to the fingers of the go-between, and how much was passed on to those in authority, does not clearly appear, but there is no doubt that the sum of 300 dollars was demanded, and paid, as a preliminary before the candidate could assume the uniform of policeman.

This practice once begun, it rapidly extended. As the initial cost was 300 dollars, each step in promotion cost a larger sum. To be made a sergeant cost 1,600 dols., while the price of a captaincy was 15,000 dollars! The police who had purchased their promotion in this fashion naturally felt that they had a vested interest in their posts. In the British army a similar system of purchase grew up, but it was one which was regulated by law and sanctioned by custom, whereas in the case of the New York police the whole system was under the ban of the law. The Lexow Committee remarked in their report upon this subject :—

> The policeman who pays for his appointment commences his career with the commission of a crime, and it is not strange that the demoralisation thus engendered should follow him in his further career. The captain who pays a fortune for his appointment finds himself compelled to recoup in order to return the moneys loaned to him by his friends by resorting to the practices which have been disclosed in the record before us. It seems incredible that men who are otherwise law-abiding and efficient should stoop to the perpetration of the monstrous and debasing practices revealed by this record, unless influenced by a system existing as the result of the

conditions hereinbefore alluded to. Nor is it strange that, in the contemplation of these practices by superior officers, inferior members of the force should have become demoralised, until the contamination has spread throughout the entire department.—Vol. i., pp. 49, 50.

It may be asked how was it that, while the evil was still in its infancy, and the force as a whole was not yet tainted through and through, its honest members did not expose the corruption which was being established in their midst? The answer is that the evil began at the top and spread downwards. Hence, it was impossible for the private constable to make a stand without exposing himself to a severe punishment for daring to be more virtuous than his superiors. The following extract from Gideon Granger's evidence will show how this pressure from above operated upon those below :—

A. I did not come to court because of the threats that were made by Mr. McClave and Mr. Nicoll, and I knew the power that a police commissioner has got, to use every bit of the department against anybody, to accomplish their own ends, and, in fact, he has boasted of that.
Q. Mr. McClave?
A. Yes, sir; endless power he has boasted of.
Q. What has he said in his boasting?
A. He said police commissioners had more power than the President of the United States had; repeatedly said that.—Vol. i., p. 1,142.

In considering the action of the police, we ought in justice to remember that they were living in a city the whole administration of which was infected by this money canker.

Mr. William M. Ivins, private secretary to Mayor Grace, by whom he was appointed City Chamberlain, estimated that in his time "assessments"—that is, money paid by candidates to "guarantee the result" of their elections—averaged £40,000 per annum. He wrote :—

"The existing system amounts to an almost complete exclusion from official public life of all men who are not enabled to pay, if not a sum equal to the entire salary of the office they seek, at least a very large percentage of it. The poor man, or the moderately well-to-do man, is thus at once cut off from all political ambition, because the only key to success is wealth or machine power. The ablest lawyer at our Bar could not secure a nomination for a judgeship unless he were able to pay an assessment of from 10,000 dollars to 20,000 dollars (£2,000 to £4,000); while a mere political lawyer, if he have the means of paying his assessment and stands well with the party leaders, can without great difficulty secure a nomination, and even an election, to an office for which he has no peculiar qualifications."

It would therefore be unjust to judge the police without making due allowance for the condition of their environment.

One of the most interesting witnesses who came before the Committee was Captain Creedon. It was in his case that the facts concerning the purchase of promotion were brought out most clearly.

Creedon was an Irishman, with a distinguished record and a high character. He joined the police force in 1864, and was made sergeant after fifteen years in the ranks. He remained sergeant for thirteen years, when he was promoted to a captaincy. Before he entered the police he had served with great gallantry in the Union army. He served with his regiment in no fewer than twenty-three engagements. He entered as a private, rose to be a sergeant, and his name was down for a first lieutenancy when he left the army. His record on the police for thirty years' service was extremely good, hardly anything being entered to his discredit. Such entries as were to be found related only to breaches of the technical rules of the force, and in no way implied any moral guilt.

Captain Creedon was put in the witness-box, and asked how much he had paid to be made a captain. He denied he had paid anything. As the facts were perfectly well known, the Committee was much startled by Captain Creedon's perjury. But after adjournment had given time for reflection, the worthy Captain came to the stand and explained that he had denied everything because he was an Irish revolutionist, and that he had such a dread and terror of being regarded as an informer, that he preferred to perjure himself rather than incur that disgrace. He was willing to sacrifice himself and risk going to gaol for perjury rather than in any way implicate any of his friends in the improper and illegal transactions in which he had been engaged.

It was carefully explained to him that he was not in Ireland, and that nothing he could possibly say on the stand could expose him to the imputation of being an informer. Having received this assurance, Captain Creedon opened his mouth and spoke.

The story he had to tell was very simple. Three times he had gone up for examination for a captaincy before the Civil Service Board. He had passed creditably every time, but notwithstanding this, he seemed no nearer to securing an appointment. His friends kept on telling him that he was simply wasting his time going up for examination after examination. He had much better stay at home unless he made up his mind to do one thing. He steadily turned a deaf ear to their representations, until at last four years after his first application, seeing that no one was promoted without bribing their superiors, he consented to fall in with the general practice. As soon as he did this, the way was made plain before him. Mr. Reppenhagen, the representative of the New York Democracy in his district, was indicated as the man to approach Police Commissioner Voorhis. Mr. Reppenhagen saw the Commissioner, and reported to the Captain that the place could be had for 12,000 dollars. Creedon had not at that time 12,000 dollars to invest in the purchase of a captaincy, but on talking it over with his friends, they agreed to make up a purse, so as to enable him to acquire the position which he coveted. While they were raising the money, Reppenhagen reappeared, and announced that a certain sergeant named Weigand had offered 12,000 dollars for the captaincy, and that if Creedon wished to secure it, it would cost him 15,000 dollars. Creedon's friends were men of mettle, and they agreed to raise the full sum. Creedon gave the subscribers notes acknowledging their subscriptions as a loan, which he afterwards repaid. The money was raised, and deposited in a bank. A Mr. Martin then appears on the scene as the confidential man of the Police Commissioner, smelling round after the 15,000 dollars as a rat noses round a cheese. For some reason or other there was a hitch in the appointment, and Creedon's friends and Reppenhagen passed some days in horrible suspense as to whether or not, in spite of the money being " put up," the appointment might go to Sergeant Weigand, while Martin was equally alarmed lest the 15,000 dollars should slip through his fingers.

The Record contains the following entries :—

John W. Reppenhagen examined by Mr. Goff: Do you remember saying to Martin further, that as long as Creedon's friends had put up more money than Weigand was reported to have put up, that it would play the devil in the organisation in that district if Creedon was not appointed ?
A. I might have said that.—Vol. v., p. 5,010.
Q. Don't you remember when you said that to Martin, that Martin said in word and in substance as follows: " I will go right down and I will see Voorhis, who is too damned hoggish about this thing." Do you remember those words ?
A. I don't remember the words.
Q. When he was in that condition of excitement, and when he struck the bar several times with his clenched fist, didn't he say those words, "That Voorhis wanted everything, almost the earth; he was hoggish, and he would go right down to New York and talk right up to him, and tell him he must do the right thing ? "
A. In substance he said that—yes.—Vol. v., p. 5,014-5.

Reppenhagen was evidently in a state of great uneasiness about securing the patronage for which the money had been raised by Creedon's friends. By way of enforcing his representations, he reminded Mr. Martin pointedly that the only chance he had of fingering any of the money was to see that Creedon's appointment went through, otherwise he would not make a cent. Thus pressed, Martin went off to see Voorhis. When he next saw Reppenhagen he assured him that it was all right, and that Voorhis had pledged his word to appoint Creedon the next Board Day. Even after this there was a hitch. It was reported that Weigand was going to be appointed after all. Reppenhagen then found it necessary to take hold of the affair with a strong hand.

"John," said he to Martin, "you had better go down yourself, and stay by the Commissioner until the appointment is made." Thus adjured, John went down, vowing that he would not leave the Commissioner until he had appointed Creedon. Then at last Creedon was duly appointed.

After this another hitch arose as to the difficulty of paying over the money. Then it was Mr. Martin's turn to be uneasy. He said he thought he had been bilked, and that the money would never be turned over. Creedon's friends, however, were men of affairs, and knew the kind of gentry they were dealing with. They had refused to hand over the money until the Captain was duly appointed. But now that Creedon was a captain at last they released the money. When Reppenhagen handed over the fifteen thousand dollars to Martin, that functionary handed him back five thousand dollars for himself. How much of the ten thousand dollars went to Commissioner Voorhis or how much of it stuck to Martin's fingers the record does not show. Here, however, was clear and unmistakable evidence as to the systematic manner in which promotions were arranged for and carried through between the Commissioners on the one hand and the candidates on the other.

There is a sequel to this story, which is so exquisitely absurd that it seems more like *opera bouffe* than a chapter from recent history. While the Committee was still engaged in ferreting out how the money was paid which secured Captain Creedon his captaincy, a startling rumour reached the Committee that the Police Board had suspended Captain Creedon from duty on account of his having obtained his captaincy by corrupt means. A bombshell falling in the court could hardly have created greater consternation.

To begin with, the Committee was a privileged body. All its proceedings were privileged. For any outside authority to act upon the testimony which it had taken without the direct authorisation of the Committee would be a contempt of the Senate. Further, the evidence given by Captain Creedon was tendered on the assurance of the Committee that no action could be taken upon it by any outside authority. They had promised him protection and immunity from persecution and prosecution, and for the Police Board to use his own admissions against him, which were privileged communications, the making of which secured him protection from any action based upon such admissions, was an indictable offence at the common law. But what made things worse was that, when the Captain left the stand, he had been addressed in eulogistic terms by counsel. This was not without cause. His candour in owning up and admitting everything had enabled the Committee to penetrate into the depths of the mystery of promotion by purchase. Mr. Goff had concluded his little speech by declaring that, " In view of everything ; in view of your splendid service to your country, and your good service on the Police Department, it is the unanimous expression of the Committee that the public interests would not be served were you to be disturbed in your present position as police captain " (p. 4,982).

Within an hour of this emphatic and public certificate of commendation, the Police Board met and suspended Captain Creedon from duty. Not a single captain or police officer of all the black regiment of clubbers and blackmailers, whose infamy had been proved before the Committee, and who had been indicted before the Grand Jury, had been removed from duty. Only when this honest officer had admitted the truth did they pounce down upon him and make an example. It is only fair to say that the Board was not aware when it suspended Creedon of the remarks that had been made by the counsel of the Committee as he left the witness stand. When they were rebuked they restored him to his post. But even with this allowance, the fact that the Commissioners should have only made one suspension, and that of a man who had confessed and repented of his wrong-doing, while they left all the other scoundrels unwhipped, was one of the most significant incidents in the whole course of the inquiry.

But after such an illustration of the methods of the Police Board, is it very surprising that until the Lexow Committee sat the authorities were utterly unable to discover any specific evidence as to the corruption into which the whole force had sunk?

CAPTAIN CREEDON.

CAPTAIN MAX F. SCHMITTBERGER.

CHAPTER IV.

THE following narrative of the career of a police captain of the City of New York is taken for the most part textually from the evidence tendered on oath by Captain Max F. Schmittberger, then in command of the Nineteenth Precinct. The police of New York were four thousand strong, divided for purposes of administration—and of plunder—into thirty-eight Precincts. Schmittberger was Captain of the Nineteenth. He gave his evidence almost at the close of the inquiry, when the essential facts were all proved up to the hilt by the evidence of a multitude of witnesses. Strange, almost incredible though it may appear that such an official should make so remarkable a confession, it is to be remembered that the facts were already known, and the only chance he had of saving himself was by turning Queen's evidence. When he took the stand under subpœna, the Chairman addressed him as follows :—

> We are here on the great State service to ascertain not only individual or specific cases of fraud or corruption, but the general system, and any witness who places himself on the stand here, no matter if he has himself been guilty of the violation of the law, if he places himself under the protection of this Committee, to serve it, to aid it in the ascertainment of those questions that the State Senate has imposed upon us, we shall consider it not only our obligation and our duty under the circumstances as Senators, individually and collectively, to do all that we can to see that that immunity which the law throws about you is safely guarded, but that he shall hereafter be protected from any of those results that that testimony might otherwise bring upon him.—Vol. v., pp. 5,311-2.

Thus adjured, Captain Schmittberger did on the 21st of December, 1894, unfold as remarkable a tale of infamy as ever was deposed on oath by an officer supposed to be responsible for the enforcement of the law. When he had closed his testimony, he said, " I have made a clean breast of everything I know." Mr. Goff, who was examining him, asked :—

> Is it not a fact that, owing to the developments before this Committee showing the corrupt and rotten condition of affairs in the Police Department, you feel justified in coming forward and stating all you know for the benefit of the people of this city and of this State? The Captain replied : " I feel that the pillars of the church are falling, and have fallen, and I feel in justice to my wife and my children that I should do this."—Vol. v., p. 5,382.

In compiling his autobiography I quote, wherever possible, textually from his own words, giving the reference in all important points to the page from which the quotation is taken.

From the Evidence of Captain Schmittberger.

I joined the police force when I was twenty-three years old, on January 28th, 1874. I had previously been a confectioner. I was married when I was admitted to the force. The Civil Service rules were not in operation then, neither had I to pay anything, for the practice of paying money for a position in the force had not commenced so early as 1874.

I was first assigned to the 19th Precinct, then the 29th, better known as the "Tenderloin." For three years I served as patrolman. In those years I discovered the importance of the political pull. The local politician, by his influence with the Police Commissioners and the chief police authorities, could generally make the sergeant his mouthpiece, and induce him to give preference and show favours to patrolmen who were friends and supporters of the politician. It was decidedly detrimental to discipline, but it was the principle throughout. A sergeant who was seeking promotion relied much more on his political pull than upon his record as a police officer.

Senator O'Connor interrupted to ask :—

Is there any recognition of merit at all in the department as now conducted, apart from money considerations or political influence?

Captain Schmittberger replied :—

To a very small extent. It is either politics or money.—Vol. v., p. 5,382.

The result has been that in the last ten years the police have deteriorated. "They are more politicians than anything else" (p. 5,316). The mischief of the political pull was increased when candidates had to pay for their appointment. They felt they had purchased their positions, and were sort of independent.

The system of purchase, which did not exist in 1874, gradually became so general that if men wanted to get into the department it was necessary to see one of the "go-betweens," a set of men of whom one Charley Grant, Commissioner McClave's secretary, was very well known. These purchase-officers made poor policemen, and they felt they had a right to more protection than the others. When they were rebuked for offences by their officers they would often defy them, basing their defiance upon the ground of political influence and power to protect them from the consequences of their act. This was especially the case with those men who belonged to political organisations, political clubs.

There was the Pequod Club, for instance, a Tammany club, presided over by Police Commissioner Sheehan, which I was pressed to join, owing to the pull it would give me if I belonged to the Commissioner's club. Several police captains belonged to it, and the tickets for the club outings, at five dollars apiece, were forced upon storekeepers and liquor dealers by the police. They also compelled all the liquor dealers in the precinct to buy Munzinger's mineral waters, for Munzinger was secretary of the Pequod.

In the Tenderloin there were a great number of disorderly houses, which were resorts for the criminals of the whole country, who came there to meet prostitutes. That precinct of New York was the centre for the criminal classes. No one interfered with them, it being perfectly well understood by the police that they were under protection, and they were under protection because they paid money for protection directly to the police captain of the precinct. This was necessary, because without his protection the officers would have closed the house. If they had interfered with a protected house, they would have been removed to another beat. Even if outrages occurred they knew they were not to interfere, as the houses had paid the captain for protection, and no interference was permitted. I heard once of an officer, of the name of Coleman, who was killed in a disorderly house, and there never has been an inquest or an arrest of any persons suspected of the crime, or any judicial inquiry whatever touching the cause of that officer's death (p. 5,328).

I was raised to the rank of a roundsman in April, 1880, because I found Commissioner Whelan's favourite dog, and I remained in the precinct till March 6th, 1883. During all that time the state of things was very bad. French women used to stand out in front of the railing in front of their houses and pull every man in as he went through the street. When citizens complained, they got no satisfaction. On one occasion a citizen who complained was ordered out quick. There was a friction—a very large one—between him and the Captain. It was even reported in the newspapers at the time that the Captain had threatened to club the complaining citizen out of the precinct.

During these early years I had a good record. I had arrested an important burglar, who had shot at me. I received honourable mention twice; I got the medal of honour from the department, and also the gold and diamond medal from the citizens of the precinct for raiding out the thieves there; I sent over 1,200 people to State prison whom I arrested myself in seven years as a detective (pp. 5,383–4).

So it came to pass that in March, 1883, I was made sergeant. I remained as sergeant for seven years, when I was made captain. I had passed at the head of the Civil Service list, and had some influential political men recommending me. I paid nothing for my appointment.

When I became captain I objected at first to the levying of black-mail. I was appointed to the steamboat squad, and I had not been there any time when detective Vail told me that he collected money from the ship companies and dock occupants or lessees, and that my predecessors always received half. I told him I did not care about a

F

thing of that kind. Vail replied, "You're a damned fool if you don't do it ; you might as well get it as well as the others " (p. 5,337). So I told him to go on and do the collecting. He brought me 190 dollars a month, and I gave him 20 per cent. commission.

At this time, in the police department when I became captain, it was an understood thing, and a matter of common understanding among the captains of the various precincts, that they were to take advantage of any opportunity that presented itself to make money out of their respective precincts (p. 5,337).

I did it—we all did it. It was the universal custom. I had a list of the men and the amounts they received. The wardman brought me half of it to the station-house. I then returned him 20 per cent. It was a poor district, and so I was not expected to send any of my share up to the inspector. He told me himself that he hardly expected anything, as there wasn't anything in the precinct. That was true, and therefore I tried to get another as soon as possible. At the end of thirteen months I was transferred to the Twenty-fifth Precinct. I brought with me my confidential collector, Gannon the detective.

When we settled down in the new station we discussed what collections could be made. We found there was nothing, only the policy shops, of which there were about ten, and the Liquor Dealers' Association. There was no difficulty about either.

The policy shops, all those in the precinct and in the upper part of the city, are under a man by the name of Parker, and if I remember right, Parker came to the station-house and saw me, and told me how many shops he had in the precinct ; that was all. He was introduced to Gannon, and Gannon did the rest (p. 5,341). He fixed the old price that had been understood for years long before my time—twenty dollars a month per shop). The Bohemian Liquor Dealers' Association were equally easy to manage. They paid eighty dollars per month.

My predecessor before he left had a talk with me about what should be given to the Inspector. He said he gave him usually from fifty to seventy-five dollars a month. He used to put the money in an envelope, and give it to an officer, who would give it to the sergeant in Inspector Williams's office. I did not take this course. I went directly to Williams and handed him fifty dollars in an envelope. He took it in his office at headquarters without a word (p. 5,343).

I was three months in that precinct. I gave the Inspector a hundred dollars one month. It was necessary to square him because it was in Williams's power to send men up there to raid those policy shops over my head ; I had to prevent him from doing that. Of course, upon consideration of receiving that sum of money every month he wouldn't do it (p. 5,344).

I had also to pay 20 per cent. to my collector. In return for this money I gave protection to the policy shops, and allowed all the liquor dealers to run open on Sunday. I was in the precinct three months, during which time I duly reported to headquarters concerning disorderly houses, gambling houses, &c., in my precinct, but I was very careful to say nothing of the ten policy shops which paid for protection. It was an understood thing the law was not to be enforced in the case of those who paid for protection.

After three months I was changed to the Twenty-seventh Precinct. In that precinct there were ten policy shops and three pool-rooms. I brought Gannon along with me. The policy shops paid as before, but the pool-rooms paid two hundred dollars a month. This was the old tariff paid to my predecessor, and continued, as a matter of course. Besides the usual 20 per cent. to the collector, I had to pay two hundred dollars per month to Inspector Williams. During the nine months I was in the precinct I handed him directly eighteen hundred dollars. He made no remark, and I would merely say, "Here is something for you." I gave him the same money I received from the pool-rooms. But in this precinct I drew no money from the saloons. There had been some trouble with my predecessor, and it had been arranged that instead of paying the police the liquor dealers were, in future, to pay direct to Tammany Hall (p. 5,349).

I was removed from this precinct because of the liquor dealers. Superintendent Byrnes ordered me to make direct *bonâ fide* excise arrests where liquor was sold on Sunday. I made over twenty *bonâ fide* arrests. The President of the Liquor Dealers threatened the officers to have them transferred if they made real arrests, and he was as good as his word. I also was transferred for the same cause. The liquor dealers pulled the leg of Commissioner Martin, who was a Tammany chief, and we were all transferred. The Superintendent whose orders I obeyed could not protect us. He simply told me to keep quiet, that the thing would right itself.

I was transferred to the Fifth Precinct, and there remained only nine weeks. There were only two pool-rooms, which yielded four hundred dollars a month, of which I gave fifty dollars to Inspector McAvoy. I put the money in a blank envelope and left it on his desk at headquarters.

From the Fifth I was removed to the Ninth, where I only remained a month. I made no collections there. But when I was removed to the Twenty-second I had better fortune : I remained there from May to December. Here I first struck disorderly houses. They paid—some ten, others twenty-five, and others again as much as fifty dollars a month. The policy shops paid the usual twenty-dollar tariff. There I collected from five hundred to six hundred dollars per month. The gambling houses were all strictly closed up.

It was while I was in this precinct that I came across Commissioner Martin, who was protecting personally a house of ill-fame kept by Mrs. Sadie West, 234, West Fifty-first Street. A body of citizens had made a formal complaint. I sent an officer down to make inquiries. Mrs. West said, "Commissioner Martin is a friend of mine, and don't you do anything until you hear from him." Next day Commissioner Martin, who was at the head of the Police Board, ordered me to send the officer back to apologise and say he had made a mistake. "Hold on, Commissioner," I said ; "this originates from a complaint of citizens." "Well," he replied, "I don't care ; I want you to do what you are told." So I had to send that officer back, and he had to apologise (p. 5,363).

That was not the only difficulty I had with the Commissioners. Commissioner Sheehan did his utmost to induce me to allow a gambling house to be opened in the precinct by one Maynard, a friend of his friend Mr. Proctor. The capital which Proctor was to bring to the gambling house was his pull with Sheehan—the Superintendent's orders were strict. So I told Sheehan, whom I met at the Pequod Club. Sheehan told me that there was a Spanish Club in that house, and I had no right to interfere with it; "if they played cards among themselves without playing gambling games that I had no right to interfere." But the Superintendent said he would break me if I allowed cards to be played there. When I told Sheehan this he exclaimed, "Well, if they cannot play, Daly can't play!" As a matter of fact Daly was not playing (p. 5,368).

During my stay in this precinct I used to take one hundred and fifty dollars a month in a closed envelope and give it to Inspector McAvoy at headquarters. One curious circumstance I remember about him. The Inspector is a very religious man, and he had conscientious scruples. He asked me one time if some of the money I gave him came from disorderly houses ; if it did he didn't want it, because he didn't want any money of that kind; I told him no, it hadn't; he drew the line there (p. 5,370).

Of course as he had been captain in the precinct himself he knew that it did come from disorderly houses, but he wished to be told it did not. I reported to headquarters that there were no disorderly houses in the precinct.

In December, 1893, I was made Captain of the Tenderloin, and have been there ever since. But the glory had departed owing to the raids made after Dr. Parkhurst's action. I did not get more than 200 dols. a month there. Georgiana Hastings's house of ill-fame I was warned not to touch, as if I did I should burn my fingers. I was informed that certain public officials were in the habit of visiting Georgiana Hastings's house—some officials that graced the Bench, and some officials that held commissions in the City of New York. One night, when a Bench warrant was sent there for execution, there were two officials, one a judge of a Court in this city—not of a Civil Court—in the house, and so that warrant was not executed (p. 5,374). She paid no protection money. She was protected inviolate by the law on account of the influential character of her customers.

Last year I made a political contribution of 100 dols. both to Mr. Martin and to Mr. Sheehan, who were both Police Commissioners and Tammany leaders in their respective districts. I had nothing much to do with handling money in payment for promotion. I acted as go-between in the case of Martens. I took 1,600 dols. of his to Captain Williams, and he got him made sergeant. Martens afterwards told me it would cost him 14,000 dols. to be made captain. On the whole, I have been four years a police captain. In that time I have been in command in six precincts, in every one of which I found the custom of collections regularly established from of old.

It would seem that the tariff was fixed : the commission to the collectors, and the proportion for the Inspector. The figures were as follows :—

Precinct.	Time of Stay.	Sources of Revenue per Month.	Collectors' Com. 20 per cent.	Inspectors' Share.	Total Net Receipts.
37	13 months.	Blackmail on ships, $190	495	—	1,975
25	3 "	{10 policy shops at $20, Liquor dealers, $80}	168	200	472
27	9 "	{10 policy shops at $20, 3 pool-rooms at $200}	1,450	1,800	3,950
5	2 "	2 pool-rooms at $200	160	150	5?0
9	7 "	{Policy shops, $20, Houses of ill-fame, $10, $25, and $50 = $500}	700	1,050	1,750
19	12 "	Houses of ill-fame, $200	480	—	1,920
46			3,453	3,200	10,657

The ransom extorted from the vicious and criminal classes of a single precinct by the police would seem to be an irreducible minimum of a thousand pounds per annum.

The Lexow Committee reported :—

The confessions summarised show the existence throughout the city of a system so well regulated and understood that upon the assignment of a new captain no conversation was necessary to instruct the precinct detectives or wardmen as to their line of conduct. Without a word they collected the illicit revenue, simplifying their duties as much as they could, either by granting monopolies of a special kind of crime to individuals, or imposing upon certain individuals who had knowledge of a particular class of crime the obligation of collecting for them, thus collecting monthly from all licensed vice and crime, and paying over their collections to the captain, deducting for their services twenty per cent. from the total. Or, rather, at first, paying the whole to the captain, and receiving twenty per cent. back from him, and thereafter making the deductions themselves. The captain, on his side, visited the inspector and paid over to him a substantial proportion of the amount collected.—Vol. i, [p. 45, 46.

THE CITIES WHERE DWELL THE STRANGERS WITHIN THE GATES.
View of Brooklyn Bridge from a roof in Broadway.

CHAPTER V.

"THE STRANGER WITHIN THE GATES."

"I WAS a stranger and ye took me in." The familiar passage needs to be interpreted in a different sense if it is to describe the treatment of the stranger by the police of New York. In the evidence of the men who practise the confidence trick, the curious fact came out that the police expressly abandoned strangers to the tender mercies of the Bunco Steerer and Green Goods dealer. These thieves were forbidden to practise their arts upon the resident population of New York. But the "guy" was fair game. The stranger from the country was abandoned to the plunderer, who indeed could count upon the active co-operation of the police—in return for a share of the loot. The stranger was taken in indeed. But not in the sense of the Bible text.

The treatment of Americans who were strangers in the sense of not possessing a fixed abode within the city limits, was bad. The treatment of the stranger from over sea, the foreign immigrant, was infinitely worse. It has been the glory of Columbia, as one of the poets declared, that her latchkey was never drawn in to the poorest and weakest of Adam's kin. The boast is no longer true. Restrictions upon the pauper immigrants from the Old World have been multiplied of late with ominous rapidity. But the foreigner had already established himself by the million within the Republic before the restrictive policy was begun.

In the Civil War, when the negroes were enrolled as soldiers in the Federal ranks, their presence was excused by the cynical remark that niggers were good enough food for powder. The foreign denizen of the New York slums is regarded in much the same light by the police of the city. Not as food for powder, but as material for plunder—squeezable folk who have no rights, save that of being allowed to swell the registration list of their oppressors. The police brigands levied blackmail boldly enough even when dealing with the cute Yankee and the smart New Yorker. But when they were let loose on the foreigner their rapacity knew no bounds. They had the power of a Turkish pasha in an Armenian province, and they used it almost as ruthlessly. They did not massacre, it is true. There was no occasion for such extreme measures. Even the Turk would not slaughter his taxable cattle if they were not guilty of indulging in aspirations after freedom. No dream of revolt ever crosses the mind of the poor wretches in the city slums to whom the policeman is the incarnate embodiment of the whole American Constitution. Back of him stands the whole Government—City, State, and Federal. What he says goes. So the foreigner—poor, ignorant, friendless—can only obey.

A witness before the Lexow Committee testified to the existence of a gang of criminals known as the Essex Market Gang, which had established a regular reign of terror in the neighbourhood. This witness, whose name was John Collins, said :—

> Last night business people spoke to me; I live nineteen years in that neighbourhood and begged of me to protect them; it is impossible to live there with the gang; they can convict any man they want to, and they can make free any man they want to, because they have got their witnesses; the leading man is Martin Engel, he owns property over 200,000 dollars, got from ruining people.
> Mr. Moss: You can see what power these men have when they have lots of men swearing to anything, and police officers to make arrests, and judges holding them and discharging them at will.
> Chairman Lexow: If the situation is such as indicated, how is it there has not been a revolt down there?
> Mr. Moss: The class of people are largely those who have come from foreign countries—countries where they have been used to that sort of thing, and supposed this Government just about the same, and, perhaps, a little worse than the place they came from; they are largely Polish Jews and Russian Jews and foreigners of that class, who have small understanding of the English language and no knowledge of our custom. Those are the class of people that are terrorised by this gang.—Vol. v., p. 4,896.

In small things as in great, the helplessness of the poor foreigner is conspicuous. Here is an instance of the way in which an Italian shoeblack was treated for daring to ask an officer, whose boots he had blacked on credit for a month until the little bill had run up to 75 cents, to settle up. The bootblack, whose name was Martini, stopped the officer, whose name was Gwinnen, as he was passing their stand, and said :—

> "Gwinnen, why don't you pay what you owe me?" so he said, "The next time you stop me on my way going across the street, I will smash you on the jaw, you dirty Italian son-of-a-bitch;" at the same time my partner got up and said, "Well, why don't you pay us?" At the same time he rushed up against my partner like a cyclone and struck him right and left with his hand; and he had him all bleeding. I tried to step in between the two of them to separate them, and this officer Looney came along from behind me and he grabbed me by the back of the neck and punched me between the eyes, and he said, "Let us pull the guinea in."
> Q. Whom did he mean by the guinea?
> A. Well, he meant us two; so we went to the station-house, and they made a charge of disorderly conduct; they claimed that we were fighting each other, me and my partner.
> Q. And both of you were cut and bleeding at this time?
> A. Yes, sir.
> Q. Were the officers in uniform?
> A. All in uniform. When they went into the station-house they told their story, and when I went to tell my story, they wouldn't listen. They heard the policeman's story, but would not let us tell ours at all. Another officer took me to the court, and Gwinnen took my partner along; when we got to the other side of the station-house, Sixty-seventh and Lexington Avenue, this Gwinnen took off his belt, doubled it in two, and struck my partner in the face two or three times.

Q. You were then under arrest?
A. Yes, sir.
Q. And on your way to the police-court?
A. Yes, sir; I appealed to the officer that had me, and I said, "Officer, tell him
that he should not hit him any more;" so after he turned around my partner was a
sight.—Vol. iv., pp. 3576-7.

The sequel of this episode is interesting. The judge, apparently
thinking the poor wretches who were brought before him all bloody
had had enough of it, dismissed the case. Strange to say, the victims
in this case endeavoured to obtain redress. They appealed to the
Superintendent, who promised that the officers should be punished.
Nothing was done. They then made another effort, raised £5 to
pay a lawyer, and began an action for assault. One officer was held
for the Grand Jury. But it was postponed again and again. The
lawyer insisted on more money, which was not forthcoming, and so
the Italians lost their £5, had their beating, and do not even appear
to have recovered their 75 cents.

The lesson thus taught, not to throw good money after bad, and
the impossibility of getting justice of a policeman, has been learned
so well that one marvels at the temerity of the brave bootblacks,
whose courage deserved a better fate.

The Lexow Committee in their Report put it on record as their
deliberate conclusion that—

The poor ignorant foreigner residing on the great east side of the city has been
especially subjected to a brutal and infamous rule by the police, in conjunction
with the administration of the local inferior criminal courts, so that it is beyond a
doubt that innocent people who have refused to yield to criminal extortion, have
been clubbed and harassed and confined in gaol, and the extremes of oppression
have been applied to them in the separation of parent and child, the blasting of
reputation and consignment of innocent persons to a convict's cell.—Vol. i.

The case which appears to have produced the deepest impression
for wanton wickedness and ingenious devilry on the minds of the
Commissioners was the attempt to plunder an unfortunate widow
woman of the name of Urchittel. Mrs. Urchittel was a Russian
Jewess, who emigrated to the United States in 1891. Her husband
had died at Hamburg, from which city she sailed for New York,
where she arrived, accompanied by her four children, the eldest of
whom was fourteen, the youngest three. But it is best to print in
her own simple language the statement of her wrongs:—

In 1891 I came to New York, a widow with four children; my husband died in
Hamburg. Being without means, I applied to the Hebrew charities on Eighth
Street for help, and they were kind enough to support me for starting a boarding-
house in 166 Division Street, and gave me for furniture and other necessaries, and,
besides 60 dollars, sent immigrants to my boarding-house. My business was
increasing daily, having thirty to thirty-five persons every week, and in eight months
I saved 600 dollars. I worked hard indeed, but I did it gladly, knowing that this
will enable me to support my children, the orphans.

The immigration having been stopped, I had to give up boarding business, and
applying again to the Charities, they supported me again, giving me 150 dollars, and
sent me to Brownsville, where I bought a restaurant and made a nice living, but

having the misfortune to lose one of my beloved children, I left Brownsville, after staying there but a little time, and came back to New York.

I bought a cigar store in 33, Pitt Street, corner of Broome, for 175 dollars, and gave the landlord 40 dollars security, and supplied more goods for 50 dollars. On the second day of my taking possession of the store a man came in and bought a package of chew tobacco for five cents. A couple of days later the same man came in, asking me for a package of chew tobacco, to trust him, which I refused, excusing myself being recently the owner of that store; I don't know anybody of that surrounding. I cannot do it. He took then out a dollar of his pocket and gave it to me for changing, and having no small change, only pennies, which he wouldn't take, I sent my one-year aged daughter to get other coin for the dollar, and handing same to the man I felt a tickling in my hand caused by the quarter of the dollar in the hand of the man, and I said good-bye to him.

On the evening of that day another man came in the store, and told me that the man who was before asking for chew tobacco without money is a detective, and that he has a warrant to arrest me, and I can avoid the trouble by giving the detective 50 dollars, and refusing to do it, I will be locked up, and my children taken away from me till the twenty-first year. Not knowing to have done anything wrong, I laughed at the man, and told him that I wouldn't give a cent to anybody, and if that man should come in again, I will chase him out with a broom.

The other night, at 11 o'clock, the children being asleep already, the same man who asked me to trust him the chew tobacco, and after which I learned he was a detective, named Hussey, came in with another man who took away my cousin that came to see me in that night, and the detective remained with me alone in the store: he told me then that he knows that I keep a disorderly house and saved 600 dollars of that dishonest business. If I wanted to escape being arrested, he wanted 50 dollars. I opposed to his assertion, and protested against his wanting money of me, saying that I ever made a living by honest business, but he wouldn't listen to me, and in spite of my protesting and the crying of my children, I was forced to leave my store and follow him.

As we were two blocks away we met Mr. Hochstein, and crying, I told him all my trouble, and how I don't know anything about the false accusations. It was of no avail: Mr. Hochstein told me that the detective wants 75 dollars, but he will try to settle it with 50 dollars, but without any money nothing can be done for me, and gave me also his advice, to pay 10 dollars monthly to the detective I wouldn't be troubled at all, and that I should resume my business unhindered. I repeated again that I don't know anything about dishonest business, but it was no use talking more.

I was dragged from corner to corner till three o'clock in the morning, insisting that I had money with me, 600 dollars I kept it in my stockings. Weary and tired out, I sat down at the corner of Essex and Rivington Streets at a dry goods store and took off my stockings, showing that I had no money in them. "If you don't want to give the money," said the detective to me, "I can't help it, you must follow me to the station-house." Being convinced that it is impossible that I should escape without giving money, I took out 25 dollars of my pocket, the only money I had, and handed them over to the detective standing by a window, which money was parted between Mr. Hochstein and himself, he taking 13 dollars and Hochstein 12 dollars.

They went with me to Essex Street, and, sending me in through a gate in the house, where I was kept about two minutes, they sent me home after with the warning to be prepared with fifty dollars. At seven o'clock in the morning the detective, Hussey, came to my store asking for the money. I cried again and begged him to let me go, that I am not able to give him any more money; but he didn't want to hear me any more, and I had to follow him. By the signal of a whistle a man came near me, and the detective gave me over to him with the remark not to let me go till I have the fifty dollars. The name of that man is Mr. Meyer. I went with him to Mr. Lefkovitz, manufacturer of syrups, 154, Delancy Street, and to Mr. Frank ———— for selling the store even for the fifty dollars, but they didn't want to buy it, seeing the man after me and fearing trouble. After trying in vain to sell the store the detective said to Mr. Meyer, "That bad woman don't want to give the money. Take her to the court," and I had to stay at the trial.

Two bad, disreputed boys were engaged by the detective, Hussey, for witness. The one said that he gave me fifty cents for gratifying him, and the other said that he would give me forty cents, and I did not agree asking fifty, and thus I

MRS. URCHITTEL.

was detained in default of five hundred dollars bail. Having been sitting in the court the detective, Hussey, came in to me on the same day at four o'clock P.M., and told me that my children are already taken away from my house, and if I can give him the fifty dollars he can help me even now.

Hearing the distress of my poor children, I cried loudly, and a lady took me to a dark room, where I was locked up. Unable to procure bail, I was imprisoned for three days, and sent after to the Tombs, where I had to stand trial.

There were about fifty persons to witness that I had always made an honest living, but they were not asked at all, and being wholly unable to understand the English language, I couldn't defend myself. The lawyer, who was sent from the Hebrew Charities, came too late, and had to give only the certificate of the society, testifying that I was supported by them, and led a decent living. It came too late, and I could not talk any more.

I was fined fifty dollars. My brother sold my store for sixty-five dollars, and paid the fine.

I ran then crazy for my children, for I didn't know where they were. Meeting the detective he told me that they are in the hands of a society in Twenty-third Street. I ran there, but no one knew of my children. Finally, after five weeks, I received a postcard of my child, that the children are at One Hundred and Fifty-first Street and Eleventh Avenue, and when I got there, and begged to give me back my children, none would hear me.

Grieved at the depths of my heart, seeing me bereaved of my dear children, I fell sick, and was laying six months in the Sixty-sixth Street hospital, and had to undergo a great operation by Professor Mundy. After I left the hospital, I had the good chance to find a place in 558, Broadway, where I fixed up a stand by which I am enabled to make a nice living, to support and educate my children. I went again to Twenty-third Street, begging to release my children, and that was denied again. My heart craves to have my children with me.

I have nothing else in the world only them. I want to live, and to die for them. I lay my supplication before you, honourable sir, father of family, whose heart beats for your children, and feels what children are to a faithful mother. Help me to get my children. Let me be mother to them. Grant me my holy wish, and I will always pray for your happiness, and will never forget your kind and benevolent act towards me. Your very humble and faithful servant, (Signed) CAELA URCHITTEL.—Vol. iii., pp. 2,961–4.

The piteous plea of this bereaved mother produced a great effect upon the mind of the Committee. The children had been taken away by the Society for the Prevention of Cruelty to Children, under an Act which had been passed with the best intentions in the world, but which, as the case of Mrs. Urchittel showed, was only too facile an instrument in the hands of the corrupt police. It will be noticed that in her evidence she said that "two bad, disreputed boys" were engaged to swear away her character. The allusion was a reminder of the fact that one of the worst developments of the system under which the police became bandits was the organisation of a band of professional perjurers, who would swear anything the police cared to tell them. Mrs. Urchittel's character was irreproachable, yet on the evidence of these scoundrels she was convicted of keeping a house of prostitution. The man Hochstein, who divided the plunder with the detective, was a saloon-keeper, and a prominent politician in the district, who figures very conspicuously in the evidence of other witnesses before the Committee. No sooner had Mrs. Urchittel given her evidence than two men came to her and warned her that if she were to commence with Mr. Hochstein she would get into trouble, and be sent to prison for two years.

The efforts of the Commissioners to secure the return of the children to their distracted mother were for a time thwarted by the provisions of the law which is so hidebound and imperative in its terms that no judge would venture to interfere with the commitment of the police magistrate. Mr. Goff called attention to the fact that "the condition of the law in New York City is that, upon the *ipse dixit* of one man, children can be taken from their protectors, fathers and mothers, and secreted away in some institution, and there is no power invested in any court or in any official to compel him to reveal where the children are or to restore them." The sensation occasioned by this case was so great that the Commission were able towards the close of their sittings to announce the gratifying intelligence that they had at last succeeded in securing the release of the children, who were then, after more than eighteen months, handed over to their mother. The opinion of the Commissioners on the case was embodied in the following terms, which I quote from their Report :—

Oppression of the lowly and unfortunate, the coinage of money out of the miseries of life, is one of the noteworthy abuses into which the department has fallen . . .

The evidence of many witnesses shows the existence of a wonderful conspiracy in the neighbourhood of Essex Market police-court, headed by politicians, including criminals, professional bondsmen, professional thieves, police, and those who lay plots against the unwary, and lead them into habits of law-breaking, or surround them with a network of false evidence, and then demand money as the price of salvation, and if they do not receive it, drag their victims into court and prison, and often to a convict's cell. . . .

In another case, Mrs. Urchittel, a humble Russian Jewess, ignorant of our tongue, an honest and impoverished widow with three small children, whom she was striving to support, was falsely accused by a precinct detective of keeping a disorderly house in the back room of her little store where she and her little children slept, and he demanded a sum of money which she could not pay, whereupon he took her from her home, dragged her through the streets until three o'clock in the morning, pulled down and searched her stockings for money, until she in despair produced all that she had saved for her month's rent. This being insufficient, he gave her a short time to obtain the balance, and she tried to sell her store, but failed, and then he arrested her again, lodged a false and infamous charge against her, fastened it upon her by the testimony of miserable tools whom he had employed for the purpose, and secured her conviction. Her children passed into the hands of the Society for the Prevention of Cruelty to Children. Her fine was paid by selling her store, and she was released, only to fall into a severe and lingering illness. When she recovered her home was gone, her children were gone, and she was penniless.

Many cases of similar oppression are found on the record.—Vol. i., pp. 43, 44.

Is it any wonder that the Lexow Committee reported under the head of "Brutality," as it existed in the police force :—

This condition has grown to such an extent that even in the eyes of our foreign-born residents our institutions have been degraded, and those who have fled from oppression abroad have come here to be doubly oppressed in a professedly free and liberal country.—Vol. i., p. 30.

This is how " Liberty enlightens the world " from her eyrie in the Island of Manhattan.

AUGUSTINE E. COSTELLO.

CHAPTER VI.

SAID Mr. Goff at one of the sittings of the Lexow Committee :—

We have, Mr. Chairman, called attention heretofore to what may be justly termed "slaughter-houses," known as police-stations, where prisoners in custody of the officers of the law, and under the law's protection, have been brutally kicked and maltreated, almost within view of the judge presiding in the Court.— Vol. iv., p. 3,598.

Slaughter-houses is not a bad term. The cases in which witnesses swore to violent assault on prisoners in the cells by policemen were numerous. That which immediately provoked this observation was a typical one of its kind.

One Frank Prince, who had been keeping a disorderly house in Ninety-eighth Street, had the temerity to refuse to pay the 100 dollars a month blackmail which had been demanded by the police. His house was raided, and he was taken to the station-house. He was accused before the Captain of having said that he would make him close the other disorderly house in the district, which presumably was under the Captain's protection. Now not to pay blackmail yourself was bad enough; but it was far worse to threaten to dry up the contributory sources of police revenue. The poor wretch denied that he had ever uttered such a threat. "Take him into the cell and attend to him!" said the Captain Prince was marched out by the wardman, who was also blackmail collector for the precinct. When they reached the cell, the turnkey and the wardman kicked him through the doorway, and then following him in fell to beating him about the head with a policeman's billy. They kicked him violently in the abdomen, inflicting permanent injuries, and declared he deserved to have his brains knocked out. Such was the "attendance" prisoners received in the police cell to teach them the heinousness of refusing to pay ransom to the banditti of New York. This case by no means stood alone.

The most remarkable case of police brutality to prisoners under arrest, and which is one the best attested in the collection, is that of the Irish revolutionist, Mr. Augustine E. Costello.

The story of Mr. Costello was wrung from him very reluctantly. He was subpœnaed on behalf of the State, and confronted with the

alternative of being committed for contempt of Court or of being
committed for perjury. Mr. Costello, being a revolutionary Irishman,
had a morbid horror of doing anything which could in any way
lead any one to accuse him, no matter how falsely, of being an
informer. The prejudice against the witness-box often appears to be
much stronger on the part of Irish Nationalists than the prejudice
against the dock. Mr. Augustine E. Costello is an honourable man
of the highest character and the purest enthusiasm. He was one of
those Irishmen who, loving their country not wisely but too well,
crossed the Atlantic for the purpose of righting the wrongs of
Ireland. His zeal brought him into collision with the Coercionist
Government that was then supreme. He was convicted and sentenced
to twelve years' penal servitude. He was a political offender, the
American Government intervened on his behalf, and the treaty
known as the Warren and Costello Treaty was negotiated, which led
to his liberation before his sentence had expired. During his incar-
ceration in this country he was confined in several prisons, both in
England and Ireland, and thus had a fair opportunity of forming a
first-hand estimate of the interior of British gaols and the severity of
our prison discipline. He was treated, he reported, with a great deal
of rigour, but he was never punished without warrant of law, and was
never pounded or assaulted. It is characteristic of the Irish political
convict that, when Mr. Costello was asked about this before the Lexow
Committee, he carefully inquired whether his answers would more
or less justify "the people on the other side," and it was only on
being assured that it would do no such thing that he reluctantly
admitted that he had never experienced as a convict in British gaols
anything like the brutality with which he had been treated by the
New York police.

Mr. Costello's story, in brief, is this. About ten or a dozen years
ago he was on the staff of the *New York Herald.* By his commission
he was attached to the police headquarters, in which capacity he was
necessarily brought into the closest relations with captains and
inspectors. He discharged his duties with satisfaction to his
employers, and without any complaint on the part of the police.
Two lawyers of good standing, who were called as witnesses, testified
that they had known him for years as a thoroughly honourable man,
a newspaper man of talent and ability; one whose word they would
take as soon as that of the President of the United States. Every
one who knew him spoke in the highest terms of his veracity and
scrupulous regard for accuracy.

Mr. Costello in 1885 conceived the idea of publishing a book
about the police under the title of "Our Police Protectors." His
idea was to hand over 80 per cent. of the profits of the work to the
Police Pension Fund, retaining 20 per cent. as compensation for his
work. The book at first was very successful. The police sold it

FOURTEENTH STREET, NEW YORK.

G

for the benefit of the Pension Fund, and the profits were duly paid over by him to the fund in question. But just as the book was beginning to boom, the Superintendent of Police brought out a book of his own, entitled "The Great Criminals of New York." No sooner had it appeared than the police withdrew all their support from Mr. Costello's book, declared they had nothing to do with it officially, and left him stranded with the unsold copies on his hands. Mr. Costello appears to have regarded this as natural under the circumstances. He entered no complaint of the way in which he had been treated over "Our Police Protectors" by the department, for whose Pension Fund the book was earning money, but at once set himself with a good heart to bring out another book of a similar character about the Fire Department.

Mr. Croker, who was then a Fire Commissioner, and his two colleagues gave Mr. Costello a letter certifying that the Fire Department had consented to the publication of his history in consideration of his undertaking to pay into the Fire Relief Fund a certain portion of the proceeds of the sale of the book, for the publication of which Mr. Costello had been given access to the records of the department. Armed with this letter, Mr. Costello set to work. He printed 2,500 copies of the book, with 900 illustrations. The book itself was bulky, containing as many as 1,100 pages, and costing nearly £5,000 to produce, an expenditure which he had incurred entirely on reliance upon the support of the Fire Department promised him in the letter written by Mr. Croker and his fellow commissioners. But again an adverse fate befell the unfortunate Costello. Just as the book was beginning to boom, another man named Craig, who had a pull at the Fire headquarters, got out a very cheap book, called the "Old Fire Laddies," which he ran in opposition to Mr. Costello's expensive work. The Fire officials backed the man with a pull against Mr. Costello, who had no pull. Friction arose, and the Fire Department withdrew the official letter on the strength of which Mr. Costello had gone into the work.

But the power of the pull was to make itself felt in a still more painful fashion. Mr. Costello had several agents canvassing for orders for the book, and for advertisements. He did his best to obtain from those agents the Croker letter, and succeeded in doing so in all but two or three cases. As he had already spent his money, the only thing he could do was to continue to push his book. His agents, no doubt, when canvassing made as much capital as they could out of the credentials which Mr. Costello had originally received from the Fire Department. This was resented, and it seems to have been decided to "down" Costello. The method adopted was characteristic. The Fire Commissioners and the Police were two branches of Tammany administration. When Mr. Costello's canvassers were going about their business, they were subjected to arrest. He had as many as

half-a-dozen of his canvassers arrested at various times. They were
seized by the police on one pretext and another, locked up all night
in the police cell, and then liberated the next morning, without any
charge being made against them. The application of this system of
arbitrary arrest effected its purpose. The terrorised canvassers
refused to seek orders any longer for Mr. Costello's book. One or
two, however, still persevered. In November, 1888, two of them,
who had retained the original certificate, were arrested in the First
Precinct at the instance of Captain Murray of the Fire Department,
who said that they were professing to be connected with the Fire
Department, with which they had nothing to do.

Mr. Costello, accompanied by his book-keeper, Mr. Stanley, went
down to the police-station to endeavour to bail his canvassers out.
Mr. Costello had no fear for himself, as he believed Captain
McLaughlin was his friend—a friendship based upon the Captain's
belief that Mr. Costello's influence had counted for something in
securing his captaincy. Mr. Costello complained of the repeated
arrests, and declared that he would not let it occur again if he could
help it. Captain McLaughlin showed him the books that had been
taken from the imprisoned canvassers, in one of which there was a
loose paper containing the memorandum of sales made on that day,
and a copy of the Croker letter. Mr. Costello at once took possession
of the letter, which he had been trying to call in for some time. He
showed it to the Captain, and then put it in his pocket, telling the
Captain that if it was wanted, he would produce it in court the next-
day. The Captain made no objection, and they parted, apparently on
friendly terms.

Mr. Costello had supper, and then went off to the police-head-
quarters at seven o'clock, in order to secure an order for the release
of his canvassers. Suspecting nothing, he walked straight into the
office, where he found himself confronted by Inspector Williams.
This Inspector was famous for two things : he had the repute of being
the champion clubber of the whole force, and it was he also who
first gave the *soubriquet* of "Tenderloin" to the worst precinct in
New York. The origin of this phrase was said to be a remark made
by Inspector Williams on his removal from the Fourth to the
Twenty-ninth Precinct. Williams, who was then captain, had said,
"I have been living on rump-steak in the Fourth Precinct; I shall
have some tender loin now." Mr. Costello picked up this phrase,
applied it to the Twenty-ninth Precinct, coupling it with Williams's
name. Williams never forgave Costello for this, and on one occasion
had clubbed him in Madison Square.

When Costello saw the Inspector, he felt there was a storm brewing,
for Williams was in one of his usual domineering moods. The
moment Mr. Costello entered, the Inspector accused him of stealing a
document out of Captain McLaughlin's office, and detained him for

five hours. It was in vain that Mr. Costello explained that the document which he had sent home by his book-keeper, and placed in his safe, was his property, and would be produced in court when it was wanted. During the five hours that he stayed there he noticed what he described as "very funny work" going on. The Inspector was telephoning here and there; detectives were coming in and whispering, as if receiving secret orders; and at last, at midnight, two detectives came in and whispered a message to the Inspector. Thereupon Williams turned to Costello, ordered him to accompany the detectives, and consider himself under arrest. A foreboding of coming trouble crossed Costello's mind. He asked his book-keeper to accompany him, as he felt that there was something going to happen, and he wanted him to be an eye-witness. This, however, did not suit his custodians. On their way down to the police-station one of the detectives said to Stanley, "You get away! We do not want you at all." Costello said, "Well, if you have to go, you might look up Judge Duffy. I may want his services as well as these men." Stanley left, and Costello, with the two detectives, made his way to the police-station.

It was getting on to one o'clock in the morning. Costello was carrying an umbrella, as it was raining, when they came in front of the station-house. The door was wide open, and the light streamed on to the sidewalk. Just as he was placing his foot on the step he saw two men come towards him. The bright light cast a shadow, and in that shadow he saw Captain McLaughlin raise his fist and deal a savage blow at his face. He instinctively drew back his head, and the Captain's brass-knuckled fist struck him on the cheek-bone, knocking him down into the gutter. The detectives stood by, indifferent spectators of the scene. As Costello lay half-stunned and bleeding in the muddy gutter, Captain McLaughlin attempted to kick him several times in his face. Fortunately, his victim had retained hold of his umbrella, and with its aid was able to keep the Captain's heavy boots from kicking him into insensibility.

He struggled to his feet, when Captain McLaughlin went for him again. What followed is best told by the transcript from the evidence before the Lexow Committee:—

Augustine E. Costello examined by Mr. Moss. I said to Captain McLaughlin:—"Now, hold on; I am a prisoner here; this is a cowardly act on your part; if I have done anything to offend the laws of the State there is another way of punishing me; this is not right." You could hardly recognise me as a human being at this time; I was covered with blood, mud, and dirt, and had rolled over and over again in trying to escape the kicks that were rained at me. I hurried myself as fast as I could into the station-house, thinking that would protect me; all this time I was being assaulted, the two detectives stood over me.

Q. What were their names?

A. I cannot recall it just now, but I can get their names later on; two wardmen of that precinct; there was a second man with the man who assaulted me; that man, I may tell you, was Captain McLaughlin.

Q. What do you mean; on the sidewalk?

A. On the sidewalk; the man with him, standing right off the kerbstone on the street; and when I got into the station-house, I asked to be allowed to wash the blood off myself, and I was feeling more like a wild beast than a human being.

By Mr. Moss :—Tell us what he did?

A. McLaughlin put himself in all sorts of attitudes and tried to strike me, and I dodged the blows.

Q. Was that in the general room of the station-house?

A. Yes. Captain Murray, of the Fire Department, was present at the time; he made the complaint against the two men.

Q. You were a prisoner, and standing in the middle of the station-house floor while McLaughlin was raining blows at you?

A. Yes. "Now," I said to him, "McLaughlin, look here, I never felt myself placed in the position that I do to-night; no man has ever done to me what you did to-night, and I advise you to let up. Standing here, if I am assaulted again, you or I will have to die; one man of two will be taken out of this station-house dead, and so, stop." At this time I had my fighting blood up, and had recovered from the collapse I was thrown into. I said, "You may think me not protected here; but I have a good strong arm, and if you assault me again, as sure as there is a God in Heaven, I will never take my hands from your throat until you kill me or I kill you." He kept on blustering, but never struck me again.

Q. What was the nature of the punishment?

A. He had brass-knuckled me.—(Vol. iv., p. 4,527).

Q. You say he desisted at that moment?

A. He desisted at that moment when I said he or I would have to die if he did not stop. I was then allowed to go into his private room and wash some of the mud and gutter off my face and hands. I could not wash the blood off, because that was coming down in torrents; and when I was going downstairs, somebody kicked me or punched me severely in the back, and I feel the effects of it yet at times, and I suppose I always will. Then I was thrown into a cell bleeding, and by this time a second collapse had come over me, and I must have fainted in the cell.

Q. Did McLaughlin go into the cell?

A. No; he came down after me, after I was locked up, and made it clear he gloried in the fact that I was in that condition. So, fearing that some one would open the cell door during the night, when I would be in a faint—because I felt very weak from the loss of blood—I took out my note-book and wrote in it, "If I am found dead here to-morrow, I want it known I am murdered by Captain McLaughlin and his crowd." I hid that in my stocking, that piece of bloody paper. I kept it for a long time, and I tried to find it to-day, but could not put my hands on it, and am very sorry I cannot put my hands on it.

Q. Were you persecuted any more that night?

A. I was persecuted in a way that they would not give me any water.

Q. Did you call for water?

A. Yes, and it was denied me; everything was denied me. From loss of blood and all that I became unconscious; and about five o'clock in the morning, when I could get a little rest, I was routed out from my bed and told to get ready; then I asked the privilege of getting something to brush off my clothes and my shoes, and after paying a little for it, I did get it; and I was taken out by these two same men that had arrested me. Now, before I proceed any further, will you let me go back a little?

Q. Yes.

A. All the five hours I was kept a prisoner at police headquarters with Inspector Williams standing over me, I might say, with drawn baton, two detectives were up at my house, which shows this was a put-up job and conspiracy to degrade me; from quarter after seven or half-past seven, from the time this happened two detectives were up at my house bullying my wife and scaring her to death, and all this time they knew I was down in the hands of Inspector Williams. Inspector Williams told me this with great glee as I was about to be taken away. I said, "You must have no heart." I said, "I don't mind the persecution I have been subjected to, but I don't wish to have that inflicted on my wife and children; they will go crazy. I beg you to telephone the station-house, and have those brutes taken out of my house;" and he did, but they were there up to midnight, and all these five hours in my house bullying my wife and sending my children into hysterics.

Q. You went to Court the next morning, did you ? "
A. Yes, sir. I begged then of the men that they would allow me to buy a pair
of glasses more or less to conceal my lacerated face. I was in a terrible state.
They refused until I got very near the place and I said, " I will make trouble for
somebody if I go in this condition ; " and they let me buy a large pair of blue
goggles, and I sent for Counsellor Charles T. Duffy, who is at present justice of the
peace in Long Island City, and I told him what happened to me, and he said,
" These people are too much for me ; I will go and get somebody to assist you.
What do you think of Mr. Hummel ? " I said, " Do what you like about it ; have
Mr. Hummel." I paid him a retainer fee, and he said, " These are infernal brutes,
and we ought to break them." I said, " I am prepared to do what you tell me."
When the case was brought up it was laughed out of Court ; there was no case for
me or my men. They first had me to get bondsmen before the thing was tried ;
but there was no case tried—there was no case to try. Hummel said, " What have
you against this man ; he has not destroyed any documents."—Vol. iv., p. 4,520.

Mr. Costello was taken home, and laid up in bed for five days.
His face had to be sewn up. The doctor, who, by-the-bye, was
Mr. Croker's brother-in-law, certified that the injury to the face
had been produced by brass knuckles, the cut being too severe
to have been produced by the simple fist. He was threatened with
erysipelas, but, fortunately, recovered.

I should have mentioned· that while Mr. Costello was being
taken into the station-house all bloody and muddy, his book-keeper
came to obtain access to him. Captain McLaughlin stopped him,
pulled open his overcoat, and searched his pockets.

"What is this for ? " cried Stanley. The Captain made no
answer, but continued the search. " What does this mean ? " angrily
asked Stanley.

" You know d—— well what it means," was the reply.

" I do not understand you," said Stanley. " What is it for ? "

" Open the door," said the Captain to an orderly, " open the door."
The orderly opened the door. " Now," said the Captain, " get the
Hell out of here ! " and the book-keeper was promptly forced right
out, and left on the sidewalk to reflect upon the irony of events
which had subjected the author of " Our Police Protectors " to such
treatment.

It is a very pretty story, and one which naturally provokes the
inquiry as to how such things could be practised with impunity.
Mr. Costello himself said that if there had not been so much
Celtic blood in his veins there would have been several funerals in
New York, for he was not only a Celtic Irishman but a Catholic
Irishman, and murder was repugnant both to his religion and to his
nature. Other redress than that which could be gained by your own
right hand it was impossible to obtain, for it was this witness who
made the famous remark previously quoted. Senator O'Connor
asked him, " Did you ever take any proceedings against these men ? "
and the witness replied, " I never did, sir. It is no use going to law
with the devil and court and hell ! "

He probably thought himself lucky that he had escaped without
permanent disfigurement. One Thomas J. Standant was less fortu-

nate. A policeman named Schillinberger, of the Eleventh Precinct, who was a very athletic man, struck Standant a tremendous blow with his fist, which was not, as in McLaughlin's case, provided with brass knuckles. Standant's nose was smashed, the blood poured from his eyes and ears, and he was carried to the hospital, where he had to submit to various operations before he recovered his eyesight and hearing. He was badly disfigured for life. When he brought an action against the policeman for assault, the officer was defended by the Corporation Counsel. Schillinberger, although indicted by the Grand Jury, was never suspended for a moment, but continued on duty during the whole of the sittings of the Commission.

In another case a witness was produced who could hardly speak intelligibly. On Thanksgiving morning he had bought a couple of crabs from an oyster stand, the owner of which had apparently paid blackmail, and was therefore under the protection of the police. When the policeman on the beat heard the altercation between the customer and the protected oyster stand keeper he walked up to the witness and, without a word, delivered a smashing blow upon his mouth. Two front teeth were splintered up into the gum, inflicting so severe an injury that it was two days before the swelling abated sufficiently for the dentist to be able to cut away the teeth, and four days before the roots could be touched. The dentist declared that the officer must have had something in his hand, either brass knuckles or some other weapon of that kind, to splinter the teeth so badly. But in all those cases the fist seems to have been the favourite weapon.

The only other case that I shall refer to is that in which the policeman used his club. There was a fight in the hallway of a house, and one Frank Angelo had stepped in to try to part the combatants. Up came a policeman of the name of Zimmerman, who rushed into the midst of the *mêlée*, and striking Angelo heavily with his club, knocked his eye out. The eye hung down on the man's cheek, and had to be subsequently removed. Angelo, all bloody, with his eye in this ghastly position, was arrested by his assailant, and taken to the police-court. The poor fellow, not knowing what would befall him, sent for a lawyer, who first of all charged him £10 for his professional services, and then said that the only way for him to get out of the scrape was to pay the officer £5, which he accordingly did. The judge asked him no question, and discharged the case. It is needless to say that Angelo brought no action against the policeman. There was no justice, he said, in New York. Justice there was indeed—hideous, diabolical, devil's justice. It is bad enough to have your eye knocked out with a policeman's club in the street when you are endeavouring to prevent a fight, but it is worse to have to pay that policeman £5 for having performed that operation, and an additional £10 to a lawyer to induce the ruffian to accept the money.

After reading this, it is not surprising that Mr. Goff, now Recorder of the City of New York, publicly declared, after a careful examination of the records of the Police Department for three years, that it could be proved that the police force was to all intents and purposes and in practice exempted from and above the operation of the law of the land. Mr. Goff, after saying that in three years only one policeman had been convicted for an assault upon a citizen, and remarking that the air of the trial-room at police headquarters was blue with perjury, continued thus:—

> The members of the police force of this city commit offences of the grade of felony and misdemeanour, and they have gone for years unpunished and unwhipped for those offences, which, if committed by citizens, would have resulted in fact in sentence to State's prison, and to the penitentiary. In other words, the operation of the law of this State, so far as it applies to the citizens of New York, and to all persons as it should, stops short of the police force. Felonious assaults have been committed upon citizens by policemen, which if committed by a civilian would result possibly in four or five years' sentence in Sing Sing, and all the policeman need apprehend is, a charge against him, with a possible conviction finding him guilty of assault, and a fine, for instance, of ten days' pay. A police officer of this city can brain a citizen with a club, and he may reasonably expect that all the penalty he will have to pay for that is about the sum of thirty dollars, while an ordinary citizen, if he commits that offence, is almost certain to go to State's prison. —Vol. iii., p. 2,826.

This is not a case of one law for the rich and another for the poor. It is one law for the citizen and none at all for the policeman.

Some of the evidence taken as to the action of the police supplied the Committee with very sensational episodes. One witness, for instance, a truckman, of the name of Lucas, appeared before them with his head in a frightful state of disfigurement. The man had been drunk, and gone to sleep on a doorstep, when he was robbed of four dollars. On waking up, finding that he had lost the money, he asked a policeman if he could find out anything as to who had robbed him. This seemed to offend the officer, for he struck Lucas in the face, knocked him down in the gutter, and then standing over him, belaboured him unmercifully with his club on his face and head. "For God's sake!" cried the man, "do not kill me altogether." A young man, a stranger, coming past, seeing the outrageous nature of the assault, asked the policeman to stop. Thereupon another policeman in citizen's clothes ran up, knocked him down, jumped on him, and then marched Lucas and the stranger off to the police-station. The blood running down Lucas's neck, drenched his shirt, and one of the picturesque incidents of the inquiry was the production of the bloody shirt before the senators. The man was bleeding so freely that the sergeant of the police-station had to sew up the top of his head. It took twenty-seven stitches to sew up the wound opened by the policeman's club. When he got into the police-station he was again assaulted, and had he not run for the sergeant, he was of the opinion that he would have been killed altogether. The next morning, he was brought before the judge, and discharged. Nothing seems to have been done to the officer.

The Committee summed up the whole case in the following sentences:—

It was proven by a stream of witnesses who poured continuously into the sessions of the committee, that many of the members of the force, and even superior officers, have abused the resources of physical power which have been provided for them and their use only in cases of necessity in the making of arrests and the restraint of disorder, to gratify personal spite and brutal instincts, and to reduce their victims to a condition of servility. . . .

Besides this exhibit of convicted clubbers, still wearing the uniform of the force, there was a stream of victims of police brutality who testified before your committee. The eye of one man, pushed out by a patrolman's club, hung on his cheek. Others were brought before the committee, fresh from their punishment, covered with blood and bruises, and in some cases battered out of recognition. Witnesses testified to severe assaults upon them while under arrest in the station-houses. The line of testimony might have been endlessly pursued by your committee . . . We emphasise this finding of brutality because it affects every citizen whatever his condition, because it shows an invasion of constitutional liberty by one of the departments of government whose supreme duty it is to enforce the law, and because it establishes a condition of affairs gravely imperilling the safety and the welfare of the people in their daily avocations.—Vol. i., p. 31.

INSPECTOR WILLIAMS, CHIEF CLUBBER OF THE FORCE.

AMERICAN TRACT SOCIETY'S DEPÔT.

(New York is a city whose Buildings are as colossal as the Corruption of its Police.)

CHAPTER VII.

THE Confidence Trick is perhaps the form of crime that would most naturally commend itself to the police banditti of New York. For the force was engaged all day long in playing a gigantic Confidence Trick upon the citizens. The gold brick which the swindlers sold to the credulous countryman was hardly more mythical than the enforcement of the law which was supposed to be secured by the organisation of the City police. It is therefore not surprising to learn that the police were hand-and-glove with the gang of swindlers which, under King McNally, carried on the Green Goods trade in the City of New York. It was one of the most lucrative of all the crimes which were carried on under police protection, and one of the safest. Few of all the stories told before the Lexow Committee display quite so unblushing a co-partnership between the law-breakers and the law officers as was revealed in this Green Goods swindle. The rascality of the rogues was so audacious that it provokes a laugh. For it is possible to carry impudence to a point where indignation is momentarily submerged by the sense of the ludicrous. Sheer amazement at the existence of such preposterous villains begets such a sense of its absurdity, that any censure seems as much out of place as in the nonsense tales of the nursery. Yet when the grotesque impression subsides, it is difficult to find terms strong enough to characterise this systematic misuse of the powers created for the protection of life and property and the due observance of the law for the purpose of facilitating fraud and of aiding and abetting and protecting swindling.

The evidence taken before the Lexow Committee contains a mass of materials for an exhaustive description of the criminals of New York, and the various methods by which in 1894 they preyed upon the public; but the person who undertakes the compilation of such a work is not to be envied. The Report of the Committee is a very striking illustration of the wickedness of issuing books without indexes. Here we have five bulky volumes of evidence without even an index of the names of witnesses. There is no subject-index of any kind. Witnesses are called and recalled in bewildering confusion. Nevertheless, even the most cursory perusal of the evidence brings to light a great many interesting and extraordinary facts as to the organisation of the criminal classes of the city.

Green Goods are forged or counterfeit bank notes. The pretence is either that there has been an over-issue of certain denominations of paper money by the Treasury, or that the plates have been stolen from the Government, and by this means it is possible to offer to sell ten dollars for one.

McNally, the King of the Green Goods men, employed at times a staff of thirty-five men. He began his career some twenty years ago as a bully who was kept by a prostitute. He swindled out of all her money a mistress of his who kept a restaurant, and started an Opium Joint. He then embarked in the Green Goods business, kept his carriage, and made his fortune.

The men who work this Confidence Trick seem to have carried their organised system of swindling to a very high pitch of perfection. Their master-stroke, however, was the admission of the police to a working partnership, which enabled them not merely to carry on their swindling with impunity, but also stood them in good stead whenever a victim had to be bullied and driven out of the city. King McNally was, unfortunately, not available for examination, owing to his precipitate departure for foreign parts as soon as the inquiry began. The Committee, however, was able to secure evidence which brought out very clearly the main lines of their operations.

The chief witness was one William Applegate, whose sister accompanied McNally in his hurried departure to Paris. Applegate had been employed for three years as one of the gang. He began when nineteen as a circular-folder, for which he received 8s. a week. These formed the foundation of the Green Goods business. A Green Goods gang in full operation is constituted as follows :—

(1) The Backer or Capitalist, who supplies the bank roll—a roll of 10,000 genuine dollar bills, which are shown to the victim. He receives fifty per cent., out of which he pays the police, and so guarantees the protection of the gang.

(2) The Writer, who addresses the wrappers in which the circulars, bogus newspaper-cuttings, etc., are enclosed. He receives the other fifty per cent., out of which he has to pay the percentage due to the rest of the gang.

(3) The Bunco Steerer, who is sent to meet the victim at some hotel, fifty to a hundred miles distant from the city. He is the messenger who gives the victim the pass-word, and then leads him to the Joint or den where the swindle is completed. He receives five per cent. of the plunder.

(4) The Old Man, a respectable-looking old gentleman, who says nothing, but who sits solemnly in the Joint when the "beat" is being carried through. He receives five dollars.

(5) The Turner, who is represented as the son of the old man, and does the selling of the bogus notes. His fee is ten dollars.

(6) The Ringer, a confederate behind the partition, who dexterously replaces the good money shown in the bank roll by the bundles of bogus notes. His fee is five dollars.

(7) The Tailor, who remains on guard at the railway station, personating a policeman, for the purpose of bullying any victim who discovers he has been swindled, and returns to try to recover his money. This gentleman is also paid five dollars a victim.

With this staff, and the protection of the police, the Green Goods business can be carried on very successfully. McNally used to take as much as £1,600 in a single day. Fortunes of £40,000 were accumulated by the leading backers, although McNally's pile was not estimated at more than £20,000.

The first step is the obtaining of directories and the arranging for the despatch of circulars. The circulars were of the familiar kind, printed as if typewritten, and addressed by a staff of writers, of whom McNally had eight or ten kept constantly at work. Enclosed in the envelope with the circular were slips printed as if they were cut out of newspapers, the same with intent to deceive, the slip being carefully written by Mr. McNally, or some member of his gang, for the purpose of giving the reader to understand that the offer of the circular was *bonâ fide* and reliable. These were sent out by thousands, the printer executing orders for 200,000 sets at a time. A slip was also included giving the address to which a telegram should be sent, in order to secure the advantageous offer made to the victim by the circular. These addresses were usually vacant lots in the city, but arrangements were made by bribing the officials of the telegraph company to hold all telegrams sent to such fictitious addresses until called for.

The business was carried on a kind of mutual partnership basis. It was worked somewhat in this fashion. A writer would send out 10,000 circulars or more a day. One, or perhaps two, of those would hook a victim, who would telegraph, making an application for the money offered him at such tempting terms. This victim would belong to the writer of the circular by which he had been caught. Having thus hooked a victim, he had to be landed, and for this purpose he had to be brought to town and personally conducted by a bunco steerer to the den or joint, where three confederates fooled the victim to the top of his bent, and usually succeeded in fleecing him by one form or another of the confidence trick.

The victim, who was known as a "Come On" or as a "Guy," was swindled by a variety of methods. One favourite plan was to undertake to sell the credulous rustic 10,000 dollars for 650 dollars. For less than 650 dollars he was told he could not have the "State rights." The monopoly for his own State was promised to the favoured individual, whose 650 dollars had to be paid down on the spot. A locked box was then given him, within which he was assured there were 10,000 dollars in coin. In reality, there was a brick, which was all the poor victim got for his money.

Another method of swindling was thus described by the witness Applegate when under examination by Mr. Goff :—

Q. I hand you two tin boxes ; do you recognise those as belonging to McNally ?

A. Yes, sir.

Q. Were those boxes used in his business?

A. Yes, sir.

Q. Here is a third one, and a fourth one; what were those four boxes used for ?

A. They would put the money in one box for the man, in a box like that, and that would be a deal of from about 300 dollars to 500 dollars ; they would put the money in this box and it would be in front of the victim, and in the meantime a duplicate box would be behind the partition, and in the duplicate box there would be a brick and some paper, and they would put the money in this box here on the desk and lock it up before the victim; it would be on the back of the desk like that, and then Billy Vosburgh would say, "Get that book," and with that they would lift up the desk and that would hide the box from the victim, and then Walter McNally, who did the ringing, would open his trap door and take this box in and put the other box out ; it would all be done in a second.

Q. I will now hand you this fifth box ; what is that used for?

A. That was used for the bank roll.

Q. What is there—is there a false lid to that ?

A. No ; there is one, yes.

Q. How was the bank roll brought into play there ; explain about that ?

A. The bank roll would be laid right in there, 8,200 dollars ; it would be laid there. There was supposed to be 8,200 dollars done up in packages, with three elastics around them.

Q. Now, I hand you this book, and ask you if those were the packages there were exchanged for the genuine packages ?

A. Yes, sir ; these were, as we called them, the dummies.

Q. Explain how they were operated ?

A. You see this is a package supposed to be of 5 dollar bills. There would be a good one on the top, and a good one on the bottom, and here would lay the same package of genuine money, and Walter would count out, say, 200 dollars in 5 dollar bills, which would be so much, and he would say, to save time, "We will measure the packages together, and, instead of counting each and every bill, we will put the packages together," and the victim would think there was the same amount of money in each one, and then, through sleight-of-hand, he would put these in the box, and the good money on top; and if the victim wanted to see the packages again he would show them, and the one on top would be good money ; and if the victim is a hard victim, he might want to take the money with him, and then Walter would shift these packages, and, therefore, he got about 60 dollars for 500 dollars or 1,000 dollars.

Q. And the victim would get those packages that we now exhibit, instead of the packages containing the good money that he has seen ?

A. Yes, sir.

Q. There were many of those in use, were there not ?

A. Yes, sir, we would never take the elastics off these ; we would just take the elastics off the good money.

Q. Here is a box with a heavy weight; see what is in this box ?

A. I guess that is a brick (witness takes out a brick wrapped up in paper); that is what he would get for his 650 dollars; for a 300 dollar deal he would get half a brick ; for 10,000 dollars it would have to be heavier than for a less amount.—Vol. iii., pp. 2,575-6.

In connection with McNally's gang there was an Art Gallery fitted up adjoining a saloon used sometimes as McNally's

headquarters. The chief feature of this Art Gallery was a great
number of pictures representing treasuries filled with all kinds of
money. " Here," said the Steerer to the Guy, " is the picture of
what you will get in reality." The effect upon his imagination of
these painted representations of enormous treasure in gold and silver
predisposed the victim to part freely with his money, and believe the
plausible friends who so kindly proposed to point out to him so short
a cut to a fortune. McNally had a private carriage also, with a
footman in livery. " The carriage racket," as it was called, was thus
described by Applegate :—

Q. Now, proceed and describe the operations of the carriage?
A. Well, previous to the steerer and the guy coming to the carriage, there would
be a satchel put there, a little red satchel.
Q. In the carriage?
A. In the carriage, with a brick and paper in it; there would also be two or
three satchels without anything in it on the seat of the carriage. Walter Haines
would get in with the guy. Walter Haines would have the money in the bag, the
bank roll, and he would put the money in the satchel, a duplicate satchel to the
one that had the brick in it; he would put the money in the satchel, and after the
guy had paid Haines his money so—we never received theirs before we gave them
ours, and after he made the deal and everything was all right, Haines would say,
" I will go to the depôt," and the steerer would grab the satchel and run out, and
Walter Haines would slip the money in the cab, and Haines would say, " The steerer
will go with you," and he would go away with the steerer.
Q. Were there any cases in which they discovered the fraud before they left the
State?
A. No, we worked kind of snug; when we were working the carriage racket we
worked a little on the snug.
Q. What is that?
A. We did not have the protection we ought to have had, and the steerer then
would have to go with the guy and keep the satchel and see the guy on the train,
and, after he got on the train, he didn't care a darn where he went.
Q. And he did not have the facilities as in the turning joint?
A. No, sir; we would not give him the satchel until he got on the train, and
would say, " We will give you this at the proper time and place."
Q. Weren't you in the habit of giving to the guy keys?
A. No; we generally threw the key away and told him to cut it open; not with
the satchel; with the box we gave him keys.
Q. Was there any design in giving the keys with the box?
A. We never gave him the key which fitted the box.
Q. So when they got on the railroad——
A. When a guy gets a box like that there will be some combination on it, and
he will get the wrong key, and he don't know how to get out of it.
Q. And you always made sure to give him a key that would not open the box?
A. Yes, sir; the reason of that is that we gave him a key that fits the box with
the money in, and that would not fit the box that had the brick in.—Vol. iii.,
pp. 2,613–5.

There were many ways of swindling the unfortunate guy. When
once they are hooked, they can be played with to almost any extent.
In this, as in higher regions, the saying holds good—

Faith, fanatic faith, once wedded fast
To some dear falsehood, hugs it to the last.

A guy will pay his money down and expect the notes to be sent to
his order. When they fail to turn up, he will come back and buy
some more, which are to be expressed to him. When they do not

arrive, he will come back the third time and do another deal, and see them checked at the station with his ticket. The baggage-man is accused of stealing the money, and the guy comes up for a fourth time. In this final purchase he never allows the box or bag to go out of his own hands. Not until he opens the precious parcel and finds the brick or counterfeit notes or rolls of paper, does it dawn upon him that he has been done.

The need for great secrecy and the importance of getting a long way off the city before opening the box do not seem unreasonable to a man who knows that he is engaged in a more or less fraudulent transaction. It is the knowledge of the guy that he is doing a more or less crooked business which enables the gang to plunder him with such impunity.

Some such methods are probably familiar to the police of all the cities in the world, but that which was peculiar to New York was the arrangement made for carrying on this business, not merely with the cognizance of, but with the active co-operation of the police. This partnership was so close that in McNally's case all the business was carried on in conjunction with a police captain of the name of Meakin, who had as his agent at headquarters a detective of the name of Hanley. It is difficult to repress a smile on reading, at the very opening of Applegate's evidence, how things were worked.

Every now and then, when the newspapers made too much fuss concerning the scandals of the Police Department, the authorities would order what is known as a "general shake-up"—*i.e.*, the captains would be shifted all round, the assumption being that a new broom would sweep clean, and that by changing the captains from one precinct to another the abuses that had created any fuss would be rectified. Unfortunately the whole system of blackmail and corruption was so elaborately organised that the shifting of the captains made no change. Each newcomer succeeded to the business, and carried on the collection of blackmail without losing a single day. "Business carried on as usual during alterations" might have been posted up over every police-station in New York; but in the case of Green Goods men, their business was too profitable to be lost by the captain who had once got hold of it. The consequence was that, when the shake-up took place, and Captain Meakin was transferred from the "down-town precinct" to Harlem at the other end of the island, he carried all the Green Goods men with him up to his new station. As soon as the order was given that the shake-up was to be enforced, Captain Meakin sent word to McNally that he must follow him to Harlem. McNally thereupon told all his writers, Bunco steerers and Turners that they must pack up their traps, and follow the Captain to the precinct to which he had been transferred. The notice was short, and for a moment it seemed as if the smooth course of the Green Goods business would be interfered with, for

several victims were on their way to the rendezvous fixed by the
writers in Captain McNally's old precinct. The resources of roguery
are not so easily exhausted; the Bunco steerers were ordered to
bring their victims from the down town precinct to some saloons in
Harlem until the gang had arranged with the Captain as to where
the victims were to be plundered in the new precinct.

The saloon in which the confidence trick was played, and the
room in which the victim was relieved of his money, was known as
the "Joint," or the place where they "beat the victim." The first
thing necessary was, therefore, to find out a saloon that would be
available for the purposes of the gang. Captain Meakin was a
man of resource. He and his wardman met McNally at a drug
store, and arranged with a saloon-keeper of the name of Hawkins
that the joint should be opened in his saloon. The arrangement
made with Hawkins was that he should have a sovereign for every
man that was fleeced at his place.

Very little time was lost in bundling the boxes, with the bricks
and all the other paraphernalia of the craft, into an express waggon.
The King drove up in his carriage with the bank-roll and
his liveried coachman, while the Turners followed by the Elevated
Railway. As soon as the arrangement was fixed up with the King
and the Captain and the Saloon-keeper, the signal was given, and
the victims, who were planted at various saloons in the neighbourhood
by the Bunco steerers waiting until the Police Captain and the King
had fixed up arrangements as to the joint, were brought down and
fleeced. Thus, without the loss of a single day the business was
transferred, and was running merrily under the protecting ægis of
Captain Meakin and his police.

For four months this went on, until at last the scandal became so
great that the Police Commissioners received representations from
the inhabitants, and it became evident that the Hawkins saloon
would no longer serve as headquarters. A friendly communication
was sent to the thieves by Detective Charlton. He told them
that they would have to quit, but at the same time he obligingly
suggested that the saloon of a man named Day in the immediate
neighbourhood would be quite as convenient, and would serve
equally well as a place for "beating" their victims. To Day's saloon,
therefore, the Joint was transferred, and business went on for five
months, ten or twelve writers being busily employed in sending out
circulars, as many as fifteen thousand being sometimes despatched in
a single day.

At last an order was issued from headquarters ordering the arrest
of all the Green Goods men of New York. This looked serious,
but when you have a friend in the force you do not get arrested,
excepting as a friendly put-up job. When the order was issued from
headquarters, Detective Charlton was sent by Captain Meakin to

inform McNally that they were going to raid the Joint, and advised him to remove all the stuff before the police arrived. This timely hint was promptly acted upon, and when the place was raided nothing was found. The Green Goods men in the meanwhile had transferred themselves to Jersey, which, being a foreign State, was beyond the jurisdiction of the Superintendent. But everything was done to make their sojourn in Jersey pleasant; Captain Meakin gave them a recommendation to a detective in the Jersey force, who saw to it that they were not interfered with. In return for those services, Captain Meakin received from McNally £90 a month, the tariff being fixed at £10 per writer. The money was paid to Detective Charlton, who handed it over, no doubt after collecting his commission, to the Captain.

If the matter had only stopped here, the case of the Green Goods men would not have differed materially from that of the disorderly houses, which all subsidised the police, and were protected in return. But in the case of these swindlers, who elevated the confidence trick almost to the level of a fine art, there was a further development. If any of the writers were behind in their payments to the King, McNally promptly denounced them to the Captain, and the defaulting writer was as promptly arrested. By this means discipline was enforced in the gang and all bad debts avoided. Again, if any writer refused to follow McNally to the district where he wanted him, or in any other way allowed his personal preferences to interfere with the orders of the King, he was denounced and run in by the obedient, uniformed myrmidons of his majesty.

In order to enforce discipline over the whole of New York City, it was necessary to supplement the arrangement with Captain Meakin by a similar understanding with an officer at the headquarters department. This officer was Charles Hanley. "He was McNally's right hand man, and any time he got into trouble or his men got into trouble, the first man he sent for was Hanley; and Hanley was always sent for." He represented the Detective Bureau, and his services were necessary when any unfortunate victim, discovering that he had nothing but a brick in his box, came back to the city and made complaint. A considerable number of the guys, or the victims, never came back, being too thoroughly ashamed of their folly to face an exposure; but a certain proportion did. These "Come-backs," as they were called, naturally applied to the Detective Bureau at the police headquarters, and there they were taken in hand by McNally's partner. Applegate explained the working of this system as follows :—

In cases of a come-back of any kind; in case a man has been swindled who has found the brick in the box before he has left New York; and as a rule he would go to the central office and make a holler; Hanley would always seem to be the detective that would get the man in charge; the man would be brought up town to try and identify the people, which he never could do; then we always got the tip to go away; the man would be brought down town and chased out of town as being a counterfeiter; and they would pay 500 dollars, and 250 dollars would go back to the police; the police claimed half of the deal.—Vol. iii., p. 2,590. ·

The method, it will be seen, was extremely ingenious. The swindlers had passed forged notes upon their victim. When he made a complaint, he was promptly arrested or driven out of the town by the confederates of the gang in the police for having counterfeit notes in his possession! No wonder things went " nice and easy." Applegate described one scene which had evidently afforded the gang great amusement. A victim, who had been swindled, and had applied to the police for redress, was handed over in the usual course to Hanley, who took him up town to the saloon where he had been robbed, to see if he could find the Bunco steerer who had inveigled him into the Joint. Applegate himself acted as the go-between on that occasion. He warned the Steerer to keep out of the way, and then asked Hanley to bring the Guy down past the windows of the saloon, where the men who had swindled him could have some fun in watching him as he was trotted about the street on a false scent. By some strange mistake, and despite all warnings, the Steerer ran into the Detective and the Guy; but even this difficulty was overcome, for a few words from the Detective put it all right, and the Steerer went off without being arrested. For his part in that little comedy Hanley got one-half of the money of which the man had been swindled. In this case Hanley's share of the plunder amounted to £50. The victim was chased out of the town under the threat of arrest and imprisonment for having counterfeit notes in his possession.

"You see," said the witness, apologetically, "the guy is a guy, and you can do almost anything with him." It is certainly not difficult, when you have the police to stand in whenever you get into a tight place.

The only terror which seemed to haunt the mind of the Green Goods men was that of being shot down by some sharper who made himself up as a guy in order to possess himself of the bank-roll of genuine money. Appo, a man who spent most of his life in picking pockets when he was at liberty, and in doing time in gaol when he was caught, had a rough experience of the murderous possibilities that the Green Goods man has to face. On one occasion a Tennessee detective made himself up as a country bumpkin. When the critical moment came, he clapped his revolver at the head of Appo, shot out his eye, lodged the bullet in his skull, from which it was never extracted, and made off with all the money at that time on Appo's person. When examined before the Committee, Appo thus explained the *modus operandi* by which Green Goods men occasionally got cleaned out and murdered in the bargain. He said:—

...I take a man; I rig him up; I say, "Do you want to make 5,000 dols. or 10,000 dols.?" "Yes, sir." "Well, you go up to a hotel room, and I will touch the wires to a party band, bring him there with his bank roll, and you play guy: when he comes in and shows his goods, take your gun, stick him up, and take his money away from him. If he goes to make a kick, shoot him; he cannot do that much; the law will protect you; see how Tony Martin got killed there in Brooklyn; them men got out; it was cold-blooded murder—wilful, deliberate, premeditated murder. Fixed up? My case was fixed up there in Poughkeepsie; the man sneaked up behind me in cold blood and shot me, and sent me to State prison for three years and two months.—Vol. ii., p. 1640-1.

Another ingenious precaution which was taken by McNally was to have the detectives at the various railway stations surrounding New York in his pay, so that in case any Guy were to discover that he had been swindled, and make a fuss at the station, he could be promptly arrested for holding counterfeit money, and so bullied as to make him thankful to get home without saying more about it. The detective at the Central Depôt was paid £10 a month for his services.

The facts as they were detailed before the Lexow Committee were proved by such overwhelming evidence that the chief criminal, Captain Meakin, of the police force, was seized with an illness which rendered it impossible for him to appear in the witness-box. Perjury to an unlimited extent was familiar enough to the police captains, but the evidence about the Green Goods gang was too strong even for a police captain to brazen it out. So it came to pass that Captain Meakin was too dangerously ill during the sitting of the Committee for his evidence to be taken even at his own bedside.

The Lexow Committee reported on the subject as follows:—

It appears conclusively that a heavy traffic of this kind has been systematically carried on by these swindlers, who, in exchange for protection, shared a large part of their ill-gotten gains with the police . . . The evidence indicated that the first step in the initiation of business of this character was to establish relations with the captain of the precinct in which the work was carried on.

It appears, moreover, that men notoriously engaged in the swindling or confidence business had their headquarters in the city, known to the police, where they might be ordinarily found, and that those who were receiving protection plied their trade unmolested, while others, who had not been fortunate enough to establish relations with the police, or those who intruded upon districts not assigned to them, would be warned off, and in case of failure to obey would be summarily dealt with. —Vol. i., p. 39.

Strange and incredible though it may appear that the police should actually join hands with the criminals of the type of the Green Goods gang, it was entirely in keeping with the principles which had been elaborated into a system in dealing with every form of robbery.

The Lexow Committee reported:—

It has been conclusively shown that an understanding existed between headquarters' detectives, pawnbrokers and thieves, by which stolen property may be promptly recovered by the owner on condition that he repay the pawnbroker the amount advanced on the stolen property. In almost every instance it also appears that the detective, acting between the owner and the pawnbroker, receives substantial gratuities from the owner of the property for the work done in his official capacity.—Vol. i., p. 40.

But there was a still worse form of co-partnership involved in the procedure adopted in robberies in houses of ill-fame. A witness of the name of Lucy C. Harriot, who at the time when she gave her evidence was an inmate of the workhouse on Blackwell's Island, but who had an extensive experience in the disorderly houses of New York, explained the system in some detail. The police, she said, were able to make robberies in what were known as panel houses, safe for the thief and profitable to themselves. When a man was robbed and went to the station-house for redress, the Captain usually sent down a wardman to the house, who made it his first duty to represent to the victim the prudence of saying nothing about it, and of avoiding what would be otherwise a painful exposure. If the victim persisted, the wardman would pretend to endeavour to find the girl, but always discovered that she had gone off to Europe, or had disappeared in some mysterious way. The matter always ended in the man being scared off. I quote the evidence as given in the Report :—

By Mr. Goff: And after the stranger is scared off, the wardman goes to the house, and isn't it a rule that the money he is robbed of is divided with the police ?
A. I have heard it ever since I have been round; that is about nine years.
Q. Where do you come in when you steal 180 dols.; where does your profit come in ?
A. If the man went away quietly, the wardman would have received 90 dols. of the 180 dols., and I would have got 45 dols. out of the remaining half.
Q. And the madam for 45 dols. ?
A. Yes, sir.
Q. And the wardman gets, in this case, fifty per cent. of the loot ?
A. Yes, sir, that is so.—Vol. i., p. 3,620.
By Chairman Lexow: How many houses have you been into to which the rule as to payment of money and the division of property applies?
A. Every one that ever I entered.
Q. How many ?
A. About two dozen, I guess.—Vol. i., p. 3,f22.
By Senator Bradley : What you say is a general custom ?
A. A common occurrence.
Q. Is that tariff fixed . . . the payment of fifty per cent. to the wardman, or the policeman, in case of panel theft ?
A. Yes.
Q. That he should get one-half ?
A. Yes, sir.
Q. And that applies to all these twenty-four houses you speak of ?
A. Yes, sir, every house I went into of that kind.—Vol. i., p. 3,623.

Excepting in the most barbarous regions of Turkey, where Pashas are sometimes suspected and accused of winking at the raids of bandits in consideration of a share of the spoil, has there ever been such a story as this ?

The principle of territorial jurisdiction is so deeply rooted in the American mind that the New York police seem to have acted upon it in all their dealings with the criminals whom they shepherded. For instance, they appear to have parcelled Broadway into blocks, allotting each block to a different thief, who, of course, paid quit rent

for his district to the police. The understanding was that the
policeman was to be free to arrest the thief if there was a complaint made by the victim, but that so long as no complaints were
made the policeman would "close the other eye," and allow the
pickpocket a free run. Mr. Goff stated that there was once a fight
between the thieves; that one trespassed upon the other's domain
and went to a pawnshop about it, and the authorities at police
headquarters threatened to send the first thief up the river if he
ever invaded the second thief's privileges (vol. v., p. 5,193).

This reverent regard for territorial landmarks is very touching.
The New York police appear to have been as much opposed to
poaching as are English gamekeepers.

DELMONICO'S.

CHAPTER VIII

AMONG its other achievements, the Lexow Committee enriched the vocabulary of our language by the word Pantata. It is a mysterious word of Bohemian origin. What it precisely meant none of the witnesses could explain. It had no exact equivalent in the English language, but there was no difficulty about understanding how it was applied in New York. Pantata, in its origin, the interpreters explain, meant father-in-law. The term was used in households to describe your wife's father, but it was also held to be the equivalent of Old Man; and one witness declared that in Bohemia, the country from which the word was exported, it is frequently applied to the Emperor-King of Austria-Hungary, Francis Joseph, who is said to be Pantata to his Royal Bohemians.

Whatever may be the original significance of the term, it was applied by the Bohemian Liquor Dealers' Association to the Police Captain of the precinct in which they did their business. He was their Pantata, and from this beginning the term came to be used as a generic title for the police official, who was on terms of family relationship with the vicious and criminal class under his jurisdiction. The New York police captain was in a special sense the father-in-law, or Father-in-the-Law, to a very numerous progeny of disreputable people. Instead of being a terror to evildoers, he became their Pantata, who looked after them with semi-paternal care, and generally acted as their Father-in-the-Law, regarding it indeed as his chief function to relax the law in their behalf in return, of course, for consideration received. So long as his dues were paid there was nothing that Pantata would not do. He could, for instance, and did, practically suspend the legislation for Sunday closing. But that is a mere trifle.

It was proved by the evidence of one witness that the Pantata police did not hesitate to issue irregular licences of their own for the keeping of unlicensed saloons, or shebeens, as we would say.

One witness, Anna Newstatel, held a licence once down to the year 1890. When running a full licensed saloon she paid five dollars a month to the police. After 1890 her licence was revoked, but in consideration of her having been a good paying subject, the police told her that she might go on selling all kinds of liquor without a licence, so long at she continued to pay her dues to them, in consideration of an initiation fee of £40 down. The following is the extract from the evidence :—

Q. What was your licence revoked for?
A. For selling liquor on a beer licence.
Q. And after your licence was revoked the police allowed you to sell everything without a licence?
A. After I paid them 200 dollars at the start and then 50 dollars a month.
Q. Now did you pay 200 dollars at the start?
A. I said I couldn't afford to do that—I would sooner rent out the saloon ; and they said if I rent out the saloon as a store, and I should live private upstairs and carry on my saloon business upstairs for half of the amount—for 100 dollars to start, and 25 dollars every month—and I should try that, and they will help me and see that I shall have customers enough to do business.
Q. In other words, they told you you must go upstairs?
Chairman Lexow : That is to say, they would reduce the amount one-half if she would do that?
Q. You sold on Sunday as well as on weekdays?
A. Yes, sir.
Q. Now, about the custom that you had. Did the detectives provide you with the custom ; did they give you custom?
A. No, they did not; they came in sometimes themselves and like this, only they never paid when they came in; only they allowed me to keep open any hour and all the time.—Vol. v., p. 4,592.

This claim to be supplied with drink whenever they felt they wanted a glass appears to have been very generally recognised by the liquor dealers of New York. Sometimes the police would pretend that they would pay, but, as a matter of fact, the principle of free drinks seems to have been very widely recognised.

In the regular saloons there was comparatively little necessity for invoking the assistance of the benevolent Pantata. He had a much wider field in dealing with the gaming houses, which flourished in every precinct in New York. According to the law, no gaming house was allowed to run. Yet, by permission of the police, there were about a thousand of them running all the time the Lexow Committee was sitting. I had better quote here the extract from the Lexow Committee's Report :—

The evidence is conclusive that with reference to this class of vice the police occupied substantially the same position as they did with respect to disorderly houses.

It was proven even that while the Committee was actually in session more than six hundred policy shops were in active operation in the city, running openly, and from day to day policy slips were secured in some shops in different portions of the city by detectives in the employ of your Committee.

Qualified witnesses swore that the general average of open shops was about one thousand. The testimony disclosed the remarkable fact that not only were these violaters of the law protected by the police in consideration of a fixed sum of 15 dollars a month per shop, but that the area of operation of each " king " was so clearly understood and carefully guarded, that any intruder would be certified to the police, and would either be compelled to refrain from competition with a licensed " policy king," or else would be arrested and condign punishment would be visited upon him.

It seems clear from the evidence that this division of territory was largely for the benefit of the police, insuring a more rapid and easier collection of the tribute to be paid the " policy king " to whom a particular district had been assigned, paying in bulk at the rate of fifteen dollars per shop for all the shops running in such district or districts.

Pool-rooms flourished all over the city in the same way. Large sums were extorted from their proprietors by the police, and they were permitted to remain unmolested, openly and publicly running, until a private citizen, Richard Croker, after a conference with a police commissioner, enforced their cessation practically in a single day. This is one of the most remarkable circumstances testified to before your Committee. And yet nothing was done or attempted to be done until the private citizen aforesaid commanded that they be closed, and they were closed, and closed without criminal prosecution.

It appeared subsequently in evidence that these pool-rooms, while running, had been assessed and had paid for police protection as high as 300 dollars a month.—Vol. i., p. 3,637.

We have too much betting in England—betting carried on with the active co-operation of the press—for any English journalist to be able to throw a stone at New York or Chicago, for the extent to which gambling is carried on in policy-shops or pool-rooms. The Turf is the great gaming hell of the Old Country, and nearly every newspaper in the land plays the part of a tout and tempter to those who wish to gamble. In New York, while there is betting enough among certain classes, the masses of the people seem to prefer other forms of risking their money.

A very curious picture is given in the evidence taken by the Lexow Committee of the prevalence of the gaming habit among all classes of the population, especially in the poorer districts. After making one or two ineffectual attempts, I have given up all hope of understanding, much less of explaining, the precise way in which gambling goes on in pool-rooms. From the explanations of the witness, the uninitiated outsider can only discern vaguely that policy is much more akin to the Italian lottery system than anything which prevails in this country. Any sum can be staked, from one cent upwards. The gambler chooses a number or concatenation of numbers. What is called a "saddle" consists of two sets of numbers, while a "gig" is composed of three. There are many kinds of "gigs," which were duly described for the edification of the Committee, the "police gig" being one of those most in vogue. In the choice of "saddles" or "gigs"—or, in other words, in the selection of numbers on which to put his money—the New York gambler is exactly like a Neapolitan, and in nothing is the resemblance more remarkable than in the respect paid to dreams. Nearly every policeman, it was declared, had a dream book, and according as he dreamed, so he would put his money upon the number indicated by the dream in his pocket oracle. I made a small collection of dream books when I was in Chicago, and came to the conclusion that the dream book was much more constantly consulted in that city than the Old or New Testament. Judging from the evidence before the Committee, dream books are equally in vogue in New York, but any accident or incident would serve to suggest a favourite combination of lucky numbers, which would be in great request until some other incident arose to suggest a new combination. You staked a cent and stood to win a dollar.

One of the most painful features of this policy gambling was the extent to which it worked downwards, even to the children. Lads coming from school would beg a cent in order to try their luck. As they could only pay by attracting customers, it was impossible to run a policy shop in secrecy. In less than a couple of days the police were perfectly well aware that a policy shop had been opened, and it was therefore absolutely necessary to secure the police in advance. This seems to have been done on strict business principles, and the partnership between the various kings or satraps, to whom the police farmed out the precinct, appears to have been very harmonious.

Bucket-shop and gambling on the tape on the prices quoted on the Stock Exchange is as common in New York as it is in London; but one ingenious method of improving on the bucket-shop was brought to light in the course of this investigation. The disadvantage of the gambling in *bonâ fide* Stock Exchange securities is that they are often sluggish, and do not go up and down with sufficient rapidity to stimulate the excitement of the gambler. In New York a bogus commission agency established a system of gambling which beat the bucket-shop hollow. Instead of waiting for the arrival of genuine prices of real stocks, the genius who ran this commission agency fixed up a tape machine in his office, and before business started in the morning wrote out a series of about five hundred different quotations for stock in purely imaginary companies. When his gamblers had assembled, he turned a handle, and wound off his tape. He made the stocks of course go up and down with the requisite rapidity, and from a gaming point of view it was in every way but one superior to the ordinary betting on the tape. The one exception, however, was a pretty considerable drawback, for the proprietor of the establishment knew in advance what figures would come out, and how the prices would fluctuate. So long, however, as he did not bet himself, this made no difference to those who wanted a flutter.

Into the ramifications of the gambling in New York it is not necessary to follow the Committee in their painstaking investigation. It did not even draw the line at the Chinese quarter; and those who wish to know all about Fantah, and the mysteries of the Button Game, will find their curiosity gratified if they read through the Report. All that need be said is that no form of gambling was carried on at New York which had not the police authorities as its protectors, and the rank and file as its patrons. Under such circumstances, it is hardly to be expected that much progress will be made in suppressing gambling in New York.

The task indeed, as every policeman knows, is one of great difficulty, even when the force is entirely free from any suspicion of complicity. Mr. Moss, who is now at the head of the police at New York, had to admit last September that, despite all his efforts, pool-rooms had been running; and, as the newspapers declared, some of the police are Pantatas still. It was, however, generally admitted that if the Pantata can be exterminated by zeal, energy, and severity, Mr. Moss is the man to do it.

MR. MOSS, HEAD OF THE NEW YORK POLICE.

ST. PATRICK'S CATHEDRAL, NEW YORK.

(Roman Catholic.)

CHAPTER IX.

IF the Police Captain was the Pantata of the Gambler, he was the Farmer-General of the Houses of Ill-fame in his Precinct. His duty, as defined by the law which he had sworn to enforce, was clear. He was bound to close every disorderly house in his jurisdiction. His practice was to let them all run—for a consideration. The Strange Woman, that pathetic and tragic figure in the streets of all great cities, whose house from of old was said to be the Way of Hell, going down into the Chambers of Death, excited in the Police Captain only the sentiment of rapacity. In his eyes she was merely an asset in his farm, and one of the most valuable.

It was when the Lexow Committee approached this part of the investigation that they found the greatest difficulties placed in their way.

During the whole of the inquiry the Police Department preserved an attitude of animosity to the Lexow Committee. This was only natural, considering that the Committee was engaged in bringing to light all the misdeeds of the Department for the last three or four years. The Committee was protected by law, and supported by public opinion; nevertheless, the police eagerly seized every opportunity that was offered them in order to embarrass the Committee's investigations, by intimidating witnesses, and sometimes by spiriting them away altogether. It was proved that policemen had gone round to the keepers of disorderly houses, and had begged them to refuse to appear, or to refuse to testify, promising as an inducement that, if they would hold their tongues, they should be allowed to run their houses freely without interference from any one. The tune which all the policemen sang was " Wait till the clouds roll by." The Lexow Committee was but a creature of to-day, while the Police Department was one of the permanent institutions of the city.

" These fellows have got no pull," said the police. " You lie low for a time, and we will protect you."

When this argument failed, they resorted to menace, threatening to close up the house, to fling the keepers into gaol, and occasionally, when these threats failed, they resorted to personal violence.

The Committee, speaking of the terrorism which was employed by the police in order to prevent witnesses testifying, said :—

In the course of the inquiry, a man rushed into the session of your Committee, fresh from an assault made upon him by a notorious politician and two policemen, and with fear depicted upon his countenance, threw himself upon the mercy of the Committee and asked its protection, insisting that he knew of no court and of no place where he could in safety go and obtain protection from his persecutors.— Vol. i., pp. 25, 26.

The most distinguished exploit of the police, however, during the whole of the inquiry was the spiriting away of the French Madam, Matilda Hermann, one of the most notable keepers of disorderly houses in the City of New York. When it was known that the Committee was after her, and that Madam, who had been plundered to the bone by the police, was by no means indisposed to "squeal"—to quote the expressive vernacular of the Department—there was a consultation among the police authorities as to what measures should be taken to close her mouth. A considerable number of people in the same way of business had been induced to migrate to Chicago, where they remained waiting until such time as the Committee adjourned, but Madam Hermann was too dangerous a witness. She required special treatment. A purse was made up for her by the police, which, when the subscription closed, amounted to 1,700 dollars. She was then under subpœna, and was expected before the Committee the next day.

At midnight, a police officer in plain clothes came to her house, bundled her into a carriage in such hot haste that she had not time to complete her toilet, and whisked her off no one knew where. For some weeks the police appeared to have triumphed, but after a time the Committee were able to get upon her track. She had been taken first to New Jersey, and then from New Jersey had been rail-roaded through to Canada. From thence, after moving about from place to place, she had been taken to a Western city, where at last she was run to ground.

When the agents of the Committee found her she expressed no disinclination to return to New York and testify. She had fulfilled her part of the bargain in keeping out of the way as long as she could. Now that she was discovered she was willing to return. In great triumph she was escorted back to the city. In order to prevent any attempt at rescue, an additional staff of men were sent to Philadelphia to meet her. The precaution was timely, for as soon as they arrived at Jersey City a last desperate attempt was made by the police to prevent her evidence being taken.

She was in the custody of the Deputy Serjeant-at-Arms of the Senate, who had a party of resolute men in his train. But notwithstanding this, no sooner had the party arrived in Jersey City than they were set upon by the Jersey police, who treated them with the greatest roughness. They threatened to break their faces, hustled them about, and endeavoured in the *mêlée* to get Madam Hermann away. The Deputy Serjeant, however, stuck to his witness, and finally he, Madam Hermann, and all his men were arrested, run into the station-house, and locked up.

The sensation which this occasioned can be imagined. Fortunately, the Committee was in session, otherwise there is no knowing whether the daring attempt to seize and remove the witness might not have succeeded. The immediate publicity, however, that was given to the case convinced the police that the game was up. The Chief of the Police and the Police Magistrate refused to lend their aid in thwarting the ends of justice, and the conspirators, led by a lawyer, who was also a senator of the State of New Jersey, drew off their gang, and reluctantly allowed Madam Hermann to be brought to New York. The story reads more like an episode from the Middle Ages than an excerpt from the proceedings of a senatorial investigation in New York State in the last decade of the nineteenth century.

The French Madam, as she was called in the precinct, was evidently regarded by the police as a gold mine. She had three or four houses, with some twenty-four or twenty-five girls, and was doing a flourishing business. She paid the police altogether in the seven years that she was running the sum of over 30,000 dollars, or more than £6,000; *i.e.*, this woman alone yielded the police a revenue of nearly £1,000 a year. Part of this money, it should be said, went to the lawyers, who shared it with the police. Every time she was raided the policeman insisted upon her taking a lawyer, and told her that if she would take the lawyer of his choice, he would not swear against her. He would swear that he was not sure of her identity. This she did, and she was discharged. Every time she took a lawyer she had to pay from £35 to £80, and the lawyer always told her that he only got part of the money, as the rest of it went to fix her detectives. Her evidence on this point was very emphatic. Whether she paid 200 dollars or 100 dollars, the lawyer only got 50 dollars; the rest went up to the police.

Q. Were you told by the lawyers that that must go up?
A. From the smallest lawyer to the biggest lawyer: every lawyer was the same.
Q. And every lawyer whose name you have mentioned told you that they had to give up to the police part of their fees they got from you?
A. Every one of them.—Vol. iv., p. 4,170.

Mrs. Hermann first went into the business from being employed as a dressmaker for the inmates of disorderly houses. She gradually added house to house, until she had four houses and twenty-five girls. She had to pay the police sometimes as much as £200 initiation fee before opening a house, and then from £60 to £100 per annum as protection money.

In addition to these payments, every policeman in the street received a dollar or two whenever he chose to ask for it. The method of exacting this payment was very simple. The policeman said nothing, but simply stood in front of the door. Of course, no one entered the house as long as he was there; therefore, as counsel put it, "in order to induce him to take a little exercise round the block, he was presented with a two-dollar bill." This little episode used to occur about twice or thrice a week. Notwithstanding these payments, she made too much money to be left alone. She was raided twice in 1890, and on the first occasion the police extracted the sum of £200 before she was allowed to reopen her premises. The next year she was prosecuted, and had to forfeit £200 bail in order to avoid a threatened imprisonment. Immediately after her return she was again arrested, and had to pay £200 to the detective, who shared it with a high official at. the Central Police Headquarters.

Her business was so profitable that she admitted in Court that she had been making between £2,000 and £3,000 a year, of which sum the police and the police lawyers seem to have had a good half. On one occasion, when she had paid £100 to her lawyer to get off with a fine of £20, she was liberated on the Friday and re-opened her house on the Saturday.

Notwithstanding the way in which they fleeced their unfortunate victim, she was still subjected, like all her class, to occasional outbursts of brutality on the part of members of the force.

When Dr. Parkhurst was making his tour of investigation through "the avenues of our municipal Inferno," the wardman was sent round the district to the keepers of all the disorderly houses to describe Dr. Parkhurst, and to tell them to look out for him in case he appeared at their house. Another experience was when she took a house in West Twenty-third Street to start it as an ordinary boarding-house. She had furnished it, and was trying to let it. Promptly the wardman of the precinct came to her and asked her "whether she did not know the law of the precinct." "You know very well," he said, "that you cannot move in here until you see the Captain." And then this estimable officer did all he could to convince her that it was idle trying to run a decent boarding-house, and she had much better open the house in the regular way. The initiation fee would be £400, £200 down and the rest to stand over until business was good. There was to be a further payment of protection money, amounting to £240 a year. She had not much ready money, whereupon the wardman suggested that she might pawn her diamonds, for, said he, "the Captain is very bad off for money."

Another very amusing thing which came out in her evidence was the argument used by a detective named Zimmerman to induce her to give him £10. He got a couple of pounds one day, and came back the next, asking for another £2. She objected, but he said, "I will be a good friend to you. I have lots of pull, and my brother has shaved the Superintendent for twenty years, and I get a great deal; I have a pull on that account." It is an interesting illustration of the way in which everything was turned to account for the levying of blackmail. But we could hardly get lower than this. The origin of pulls is mysterious; but to have a pull because your brother shaves the Superintendent is a very mysterious foundation for political influence. It is, however, but one among the many things in the evidence that remind us of Turkey. The barber of the Grand Vizier is no doubt a much more influential person than many a Pasha; and detective Zimmerman was probably right in believing that his pull was good. Everywhere, and at every turn, we are confronted by the omnipresent "pull." It confirms in the strongest way what Mr. Godkin said long ago as to the city governments in America being a system of government by pulls :—

In the ward in which he lives, the foreign immigrant never comes across any sign of moral right or moral wrong, human or divine justice. He then perceives very soon that, as far as he is concerned, ours is not a government of laws, but a government of "pulls." When he goes into the only court of justice of which he has any knowledge, he is told he must have a "pull" on the magistrate or he will fare badly. When he opens a liquor-store, he is told he must have a "pull" on the police in order not to be "raided" or arrested for violation of a mysterious some-thing which he hears called "law." He learns from those of his countrymen who have been here longer than he that, in order to come into possession of this "pull," he must secure the friendship of the district leader.—*North American Review*, 1800. ·

Mrs. Hermann was only one among a number of other Madams who appeared before the Committee, but none succeeded in exciting so much sympathy on the part of the senators. The scandalous way in which the poor woman had been fleeced, and bullied, and ultimately reduced to penury by the very officials to whom she was paying protection money, roused the indignation of the Committee. If the police had protected her in return for their fee, it would have been a different matter, but, as Senator O'Connor remarked, indignantly, in addition to paying the monthly tax, and the initiation fees, raids were got up as an excuse to enable a policeman or a class of criminal lawyers to extort money out of her. Senator Pound remarked that it was the practice to protect such women until they became wealthy, and then squeeze it out of them and leave them destitute. They say that there is "honour among thieves," but there seems to be none with the policemen who handled Mrs. Hermann.

Another Madam, whose case attracted considerable attention, was one Augusta Thurow, whose misfortunes brought her into intimate relations with Senator Roesch, and led to the appearance of that redoubtable politician in the witness-box. The relations between her and the Captain of the Precinct seem to have been on straight business lines. About a dollar a month for each girl in the house was the regular tariff. When beginning business she went round to see the Captain and told him that she was willing to do the right thing, but she had not much money, and could not pay a very heavy initiation fee. He met her fairly, and said that he would send the wardman round, and she was to do what he told her. When the wardman came he said, " You wait until after the election, and, after the election is over, you start right in and do business." After the election day he returned and said, "Now we will come to terms. Give me twenty-five dollars a month and there will be no trouble either for you or for me." Business went on smoothly until one day she received a summons to go and see the Captain. When she got there she found a number of other ladies and gentlemen of her own profession at the station-house. On being admitted into the Captain's presence she thought he wanted money. He replied, ".I am not supposed to take money, but you can give me the money;" whereupon she handed him twenty-five dollars. He then told her that he had sent for her, not in order to collect the protection fee, which was the duty of the wardman, but to give her a friendly warning that he had received orders from the Central Office to close all the disorderly houses in the precinct. He hoped, therefore, that she would do her business very carefully, otherwise they might raid her from the Central Office. This was an incident which was constantly occurring. The Central Office, stirred up by newspaper reports, or by the representations of decent citizens, issues orders for enforcing the law. The police captains, instead of executing the orders of the Central Office in the spirit as well as in the letter, send word round to all those concerned warning them to be on the alert. By this means the Captain of the Precinct effectually nullifies the orders issued from the Central Office, and, even if the Central Office make a raid on their own account, they find nothing to seize.

It was shortly after this visit that Mrs. Thurow made her first acquaintance with a redoubtable policeman of the name of Hoch. Of all the collectors or wardmen who figure in the evidence, Hoch enjoys the most conspicuous notoriety. He was no sooner entrusted with the collections in that district than he insisted upon raising the fees for protection. " A ranch like that," he said, " is worth seventy-five dollars a month, and here you are only paying twenty-five dollars, and give me only five dollars, although you promised me ten dollars."

" Hoch," she replied, " I cannot afford it."

Q. What did he say when you said you could not afford it?
A. He says, " You have got the house, and why don't you make money? It is your own fault ; and that house is situated in the right spot, and you can do all the business you want and we won't interfere with you, but you must do better than this.
Q. Did he make any threats then to pull you, if you did not pay a higher rate ?
A. He said, certainly, if I could not do better than that, he would raid the house.—Vol. i., p. 1,055.

This alarmed the Madam, and off she went to her husband, who was sent in quest of Judge Roesch, the leader of the Seventh Assembly District, an ex-senator. "I will go and see somebody, and fix the thing up," said Roesch. "But it will cost about one hundred dollars." The money was paid, and she did business right away.

Some time after this she was pulled by another detective. She expostulated against the injustice of being run in, although she was paying protection money, whereupon the detective remarked senten-tiously, "Somehow or other you did not hitch with the Boss." She went round to the station-house, to find out what was wrong. The Captain told her that she had to find another house in the precinct, and he would protect her, but he would not stand the house in which she was any longer. The cause of this she discovered when she was told that she could not open the new house until she paid an initiation fee of £200 for the Captain, and £50 for Hoch.

It is not quite clear how it was that she got at cross purposes with the police, but one remark made by Hoch would seem to indicate the existence of an incipient jealousy between the police and Tammany Hall.

Augusta Thurow told the Committee that she said to Hoch :—

"I cannot afford to pay more than I am paying ; you people treat me so terribly, and I had to go to Roesch, and I had to pay him for his trouble." He said, "What did you pay him ?" I said "Never mind what I paid him." He says, "That is how it is with you ; you people get us angry ; you give money to the politicians that belong to the police."—Vol. i., p. 1,080.

The Chairman asked her to repeat exactly what he said ; and she answered, "He said, 'You give the money to the politicians that ought to go to the police. Are the politicians doing for you, or are we doing for you ?'"

The evidence of the two Madams, and of a great number of other keepers of disorderly houses, proved beyond all gainsaying that the police were in partnership with the prostitutes, and that the first-fruits of the harvest of shame were paid to the Captain of the Precinct. The Report of the Lexow Committee thus sums up the result of their investigations :—

The testimony upon this subject, taken as a whole, establishes conclusively the fact that this variety of vice was regularly and systematically licensed by the police of the city. The system had reached such a perfection in detail that the inmates of the several houses were numbered and classified, and a rateable charge placed upon each proprietor in proportion to the number of inmates, or in cases of houses of assignation the number of rooms occupied and the prices charged, reduced to a monthly rate, which was collected within a few days of the first of each month during the year. This was true apparently with reference to all disorderly houses except in the case of a few specially favoured ones. The prices ran from twenty-five to fifty dollars monthly, depending upon the considerations aforesaid, besides fixed sums for the opening of new houses or the resumption of "business" in old or temporarily abandoned houses, and for "initiation fees" designed as an additional gratuity to captains upon their transfer into new precincts. The established fee for opening and initiation appears to have been five hundred dollars.

Thus it appears that transfers of captains, ostensibly made for the purpose of reform and of enforcing the discontinuance of the practice, the prevalence of which seems to have been generally understood, resulted only in the extortion from these criminal places of additional blackmail.

As an evidence of the perfect system to which this traffic has been reduced, your Committee refers to that part of the testimony which shows that in more than one instance the police officials refused to allow keepers of disorderly houses to discontinue their business, threatening them with persecution if they attempted so to do, and substantially expounding the proposition that they were for the purpose of making money to share with the police. As an evidence of the extraordinary conditions to which this system had given rise, it is proper to call your attention to the fact that in a number of cases women, who, as keepers of disorderly houses, had paid thousands of dollars for police protection, had become reduced to the verge of starvation, while those who had exacted blackmail from them were living in luxury in houses that had been furnished out of the earnings of these women, or they were wearing ornaments of jewelry purchased by them ; and even the furniture of their houses had been paid for by those whom they had protected in the commission of crime.

The evidence establishes, furthermore, that not only the proprietors of disorderly houses paid for their illegal privileges, but the outcasts of society paid patrolmen on post for permission to solicit on the public highways, dividing their gains with them, and, often, as appears by proof, when brought before the police magistrates and committed to the penitentiary for disorderly conduct in default of bail, they compounded their sentence, and secured bail by paying ten dollars or fifteen dollars to the clerk of the court, or his agents, and were then released again to ply their calling and to become victimised as before.

The evidence furthermore shows that in some of the houses of the character described, visitors were systematically robbed, and when they made complaint at the station-house the man detailed to examine into the charge failed to arrest the perpetrator, and frightened the victim off by threats, and then returned and received his compensation, an equal division of the plunder between the thief and the officer.

The testimony taken as a whole conclusively establishes that the social evil was, and probably still is, fostered and protected by the police of the city, even to the extent of inducing its votaries to continue their illegal practices, maintaining substantially a partnership with them in the traffic, absorbing the largest part of the resulting profit.—Vol. i., pp. 33-36.

The most startling statement in the whole Report is that which is contained in the paragraph just quoted. From this it appears that the police were not merely toll-keepers on the way to hell, but if by any chance the Strange Woman wished to forsake her chamber of death, they thrust her back into it. What was it to them that she might wish to save her soul alive out of the pit ? Her duty was to stay there and earn dollars for the police. Were they not the Farmers-General of the Wages of Sin ?

Mrs. Blood, a keeper of houses of ill-fame, was compelled by a Police Captain to purchase the house of Madame Perot at some 10,000 dollars above its value, to carry it on as a house of prostitution (vol. v., p. 5,414). Another Captain smashed in the face of a man named Galingo because he had taken a house in which the Captain wished to instal a brothel-keeper from whom he expected to get £200 opening fee and £10 a month afterwards (vol. iv., p. 4,487). In other cases, witnesses who had intended to leave the business were compelled to go on running by threat of being raided and ruined if they dared to think of ceasing to earn fees for the police. The police had come to believe that they had a vested interest in every brothel; and when a keeper proposed to quit the business, he felt like an Irish tenant who is being evicted without compensation for disturbance.

MADAM HERMANN.

GANSEVOORT MARKET, NEW YORK.

"AFTER all," some readers will say, "what does it matter? These people are all outlaws; they deserve what they get, whatever it is." But the net of the New York police was exceeding wide, and the mesh was exceeding fine, and no class of the community escaped. As the sun riseth upon the evil and the just, so the blackmailer of the Police Department marked as his prey the honest and virtuous as well as the vicious and criminal. The Lexow Committee report:—

The evidence of blackmail and extortion does not rest alone on the evidence of criminals or persons accused of the commission of crime. It has been abundantly proven that bootblacks, push-cart, and fruit vendors, as well as keepers of soda-water stands, corner grocerymen, sailmakers with flag poles extending a few feet beyond the place which they occupy, boxmakers, provision dealers, wholesale dry-goods merchants, and builders, who are compelled at times to use the sidewalk and street, steamboat and steamship companies, who require police service on their docks, those who give public exhibitions, and in fact all persons, and all classes of persons whose business is subject to the observation of the police, or who may be reported as violating ordinances, or who may require the aid of the police, all have to contribute in substantial sums to the vast amounts which flow into the station-houses, and which, after leaving something of the nature of a deposit, then flow on higher. The commerce of the port even is taxed when the functions of the police department touch it, so that the shippers are compelled to submit to exactions in the city of New York that they do not meet with in any other port.—Vol. i., p. 42.

The chief sufferers, of course, were the poor and those who had no helper. They were as much at the mercy of their oppressors as the French people before the Revolution were at the mercy of their nobles. Again and again the senators expressed their amazement that a population so harassed and oppressed did not rise in revolt. Their wrongs certainly were immeasurably greater than those which led to the Tea-party in Boston Harbour and the Declaration of Independence. The chief abuse, the great grievance, might be summed up in one sentence. There was no justice for the poor. A witness of the name of Collins, speaking of the notorious Alderman, Silver Dollar Smith, and the gang by which he reigned supreme on the east side, said:—

Smith has a regular organisation; you couldn't convict them people neither; you couldn't convict them people in Court neither. It is an organisation to represent witnesses to condemn people if they have no money. If they have money to give, they are innocent; they perjure themselves if they pay money.—Vol. v., p. 4,894.

But it is not necessary to go beyond the finding of the Lexow Committee in their official Report :—

The co-ordination of all the departments of city government, under the sway of the dominant Democratic faction in that city, has produced a harmony of action operating so as to render it impossible for oppressed citizens, particularly those in the humbler walks of life, the poor and needy, to obtain redress or relief from the oppression or the tyranny of the police. Their path to justice was completely blocked. It is not credible that the abuses shown to exist have been the creation of but a short time. It is clear from the evidence that abuses have existed for many years back; that they have been constantly increasing through the years, but that they did not reach their full and perfect development until Tammany Hall obtained absolute control of the city government, and under that control the practices which have been shown conclusively before your Committee, were brought into a well regulated and comprehensive system, conducted apparently upon business principles.—Vol. i., p. 37.

The way in which the criminals in uniform and on the judge's bench acted when by any chance they could punish any one for doing what they themselves were doing all the time has already been remarked in the case of Captain Creedon, who was the only captain suspended by the Police Board during the whole investigation. A more cruel case was that of Karl Werner. This man had tried to bribe a policeman with five dollars, and was promptly arrested. Every difficulty was placed in the way of letting him have bail. At last the Court promised to accept bail, and a professional bondsman offered to give bonds for 100 dollars. His wife raised 95 dollars, and because she could not raise the additional five on the spot, the bondsman confiscated the 95 dollars, and the poor wretch was sent to gaol. The professional bondsman is one of the worst of the harpies who prey upon the unfortunate. Mr. Goff, who reported this incident to the Commission, deplored the impotence to save the victim of the bondsman and the police. " It is," he said, " simply another of the many instances of the terrible reign of terrorism " (vol. iv., p. 4,225).

Yet at the very time when Werner was being treated so harshly, the police were collecting blackmail by thousands of dollars every week. At first the Committee was incredulous. The Chairman asked once :—

Do you conscientiously believe that, notwithstanding these revelations, notwithstanding the situation that we are brought face to face with now, and what has occurred, there are police officers to-day in this city who accept blackmail ?

But he was speedily convinced that the revelations and the terrors of exposure had only reduced the amount of the blackmail levied by reducing the number of those who could be compelled to pay. The evidence of Captain Meakin's collector, Edward Shalvey, was conclusive on this point. He swore in the witness-box that he had gone on collecting, without making the slightest change, right down to September :—

Q. You collected from these several places, liquor dealers, policy shops, and houses of ill-fame as you did under the previous captain ?
A. Yes, sir.

Q. Did you ever meet with any refusal to pay from people engaged in this class of business, or did they all pay as matter of course?

A. They all paid as matter of course.

Q. So that, officer, even beneath the terrible frown of the Lexow Committee, the collections went on just the same?

A. Yes, sir.

Q. The old, old story continued, is that not so?

A. Yes, sir.

Q. And while, as a matter of fact, while there were exposures made and being testified to before this Committee since last April or May, right along the collections continued unbroken, did they not?

A. Yes, sir; not to such an extent.

Q. And the captains took the money in the same way?

A. Yes, sir.

Chairman Lexow: It seems incredible!—Vol. i., pp. 5,407–8.

"It is a tough old world, sir," as the old stager remarked to an enthusiastic young Reformer, "and takes a deal of moving." It is a very tough old world, and in the whole hemisphere there are few places tougher than New York.

The contributions paid by contractors to Mr. Croker can easily be understood. One Michael Moran, who was engaged in the towboat business, towing garbage under the Street Cleaning Department, made various subscriptions of from £10 to £30 to Tammany Hall. He was asked why he did so. He replied that Mr. Croker was the treasurer of the organisation he was doing some work for. "Tammany Hall, you mean?" asked the Chairman. "Well, I guess so," replied Moran. "Don't you know there is a distinction between the City and the organisation known as Tammany Hall?" asked the Chairman. There was no reply. But Moran evidently did not. Tammany Hall was the organisation that stood for the City. For him it was the City, and Moran said to subscribe to Tammany was the natural feeling amongst everybody that worked for the City; "one done it, and I didn't want to be left behind by anybody else; I thought I would hold my own end up":—

Q. Did any one suggest to you the advisability of giving up this money?

A. I have had conversations with other men that were in the employ of the City, and we compared notes occasionally to know what was done, and how we could keep ourselves solid.

No political contributions were made by Moran before Tammany came into power. So the Chairman asked :—

Q. How is it then that when the Department changed you felt called upon to send a cheque to Mr. Croker?

A. Well, because I didn't think I could go on and do the amount of business I I had for the City without recognising the people that were in power.

In 1892, when the Presidential Election was on, Moran doubled his subscription. Why was that? He replied :—

I compared notes with somebody in the same business that I was in myself, and found out somebody was paying a little more than I did, and I was afraid somebody in my line of business would put in a little more and I would get left.
—Vol. v., pp. 4,912–6.

When once an evil system has got itself established, innumerable other influences combine to render its extirpation extremely difficult. The Committee was much scandalised by discovering that for premises whose licence had been cancelled for immorality, a new licence was granted almost immediately. But when the President of the Excise Board was asked to explain, he said :—

> There came into consideration property interests ; we found that if licences were refused for places where business was carried on, that the banks were affected who had loaned money on mortgages, persons who had loaned on mortgages, the banks who had notes of parties in business ; the rents went to the support of persons who depended upon them solely ; the tax commissioners of the city protested to the Board of Excise against the refusal to license premises, because it reduces the value of property, and for that reason reduces the taxable values, and affected the city in that way ; real estate agents and other persons interested, and owners of property came to us and protested at the start that we ought not to refuse to allow a reputable business to be carried on on any premises, because they had been improperly conducted before.—Vol. iv., p. 4,379.

And it came to pass that no sooner was a saloon closed for vice or crime than it was opened again with a fresh licence.

The most mournful and tragic part of all these stories of oppression is that which relates to the treatment of the forlorn and desolate women who have no money with which to bribe the police. For them there is no mercy. The theory of the police, as we have seen, seems to have been that prostitutes existed for the purpose of raising revenue for the force. The women of the streets were the irregular tax-gatherers of the Department. Their vice was not merely connived at, but actively encouraged, so long as the police received their stipulated proportion of the wages of shame.

The women were the bondslaves of the Administration. By law they had no right to ply for hire ; but, in consideration of the payment of a regular ransom, they were left free to earn their precarious living.

"This is a phase," said Mr. Goff, "and a revolting phase, of a custom that exists in New York. I suppose it is the lowest form of oppression and corruption that possibly could be conceived by the human mind ; and that is, a tax upon these unfortunate women in the streets at night ; for they will not be allowed to walk the streets at night unless they pay so much to the officer, and this has been the custom in many districts of this city for years."—Vol. iv., p. 3,617.

The tariff varied.* On some profitable boats, the licence fee was

---

* The following table of some of the rates enforced by the police may be found convenient for reference :—

Pool-rooms from £10 to £60 per month.	Houses of ill-fame from £2 to £10 per month.
Policy shops from £4 per month.	Ditto. Initiation fee on opening, from £100 to £400.
Liquor dealers, 8s. per month.	
Prostitutes, outside, from 4s. a week to 2s. per night.	Price of Police appointment, £60.
Prostitutes, inside, 4s. per week.	„ of a Sergeant's post, £300.
	„ of Captaincy, £3,000.

fifty cents per night. But as a general rule the rate for "cruising" was a dollar a week. So long as she paid she was all right—always with the understanding that the policeman was to be free to arrest her if she was complained of by any whom she molested. Irregulars —occasional clandestine unfortunates—were, of course, regarded as interlopers and hunted down remorselessly. The zeal of the police-man, which was not stirred in the least by the breach of the law, rose to white heat when a woman who had not paid her fees attempted to pick up customers.

In theory, in New York—and, alas, in many other great cities —the right of a woman to freedom from arbitrary arrest without process of trial, and to redress for wrongful arrest, is absolute. In practice it does not exist. Every poor woman who is out after dark is liable to be arrested by a policeman, and to a woman friendless and forlorn there is written over the portals of every police-station, "All hope abandon ye who enter here." Before the Police Justice, the policeman's word goes. No corroborative evidence seems to have been demanded in New York. As one worthy testified before the Committee, he made arrests on general principles, and swore that his victim was loitering for purposes of prostitution. It was not necessary that she should commit any overt act, that she should molest any one, or that any citizen should complain of her molestation. It was enough that she should be loitering in the street. The oath of the policeman as to her intent settled her fate. A hurried gabble of words in a crowded court, and she was packed off to gaol.

This is the besetting sin of all attempts to keep the streets clear of immoral women by giving men, more or less immoral them-selves, absolute liberty to arrest any woman whom they please to say is loitering for purposes of prostitution. It was with a flush of pride that I came all unawares upon a reference made before the Lexow Committee to the case of Miss Cass, which made the name of Endacott a byword and a reproach in London some dozen years ago. Counsel had not got the story quite right. His version curiously mixed up the Trafalgar Square agitation with the arrest of the dressmaker in Regent Circus, but he had the main idea quite right. Scotland Yard and Mr. Matthews hit the poor girl a foul blow before the incident was ended, but it was a welcome thing to find that their belated vengeance had failed to silence the reverberations of indignation evoked by her scandalous arrest.

Americans and foreigners are often shocked at the state of London streets. Mr. Croker, I remember, expressed himself as being much horrified at the state of Piccadilly at midnight. But better a thousand times have the scandal of our streets than place the liberty of all women at the mercy of the police. The arrests of women fell 50 per cent. in London after the uproar that was made about

Miss Cass, and they are not likely to rise so long as the authorities insist upon the most just and salutary rule then introduced, that no woman shall be arrested for molesting by solicitation, unless the citizen who is molested is willing to give evidence next day in the police-court to that effect. The right of a human being to walk about the streets, to loiter about the streets, does not depend, and ought not to depend, upon the chastity of that individual. But if that principle were to be adopted as a principle of police action, it ought in justice to be applied impartially to both sexes.

Some very scandalous instances of the arbitrary arrest of innocent women, and their consignment to prison on the uncorroborated oath of a policeman, were brought before the Committee. The case of Ettie Kelter is one instance of the kind of thing that follows inevitably from making the policeman practically at once sole accuser and sole judge of the right of a woman to be at large in the streets.

Ettie Kelter was a young married woman of unimpeachable character. She had lived in Albany until August, 1894, when she came to live in New York. One Saturday evening in the following month she went out shopping, and being a stranger in the city she lost her way. She asked a gentleman to direct her to her destination. He did so. She took the wrong turning, so he called after telling her where she should go. She had hardly taken a few steps in the right direction before a young man—a policeman in plain clothes—seized her arm and dragged her off to the police-station. There he gave her in charge, declaring he had known her for years. It was in vain she protested she had never been in the city till the previous month. She was removed under arrest to another police-station, where she was locked up in a cell with a prostitute. She was terrified. She had been dragged through the street at a great rate, and no sooner was she in the cell than a blood-vessel burst. The blood gushed from her nose and mouth, scaring her companion, who thought she was bleeding to death. The blood streamed over the floor of the cell. But all the efforts of her companion failed to attract the attention of the policeman or the matron. She hammered at the door with a tin cup, but no one came. Not until the morning did the officer come to release them from the bloody cell.

Pale, weak, distracted, almost fainting, Ettie Kelter was bundled into court in the midst of a crowd of the offscourings of the streets, and brought up before Judge Hogan. She could not hear the charge, nor could she make out what the Judge said, excepting that he said something about soliciting. She did not know what it meant, but she passionately denied that she was anything but a respectable married woman who had only just come to New York. She might as well have held her peace. " Two months' imprisonment. After that, three hundred dollars bail good behaviour." This was Sunday morning.

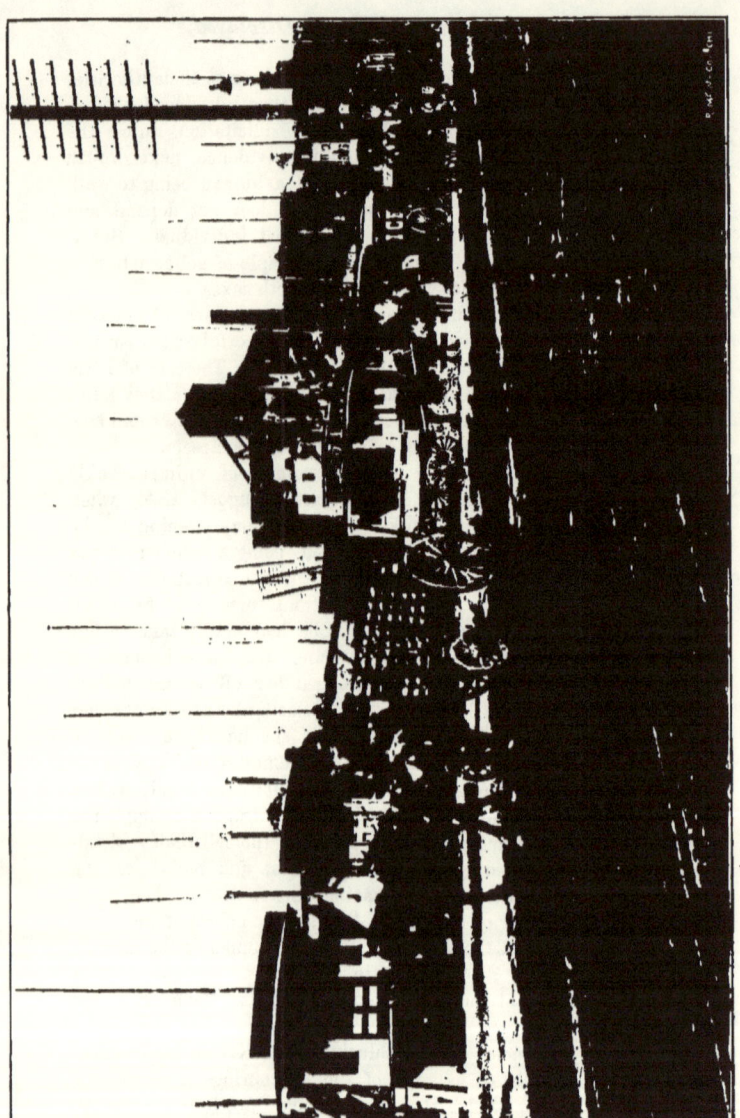

STREET SCENE IN NEW YORK; OYSTER ROW.

She was taken back to the cell, and her companion, who had been sentenced to three months' imprisonment, showed her a lawyer's card. "Send for that man," she said, "give him twenty dollars and he will get you out." Her companion did so and got out. Mrs. Kelter thought it would be better to send for her husband, who was employed as fireman on the emigrant ferryboat. The policeman who arrested her volunteered to go and tell him. But when he saw Kelter the message the policeman delivered was—

"Now you have a good chance of divorce ; I arrested your wife last night, and she has got two months on the Island."

She tried to write to her husband. But she had only two cents, and they would not give her a sheet of paper for less than five, nor would they send it out for less than fifty cents.

So the poor woman was taken to the Island, and kept there in prison for twenty-four days. At the end of that time her husband placed fifteen dollars in an envelope and handed it to Justice Hogan. His wife was released.

And that kind of infamy was going on all the time. The way in which the unfortunates were driven from pillar to post and treated as mere cattle, to be fleeced and plundered, provoked a very remarkable protest from a Police Captain who had sufficient humanity left in him to see the horror of the system which he had to administer. He was asked whose fault it was that the social evil flourished to such an extent. He said it was the fault of the law :—

Q. The law itself ?
A. Yes, sir, if you give the women the same protection by law that you do a mule and a dog you will do away with two-thirds of the houses of prostitution and women of the street.—Vol. i., p. 5,198.

In reply to the Chairman he explained how it was that houses of ill-fame were so much more difficult to deal with than gaming houses. He said :—

Because, Senator, you take the women to court, they are fined a few dollars and turned out on the street again to go and get more money, be re-arrested and pay again ; the trouble is that prostitutes are fined.
Q. Wasn't that done with gamblers as well ?
A. Well, you could get their paraphernalia and get them away, but you couldn't with the women ; a prostitute should never be fined and her money taken away from her ; those women are not bad women until they are made so ; they are dragged off the street and dragged before the court and their money taken away from them, and then drove out on the street again ; they are not bad until they are drove to it ; now, there were fully 30,000 arrests made from January 1st, 1876, to January 1st, 1878, in that little precinct alone, and I will venture to say there were not 1,500 women arrested, but arrested over and over again.—Vol. v., p. 5,213.

He was still further examined by Senator O'Connor :—

Q. I want to ask you a question or two : what do you mean to say, that if people would give the women the same protection given to mules and horses prostitutes would be fewer ?

A. What I mean by it is this : when they are arrested, instead of sending them to a magistrate to be fined and money taken from them, send them to a reformatory and inquire into their history, and you will find there are a great many of these people that you see lost in the papers. As I say, the women are not bad naturally; it is only where they are driven to it. If there was a reformatory and the money taken from them and taken care of, and put the institution under good women, good, proper persons to control that reformatory, and not abuse them, not send them to jail or abuse them, but send them to a reformatory. You will find some people from Massachusetts, some from Ohio, some from somewhere else, some from Michigan; send them to their homes, and if they are foreigners, who have not been here five years, send them back to Europe, and you will find as a general thing that the reason why the prostitutes and why the disorderly houses cannot be overcome is that there is no care taken of them ; they haven't a friend in the world. There is no friend to a prostitute ; everybody bangs her, everybody beats her; she is dragged into the station-house, taken to court, fined, and thrown on the street to get more money and bring it back.—Vol. i., p. 5,214.

These words deserve to be written up in letters of gold in every place wherever men discuss the question of abating this plague. It is the verdict of experience upon the habitual resource of the unthinking. " Go to, let us harry our sisters ! " is the first and last word of most of those who dream it is possible to promote the cause of morality by outraging the principles of justice.

Of the system in New York there is only one good thing to be said. Bad as it was, it is infinitely better than the hideous abomination of the European system of tolerated houses with their *police des mœurs* and the compulsory weekly surgical examination of their unhappy inmates. Better a thousand times even the rude, irregular tyrannies of Hoch and Koch, and all the diabolical gang of black-mailers, than elaborate all these infamies into a legalised system stamped with the seal of the approval of the State and enforced by the dread penalties of the law.

Prostitution, everywhere hateful, is at least less intolerable when it is free. When to the horrors of prostitution there is added the legalised slavery of the regulation system, you have indeed the sum of all villainies, and the abomination that maketh desolate is at last set up in the very holy of holies.

CHAPTER XI.

THE effect of law, not law written in the Statute Book, but law practically enforced among the people, is to evolve a conscience. Not without deep true meaning was it said of old time "the law is a schoolmaster to bring us to Christ." For it is the law, by its pains and penalties, which educates the individual as to the obligations of morality and the duty of well-doing. But in New York the universal practice of permitting all manner of abominations to run, provided the regular fee was paid to the police, acted as a direct depravation of public morals in familiarising the worst people in the city with a moral standard which was in itself a negation of morality. A woman of the name of Flora Waters, who kept a café with waitresses in a disreputable quarter, formulated with the utmost precision her belief that she was doing right because her money was taken by the police :—

Q. You thought the business you were doing was not wrong?
A. I thought it was all right when I paid, because they all said the money was going to——
Q. I only want to get her moral idea?
A. Because they told me the wardman did not keep the money and it goes up higher, and it had to be that way, because it was not old in this country, that people that sold liquors could keep waiters; but I thought it was nothing wrong, and everybody told me the money went all through, and everybody knew how it was worked.—Vol. ii., p. 1,363.

Here we have plainly and simply set out the inevitable consequence of any system of regulation. When the police sanction anything, it is no longer wrong to practise it. The police-court is the only Sinai of the Slum.

Bad as the police were proved to be in many instances, they were gentlemen compared with some of the Justices. The fact that such foul creatures were permitted to sit on the judgment seat and deal out sentences to men and women, the worst of whom were better than their judge, is the most melancholy feature of the whole black, bad business. This is the innermost centre of the New York Inferno.

Among the magistrates or police-court justices who figure conspicuously in this hideous drama, one Justice Koch appears pre-eminent. I prefer not to attempt to express the sentiments which are aroused by the spectacle of such a Justice dispensing justice. Miss Rebecca Fream, a mission-worker who had in vain endeavoured to secure some redress for the wrongs inflicted upon her poorer neighbours, was on one occasion ordered out of his court. She told the Lexow Committee :—

I turned to him, and I said, "Don't worry yourself; is this what you call justice?" then I said, "May God pity the poor on the east side, for with half-drunken judges on the bench whom shall they look to for justice if God forsakes them; you were half-drunk yesterday when I applied for a summons, and to-day you are so drunk you can't see out of your eyes."

Q. He made no effort to punish you for contempt of court?

A. No; there was one of the officers, and he turned and said, "By jee, I wouldn't take that from anybody." I said, "If you were in the same boat with him you would have to take it."

Chairman Lexow : Fine commentary upon the police-court procedure !

The Witness: That is nothing; that is only a drop in the bucket.—Vol. iv, p. 4,484-5.

The police-court judge seems in many cases to have been the pivot on which the whole horrible system of oppression revolved. It would need the pen of a Zola to describe adequately these shambles of the poor. There was the headquarters of the foul crew that flourished on perjury and grew fat upon using the forms of the law to frustrate its aims. It was the paradise of the professional bondsman, the blackmailer, and all the human vermin that thrive upon the misfortunes of their fellows. The worst lawbreakers of the precinct stood inside the rail beside the judge, browbeat and bullied the unfortunate accused, and practised every kind of extortion with impunity. The blackguard lawyer, hand-and-glove with the bandit policeman, found an even more detestable scoundrel than themselves upon the bench. The fiercest invectives of Juvenal would be too weak to do justice to these sinks of iniquity, in which honesty was a byword, innocence a laughing-stock, and the law merely a convenient pretext for levying blackmail.

The Committee was constantly hearing of the abuses connected with these courts, but the inquiry closed before they could be taken seriously in hand. The infamy of the system of bail, which was worked to fill the pockets of the bondsmen, led to frequent comments. On one occasion the Chairman remarked—

That seems to me to be a point that has never been properly accentuated; the commission of the police justice and the general activity of that character of man is a very great item going to show their inefficiency. Blumenthal and Hochstein's reputation was well known, and their insolvency was an established fact, and yet they went on bonds to the extent of thousands and thousands of dollars, and those bonds were even forfeited and not paid, and the men accepted again.—Vol. v., p. 4,490.

In the Report they say :—

While it was impossible for your Committee to spend much time in considering police courts, enough is shown upon the record to justify the conclusion that a very important reason why the police have been able to carry on and successfully perpetrate their reprehensible practices, is that at least some of the police justices have apparently worked in sympathy and collusion with them.—Vol. i., p. 27.

In the examination of a witness named John Collins, Mr. Moss said-

I think that the evils perpetrated by these judges, some of them, are even worse in their results than the evil practised by the police.

Chairman Lexow: It seems to me that any evil of that kind permitted by a judge is ten times worse than that committed by any other individual.

Mr. Moss: Of course, I myself have been before some of these judges for the society which I represent, and know what it was to be sat down upon, and outraged and browbeaten.

Senator Bradley: The witness says to me that the judges eat and drink with these people, and know the character of the people well.—Vol. v., p. 4,897.

The best way of bringing out this aspect of the administration of justice in New York is to set forth, without a word of comment, the substance of the evidence taken concerning the abortionists.

Abortion is not regarded in New York with anything approaching the horror that is excited by the same crime in the Old World. According to the evidence given before the Lexow Committee by an expert there were about two hundred abortionists who advertised every day in New York their readiness to kill the unborn child. It is an irregular profession that has regular practitioners. But, like all the other vices, it is a fertile source of revenue to the police. Dr. Newton Whitehead, a leading practitioner in this recognised system of ante-natal infanticide, was called before the Committee and testified as to the way in which he was at once helped and hindered by the police. Whitehead was arrested three times in six weeks. He was never tried on any one of these occasions. But he had to pay in bribing the police and feeing the police lawyer the sum of £565.

The doctor was arrested by a policeman called Frink, who insisted that he should retain for his defence a lawyer of the name of Friend. He was told that Mr. Friend had got a telephone directly from his house to police headquarters, so they informed him at once of all these cases, and he was our lawyer—the police lawyer (vol. iv., p. 4,240). Somewhat reluctantly, Whitehead sent for Friend. He had to pay him 700 dollars. Friend remarked apologetically that he would not insist on so much; but "I don't get this money myself: I have to turn over 50 per cent. of it to the police." "Our lawyer," indeed!

The policeman Frink then took his prisoner off into a small court-room, and told him, "In all these cases, Doctor, we expect to have some money off from them. Pay me 500 dollars and I will guarantee that the case will be dismissed when it is called." He paid 500 dollars and the case was dismissed, the only evidence offered incriminating, not the doctor, but a midwife, whom, however, they refused to prosecute, as "she did not have any money, and was not worth bothering with."

The lawyer, the doctor and the policeman dined together at a saloon in University Place. During dinner the policeman grew confidential :—

Sergeant Frink remarked to me that that was a very nice place; he said he knew the proprietor, and he said, "Doctor, this would be a very nice place if you ever wanted to run a young girl in here, upstairs, it would be all right; nothing would be said."—Vol. iv., p. 4,235.

A month later the doctor was again arrested. This time it cost him 475 dollars, paid to the lawyer. He was again arrested in the following month, and was held for the Grand Jury :—

Q. There was a regular raid on the abortionists at that time, was there not ?
A. Yes, sir.
Q. And all the warrants were issued by Judge Koch ?
A. All the warrants were issued by Judge Koch. Yes, sir.
Q. Do you know that any have been convicted ?
A. No, sir. It was simply a blackmailing scheme.
Q. Blackmailing by whom ?
A. I expect by the police.
Q. Who issued the warrant you were arrested on ?
A. Judge Koch.
Q. He seems to have had a monopoly on the issuing of warrants of these cases ?
A. He might have been making money pretty fast out of it.—Vol. iv., p. 4,246.

"Judge Koch," Whitehead said, " sat back in his chair, and he said he was going to make an example of me," and he held me to wait the action to the Grand Jury. He first insisted on 7,500 dollars bail, but after various interviews with the police lawyer and the police sergeant he reduced it to 2,500 dollars.

About a day or two after he had been held for the Grand Jury a lady came to see Whitehead, and said she wanted to be treated for abortion. Whitehead refused to treat her, and said that he had been so badly blackmailed :—

I told her I thought I would not practise any more ; I would leave the City of New York if they were going to prosecute me that way for nothing, and she said, " The gentleman who got me in the family way is a very influential man, and he is a judge, and can do a great deal for you, doctor." I told her I did not think he could, because I had been held for the grand jury. She insisted, and said, " Doctor, who is this man that held you ?" I said, " It was Judge Koch ;" she said, " Judge Koch ?" She said, " My God, he seduced me and got me in the family way five times, and Judge Koch paid the bill."
Mr. Goff : Proceed, doctor.
A. She left my house, and she went down to Judge Koch at Essex Market, and Judge Koch sent for me.
Q. Sent for you ?
A. Yes, sir, by her. I have got lots of proof of that: there is no need for him to wriggle out of it, for he cannot ; and I went to see Judge Koch, and he was as sweet as sugar. He told me, " Doctor," he says, " I am very sorry about this affair ; I did not know that my girl had ever been to you," he said. " I will do all I can for you—everything." He said there would not anything come of this case. " Don't you be afraid ;" the girl afterwards——
Q. Wait a while ; was there any one present ?
A. Mr. Friend here.
Q. Was present when Judge Koch said that to you ?
A. Yes, sir.
Q. Just follow the narrative: how did Mr. Friend come to be there in the room ?

Judge Koch waited for him until he came; I sat there about half-an-hour, and Koch seemed to be holding a case outside, and he waited until Mr. Friend came; he came in and saw me, and said, "I am waiting until Friend comes here."

Q. Judge Koch said?

A. Yes, sir; and when Friend came in he spoke this matter over, and Friend wanted to know what it was; he said, "It was that Alexander woman I had trouble with before."—Vol. iv., p. 4,264.

The "Alexander woman" was an actress, apparently Koch's mistress. Dr. Whitehead promised to perform the operation, but put. it off. She went away to another doctor and had the abortion brought about.

"I may say, Mr. Chairman," said Mr. Goff, in addressing the Committee at the close of Dr. Whitehead's evidence, "that of all the terrible exposures that have been testified to before this Committee, and that have shocked not only our city but the civilised world, I think the most terrible of all is that which we have heard this afternoon. I think the Committee has reached the climax of the horrible in this city."

"Satan's Invisible World Displayed," indeed!

DR. WHITEHEAD.

WALL STREET AND TRINITY CHURCH.

CHAPTER XII.

THE WORST TREASON OF ALL.

IT will be remarked, somewhat impatiently I fear, by the reader of this long and dismal series of stories of the way in which the municipal Thugs did their deadly work, But where were the citizens ? The good honest citizens, we are told, are always in a majority. They proved that they were able to elect their own City Government. Why did they not do it ? What is the use of talking about "the land of liberty," "the Great Republic," and the Democratic principle, if the richest, oldest, and most highly-educated city in the Western Continent is as impotent to use the ballot-box to protect itself as if it were a city in the dominions of the Great Mogul ?

The answer of the Lexow Committee—not by any means a complete answer—is as follows :—

The results of the investigation up to this point may . . . be properly summarised in the general statement that it has been conclusively shown that in a very large number of the election districts of New York, almost every conceivable crime against the elective franchise was either committed or permitted by the police, invariably in the interest of the dominant Democratic organisation of the City of New York, commonly called Tammany Hall. The crimes thus committed or permitted by the police may be classified as follows :—

Arrest and brutal treatment of Republican voters, watchers, and workers ; open violations of the election laws ; canvassing for Tammany Hall candidates ; invasion of election booths ; forcing of Tammany Hall pasters upon Republican voters ; general intimidation of the voters by the police directly and by Tammany Hall election-district captains in the presence and with the concurrence of the police ; colonisation of voters, illegal registration and repeating, aided and knowingly permitted by the police ; denial to Republican voters and election district officers of their legal rights and privileges ; co-operation with and acquiescence in the usurpation by Tammany Hall election district captains and watchers of alleged rights and privileges, in violation of law.

In fact, it may be stated as characteristic of the conditions shown to exist by a cloud of witnesses that the police conducted themselves at the several polling places upon the principle that they were there, not as guardians of the public peace to enforce law and order, but for the purpose of acting as agents of Tammany Hall, in securing to the candidates of that organisation by means fair or foul the largest possible majorities. They evidently regarded themselves as coadjutors of that organisation, stationed at the several polls for the purpose of securing its success whether by lawful or unlawful means, resorting to device, oppression, fraud, trickery, crime, and intimidation of almost every conceivable character . . . .—Vol. i., pp. 15, 16.

It is to be regretted that sufficient time was not at the disposal of your Committee to enable it to subject every district in the city to a rigorous examination upon the lines of this branch of inquiry, whereby a more accurate estimate of the effect of police interference might be reached. Sufficient, however, appears upon the record to show beyond peradventure that, owing to the practices above referred to during the years covered by the investigation, honest elections had no existence, in fact, in the City of New York, and that, upon the contrary, a huge conspiracy against the purity of the elective franchise was connived at and participated in by the municipal police, whereby the rights and privileges of the individual were trampled ruthlessly under foot, and crime against the ballot held high carnival.—Vol. i., p. 17.

The date of this Report, be it remembered, was January 15th, 1895. It may be supplemented by a very significant admission made by Mr. Goff, himself a Republican and now Recorder of New York. Speaking of the election frauds which he did so much to detect and punish in November, 1893 :—

It would not be just to lay the blame exclusively upon the Tammany inspectors, though, of course, being in the majority and in full control, they were chargeable with all that took place. Republican inspectors either openly co-operated with or quietly acquiesced in the perpetration of the fraud.—*North American Review*, February, 1894, p. 210.

The fraud on the ballot, to which both parties were privy, was all the more abominable because the provisions of the law against such abuses were very strict. But it is a favourite method in other countries than the United States to salve an uneasy conscience by passing a rigorous law without taking any precautions to see that it is carried into operation. This mode of relieving the feelings had been indulged in by New Yorkers in 1890, when the Ballot Reform Act passed into law. But, writing in 1894, Mr. Goff, who was Counsel to the Committee for the Prosecution of Election Frauds, said : —

Since the enactment of the reform-ballot law in 1890 no organised effort has been made to watch its operation or to detect any illegal practices. The public was satisfied with the popular catch-name of the Act, and it slept peacefully upon the assurance that fraud was no longer possible ; but the evidence obtained by the volunteer watchers, and the finding of over sixty indictments by the Grand Jury, mainly against election officials, demonstrate that false registration, false voting, and bribery are as easily and as safely practised as they ever were, and that perjury has enormously increased, owing to the number of safeguards which must be sworn away by the fraudulent voter and the collusive inspector.—*Ib.*, p. 204.

There were 1,157 polling stations in New York in 1893, and it was not possible to obtain competent watchers for all of them. But the evidence obtained was sufficient to show on how colossal a scale the frauds were practised, with the co-operation or connivance of both parties. Ballot-stuffing seems to have been common. Mr. Goff says :—

Almost without exception there were more ballots found in the ballot-box than the ballot clerk's number showed to have been delivered or the poll-list showed to have been voted, and in a great number of districts more than the registration. How they came there is to some extent a mystery ; but in some places ballots were folded in duplicate, and in others the pile of ballots on the table was added to by a sleight-of-hand performance.—*Ib.*, p. 209.

In the Thirty-sixth Election District of the Second Assembly District it was estimated that 5,000 out of the 12,770 votes counted were fraudulent. In the Seventh of the Third 567 ballots were found in the box for a district which had only 508 names on the register. Repeating and personation were almost universal. The lodging-houses played a leading part in the squalid and sordid drama. The tramps who use these dossing kens are all registered. But as they seldom pass three nights in the same place, they rarely vote where they are registered. That, however, is a mere detail. Mr. Goff says :—

The same men who registered did not, as a rule, vote upon the names given. To have them do so would require their maintenance at the lodging-house, and that would be too expensive. A more economic plan was adopted. A few days previous to election the proprietors of the lodging-houses were furnished, by the election-district captains, with lists of the names registered from their houses. Separate slips for each name were then supplied, and on election day the tramps, as they come along, were handed the slips, and they voted on the names thus given as frequently as they could get the slips. The election workers were never hard pushed to bring out the registered vote. They simply sent for the men when they wanted them, and were always supplied with the required number. Sometimes the floater forgot the name given to him or could not read the slip; sometimes a man who could not speak English wrestled with an American name, or an English-speaking man struggled with a Polish name. In all of these cases the obliging inspectors helped them out either by looking at the slip or by giving some sort of pronunciation to the unpronounceable name. In some election districts there was a rivalry as to who could vote on the most names, and the man who won the honours was an ex-convict, who voted eighteen times in two election districts of the Third Assembly District.—*Ib.*, p. 205.

The evidence taken before the Lexow Committee abounds with vivid little vignettes of how elections were conducted in New York City only four years since.

Here, for instance, is what Mr. Louis Meyer, a Republican inspector in the Third Assembly District, heard given as official directions by Police Captain Devery to a platoon of policemen on the morning of the November poll, 1893. The Union League and the City Club had decided to send watchers to the polls to detect any illegal practices. So by way of preparing for their reception, Captain Devery told the police in Mr. Meyer's hearing :—

There is a lot of silk-stocking people coming from up town to bulldose you people, and if they open their mouths, stand them on their heads.—Vol. i., p. 203, Lexow Report.

With such instructions it is not surprising that the police refused to interfere when their attention was called to the most flagrant breach of the law. Here is the story of Israel Ellis, Republican poll clerk at the Fifth Election District of the Third Assembly :—

When several voters came and they were handed sets of ballots, I wanted to get their names down, but the chairman and the officer told me it would be sufficient for me to take down the name and the vote.

I told them it was not sufficient, because if I did not do this, there would be a great deal of repeating done; and they said, "Never mind, it is none of your business; you do as we tell you; it has been carried on for a great length of time," and I still kept on protesting. And once the chairman of inspectors and another inspector said if I didn't shut up they would remove me from the board, and then the officer said if I would not stop he would take a hand in that too.

Q. The policeman said that to you?

A. Yes, sir; and then several times the repeaters came in openly, without any fear whatever, and they tried to vote, and each time I protested and challenged their votes; and one time a repeater came in and he passed the ballot clerk, he passed the chairman, but I recognised him as a repeater, and I challenged the man, and I said, "What is your name?" but the man had forgotten his name, because he was voting for the second—third—time, and so I caught hold of that man by the collar and ejected him, and the officer did not say one word; a second time a man came in to vote which I myself recognised as voting the second time in that election district; and another witness told me, whose name I do not know, that he was voting for the third time, and I waited until the man had voted, and I challenged his vote, and the man voted, and after he voted I caught hold of that man, and said, "Officer, I want you to arrest that man;" and the officer looked at the ceiling, not at me; he did not say a thing, and he did not arrest the man.

Q. Did you tell the officer what you wanted him to arrest him for?

A. I told him, the officer, that he voted for the second time to my own knowledge, and the third time to the knowledge of a witness, and wanted him to arrest him.

Q. And he looked at the ceiling?

A. He looked at the ceiling.—*Ib.*, vol. i., pp. 216–17.

One voter was allowed to vote on the Christian name John. He could not remember the other name. At the close seventy-two more votes were found in the ballot-box than there had been voters in the booth.

A similar scene was described as occurring at the Third Election District by Jacob Subin, a Republican watcher, who deposed that he had seen Mr. Rosalsky, the captain of the Socialistic Labour Party, protest against a young man who actually attempted to vote in Mr. Rosalsky's name under his very nose. Mr. Rosalsky grabbed hold of him and demanded that he should be locked up as a repeater caught in the act. Three Tammany heelers thereupon punched Mr. Rosalsky's face for him. He called upon the policeman to protect him. That worthy stretched himself leisurely and replied, "Well, I guess I am pretty busy just now. I will see you after four o'clock, and will have more time to spend." The heelers then were for mauling Rosalsky more severely; but the Tammany captain interfered, and, as an act of grace, secured his release on condition that he went right away. Rosalsky bolted for his life. After this Jacob Subin deemed it wiser to content himself with a simple protest when he saw such repeating as this:—

I have seen the Tammany Hall heelers bring in five or six men, drill them into line, and from the appearance of some of them they looked like Irishmen, and some like recent importations from Chatham Square or any of those dives, and most of those voted on Hebrew names; but the fun of it was that they could not pronounce the name under any circumstances that they were voting, and of course, as a rule, the chairman of the board of inspectors used to correct them, and in some instances they forgot their names entirely, and in such cases they went out of the line, and then the heelers would approach them and bestow such vile language upon them, and curse them and swear at them for being so stupid as not to recollect the name of the person they were voting under; and then they would drill them into line again, and I protested against them. I attempted to challenge them, and I was told unless I stopped monkeying with the regular way of doing business that I would be thrown through the window.—Vol. i., p. 303.

The appearance of the Tammany captain as master of the revels thus reported by Jacob Subin is significant. Frank Nichols, in the Twenty-

ONE OF THE MONSTER HOTELS OF NEW YORK: HOTEL MAJESTIC.

ninth Election District of the Third Assembly, where they had
eighty-four more votes than they had names on the register, took
two voters to the poll. As he was on the wrong side his men were
not allowed to vote :—

> I said, "Why can't they vote?" and they said, "No, they could not vote," and
> I said, "What was the matter of these people they could not vote?" and they
> said, "You go home; go home; you people can't vote any more," and then I was
> put out in the middle of the street, and the captain of the election district said,
> "Take this fellow away from here," and a fellow hit me in the eye with a brass
> knuckle.
> Q. Did the police do anything at all?
> A. No, sir; he would not arrest a cat that day, as long as it belonged to
> Tammany Hall; he would not arrest a cat."—Vol. i., p. 301.

Canute A. Deas, who was Inspector of Election at the First
Election District of the Third Assembly, protested fifty times in a
single day against barefaced repeating. The policeman whispered in
his ear that he meant to be fair, but he had his directions to take his
orders from the Chairman of the Board. Captain Devery drove up
and stood laughing and talking with the Tammany captain while the
legal voters were in vain clamouring to be allowed to vote. The
Republican watcher was thrown out by force under the eyes of the
policeman :—

> Q. Who threw him out?
> A. The crowd—the Tammany Hall captain of the district, who was in there;
> he was authority for everything.—*Ib.*, vol. i., p. 279.
> Examined by Chairman Lexow: When you said that the Tammany Hall
> captain was authority for everything, what did you mean?
> A. I meant that, whenever he desired to go into the polling place, he did so,
> that whatever he wanted was done; it seemed that they all worshipped him,
> bowed down to him.—*Ib.*, vol. i., p. 287.

Another witness, Ralph Nathan, described how a Republican
captain was hustled out because he swore that a voter had already
voted in four election districts, for he had followed him round and
had seen him do it. Mr. Nathan said :—

> The Tammany henchmen around the Third Assembly district have a peculiar
> method of putting a man out; you cannot make a particular charge of assault
> against them, hardly, but they push them out and hustle them out; they have
> probably ten heelers at every election district, and the polling place is generally
> narrow and small, and they can fill up a place and push you out.—Vol. i., p. 290.

Here also is a description of the method in which repeaters were
brought up when wanted. Mr. C. H. P. Collis, a prominent citizen
who acted as watcher for the Twenty-second Election District of
the Second Assembly District, deposed that he saw repeating going
on openly :—

> Q. Men voted under names that were not theirs?
> A. I cannot go so far as that.
> Q. Describe what you did see?
> A. I saw a man who sat at my side ticking off the list, and those names that
> were not ticked he would take three or four of them, men who had not voted, and
> hand them to an active worker, I supposed for the purpose of having those people

hunted up and brought to the polls, which would be legitimate; but I saw this man take them out in the street and hand them to the people there.

Q. Hand those names to the people?

A. Yes, sir.

Q. Then what occurred?

A. Then after awhile a man would come in and walk up to the polls.

Q. And would he call off one of those names?.

A. Yes, sir. In fact one man had forgotten his name and turned to the man who brought him in, and said, "What is that?"—and he told him, "John Kelly," or whatever the name was.—Vol. i., p. 130–1.

As a pendant to this scene take the following description of what happened at a previous election, where Mr. Thomas F. Harrington, Republican watcher, who had been challenging repeaters, was set upon by one Whitty, an ex-convict, as he was returning to the polling place to attend to his duties. Whitty was carrying a club and a revolver. Harrington argued with him, fearing that "they meant to inflict punishment upon me," and remonstrated against causing blood to be spilled on election day. Whitty, however, held on to his man, whereupon, said Harrington :—

I grabbed him by the throat with my left hand and went to strike him with my right, when the two officers (who had been standing watching Whitty's attack) rushed. One officer grabbed me by the coat and raised his club to strike me, and I told him if he struck me I would kill him where he stood, and a friend of mine came forward to help me, and the other officer rushed out and grabbed him, and up with his stick to strike him; they did not take hold of this Whitty at all; it was me and my friend they took hold of.

Q. And these policemen made no move to protect you in any wise in this assault, until you began to defend yourself?

A. No, sir.

Q. And then they laid hold of you and of your friend?

A. Yes, sir.—Vol. i., p. 135.

"We are in the business of carrying elections," said Boss Tweed, and a very successful business Tammany has made of it.

But what becomes of popular sovereignty, of the majesty of the ballot, of the sacred privileges of citizenship?

MR. VAN WYCK,

First Mayor of Greater New York.

From the *Journal*, New York.]

PART III.

HAMSTRUNG CÆSARISM AS A REMEDY.

CHAPTER I.

DESPAIRING DEMOCRACY.

DESPAIR is a strong word, nor can the citizens be rightly said to despair of the Republic while they are still engaged in making energetic efforts for its salvation. In the strict sense of the word, therefore, it is absurd to speak of a despairing democracy, which is still struggling to avert its threatened doom. But for democracy in the English sense of the word there is no longer any struggle in the City of New York. The ablest and the most hopeful Americans have given it up as a bad job, so far at least as city government is concerned. Hence, it is no misnomer to speak of Despairing Democracy as the natural and, perhaps, inevitable consequence of the display of "Satan's Invisible World," a few hints and glimpses of which have been afforded in the preceding chapters.

It seems but the other day that Mr. Andrew Carnegie flaunted before the eyes of his former countrymen the magnificent achievements of the principle which in city government is already abandoned in despair. Who could have imagined when reading the exultant pæan chanted by this American Scot over the achievements of "Triumphant Democracy" in the Western Republic, that within a very few years we should be called upon to chant a dirge over its grave in the first city in the United States.

Such an assertion will, no doubt, startle many readers both in the Old World and the New. It will be vehemently contested, chiefly

by those who are too deeply immersed in the roaring eddies of the
fight to be able to appreciate the significance of the drift of the
current which is sweeping them free from their ancient moorings.
But outsiders proverbially see most of the game. It is in no spirit of
exultation, but rather with a feeling of profound regret, that I note
the course which the law of evolution seems to be taking in the great
cities of the Western World. That regret is chastened and subdued
by two considerations. The first is based upon the belief in the
providential government of the universe. The second, which is more
personal to myself, is the fact that for nearly twenty years I have
been engaged in an attempt to compel hidebound devotees of parliamentary government to admit the virtue that is latent in the Russian
autocracy. I am no bigot of Constitutionalism, neither am I guilty
of the arrogant folly of pronouncing judgment upon expedients the
adoption of which the ablest and wisest men in other lands deem
to be indispensable. But the most sympathetic observer, after he has
made all allowances, cannot ignore the salient fact of the situation,
which is that by universal consent of the ablest and most practical
citizens in the foremost city of America, democracy, in the ordinary
sense of the term, has hopelessly and irretrievably broken down.

Be it carefully observed that I limit the collapse of democracy
to that application of the principle which has hitherto been regarded
as natural and almost invariable. Democratic government, as
defined by Abraham Lincoln, "government of the people, for the
people, and by the people," has in English-speaking lands, and
nowhere more so than in New England, been regarded as the
government of the community by an elective assembly—that is to
say, representatives chosen by the different localities meet together
in a common council which is entrusted with authority to manage the
affairs of the community. The House of Commons is the most
familiar type of such a democratic assembly, but every town council
in the land is based on the same principle. Nor is it only in
Britain that this principle has been applied. It has hitherto
prevailed wherever democracy has been adopted as the system
of government; whether in the French Republic, in the German
Municipalities, or in any and all of our Colonies, the same
principle invariably reappears. The centre of authority is the
elective assembly, composed of representatives of the wards or districts
or constituencies into which the city or community or nation has
been divided.

Of course, I shall be told, and justly told, that this system of
what may be called parliamentary or municipal democracy is by no
means the only form through which democracy can give effect to its
will. This, of course, is perfectly true, and that was why I was so
careful to limit and define what I meant by democracy. There is no
danger of my forgetting that democracy can exist without the usual

A VIEW IN BROADWAY.

parliamentary or municipal apparatus. Russia, although governed autocratically, is nevertheless one of the purest democracies in the world. Neither can any Englishman who lived through the Second Empire in France forget that the Third Napoleon always maintained that the Empire was the true and natural outcome of modern democracy. Nevertheless, although the Tsar of Russia rules over a democratic nation, and the Third Napoleon regarded himself as the armed guardian of French democracy, the conventional conception of a democracy in English-speaking lands has never been that of a community governed by an autocrat, but always of a community in which the centre of power lay in the elective assembly. It is this conventional theory of democracy which has been thrown overboard in New York. Hence, from the point of view of the parliamentarian or the conventional believer in government by an assembly of elected persons, the Charter of Greater New York, under which the first election has just taken place, is a more melancholy spectacle than even "Satan's Invisible World Displayed," with all its saturnalia of debauchery, violence and corruption. The Charter of Greater New York is the direct outcome, the natural fruit of the bitter experience of Tammany rule. Once more, to quote the familiar saying,—"Sin when it hath conceived bringeth forth death," and the sin revealed by the Lexow Committee has brought forth a deadly harvest in the Charter of Greater New York. Deadly, that is, inasmuch as it is fatal to the principle of vesting the government of the people in the elected representatives of the people in public council assembled. For the central principle of the Charter of Greater New York is the substitution of the authority of a Tsar-Mayor for what has hitherto been regarded as the natural authority of an elected council.

This is not a sudden and unexpected change. The evolution of an elective autocracy has been in progress for some years, but it has never before been brought into such conspicuous prominence as by the Charter of Greater New York, for that Charter is the formal embodiment in black and white of the central principle of the Second Empire, with certain modifications which accentuate rather than diminish the expression of democratic despair, of which it is the embodiment. It is this evolution of Bonapartism, of an elective dictatorship, based on universal suffrage, which is the most startling phenomenon of modern politics in the United States. The Third Napoleon never claimed to reign by divine right. His authority was based upon a mass-vote of the electors of France. His throne, although propped by bayonets, was seated on universal suffrage, and in theory he asserted, and in practice in the last years of his reign adopted, the principle that this autocracy, which originally sprang from a mass-vote of the people, needed to be renewed and confirmed from time to time by a *plébiscite* of the whole nation.

The government of Greater New York, as it has been established by the Charter under which the recent election took place, is simply the Second Empire of France re-established in the first city of the American Republic, with the limitation that the reign of the despot shall be rigidly limited to four years, after which he shall not be eligible for re-election until the expiry of another term of an equal duration. That this in no sense is an exaggeration, but a simple literal statement of facts perfectly well known in the United States, I shall shortly proceed to show; but before doing so it is well to note some of the circumstances which led up to this extraordinary evolution of autocracy on Republican soil.

CANDIDATE VAN WYCK IS SAID TO HAVE POLLED THE SOLID VOTE OF THE
CYCLISTS OF GREATER NEW YORK.

MR. SETH LOW.
First Year-Mayor of Brooklyn.

CHAPTER II.

THE TSAR-MAYOR.

THE parallel which instinctively occurs to the mind of the observer is one of somewhat evil omen for the future of the American Commonwealth. The Roman Republic evolved the Empire very much in the same way that the Tsar Mayoralty of Greater New York has been evolved from the institutions which preceded it. The Roman Empire was not based upon a *plébiscite* of the citizens, but equally with the New York Mayoralty it ignored the principle of hereditary right. Occasionally the Imperial purple passed from father to son, but for the most part the throne was filled by the only kind of election possible in those days. The Emperor was the choice of men who wielded, not ballots, but swords.

A study of the corruption and despair which produced the Roman Empire will supply many curious parallels to the existing state of things in America. In ancient Italy, as in modern New York, elective institutions had been abused until the best citizens despaired of the Republic. The Third Napoleon, in his history of Julius Cæsar, writes concerning the way in which elections were managed in ancient Rome in terms which curiously resemble those employed by the Lexow Committee in explaining how elections were worked in modern New York:—

> The sale of consciences had so planted itself in public morals, that the several instruments of electoral corruption had functions and titles almost recognised. Those who bought votes were called *divisores*; the go-betweens were *interpretes*; and those with whom was deposited the purchase-money were *sequestres*. Numerous secret societies were formed for making a trade of the right of suffrage; they were divided into decuries, the several heads of which obeyed a supreme head, who treated with the candidates and sold the votes of the associates, either for money, or on the stipulation of certain advantages for himself or his friends. These societies carried most of the elections, and Cicero himself, who so often boasted of the unanimity with which he had been chosen Consul, owed to them a great part of the suffrages he obtained. . . .
>
> This all was struck with decadence. Brute force bestowed power, and corruption the magistracies. Numerous elements of dissolution afflicted society; the venality of the judges, the traffic in elections, the absolutism of the Senate, the tyranny of wealth, which oppressed the poor by usury, and braved the law with impunity.—"Julius Cæsar," by Napoleon III., vol. i., p. 3.

As a way of escape from the disasters which afflicted the Republic, there emerged in natural process of evolution, first, the dictatorship of Sylla, then the triumph of Marius, afterwards the ascendency of Cæsar, which led directly to the foundation of the

Empire by Augustus. We are not within sight of the Augustan Empire in the United States, but the same causes which in the natural course of time ripened the Empire of the Cæsars are to be seen in full operation on the banks of the Hudson. The United States is happily at present without the legionaries whose supremacy enabled a succession of military commanders to establish the Roman Empire upon the grave of the Roman Republic. That element of danger may not be wanting in time to come. The growth of imperial ambitions at Washington is one of the most plainly marked signs of the times. A spirit which to-day annexes Hawaii, threatens Spain, and defies Europe with the Monroe Doctrine, will certainly be driven to increase its armaments or to abate its ambitions. These things, however, belong to the next century. Sufficient unto the day is the evil thereof.

The system of the Tsar-Mayor first came into operation at Brooklyn in 1882. It sprang, as did the Second Empire, from the timidity of the citizens. Mr. Seth Low, the first Tsar-Mayor, writing in the last edition of Bryce's " American Commonwealth," points out this very clearly. He said :—

> The aim of the Americans for many years deliberately was to make a city government where no officer by himself could have power enough to do much harm. The natural result of this was to create a situation where no officer had power to do good.

·· The idea of allowing citizens in their wards to elect representatives, who should wield all the powers vested in English, French or German town councils, was regarded by Americans as savouring of suicidal recklessness. To trust the elected representatives of the people in an American city, as we trust the town councils of Birmingham and Glasgow, seems rash and reckless to the American statesman. A very thoughtful writer in the *Annals of the American Academy of Political and Social Science* four years ago, singled out the English municipal system as one which no sane American would dream of applying to a great American city. He said :—

> It may be safely said that this whole organisation of the Birmingham government is an exaggeration of the features which have had the worst effects in the United States. It must make the mouth of a Tammany chief water to think of such a simplification of his labours and increase of the opportunities for plunder.

Notwithstanding this, American observers have followed Mr. Chamberlain in declaring that Birmingham is the best governed city of the world. That, however, in no way reassures the American pessimist, who has put on record his conviction that " the vicious principles evolved in English municipal government will overcome any safeguard, and that it is only a question of time when English cities have a taste of what New York has been through." The result of this deep-rooted conviction in the American mind, that the elect of the people is certain to steal if he gets a chance, was that city governments came into existence dominated by the one desire to paralyse in advance the city council, to limit its opportunities of stealing, and place it more or less at the mercy of the State Legislatures. The result of this system born of cowardice and lack of faith was to transfer almost all power in New York from the city authorities to Tammany Hall. Tammany, in theory at least, was broad based upon the people's will, nor was there any limitation to the authority of the Boss.

After a time the absurdity of this system, and the ruinous results which followed, forced upon the minds of the more intelligent citizens the fact that something must be done, and that at any cost. Some centre of local authority must be created which could be trusted not to steal. Mr. Seth Low explains and defends the establishment of the Tsar-Mayor on the theory that cities in their organic capacity are more accurately described as large corporations than as small states. He says :—

The better results flowing from this theory are easily made clear. Americans are sufficiently adept in the administration of large business enterprises to understand that, in any such undertaking, some one man must be given the power of direction and the choice of his chief assistants ; they understand that power and responsibility must go together from the top to the bottom of every successful business organisation. Consequently, when it began to be realised that a city was a business corporation rather than an integral part of the State, the unwillingness to organise the city upon the line of concentrated power in connection with concentrated responsibility began to disappear. The charter of the city of Brooklyn is probably as advanced a type as can be found of the results of this mode of thinking. In Brooklyn the executive side of the city government is represented by the mayor and the various heads of departments. The legislative side consists of a common council of nineteen members, twelve of whom are elected from three districts, each having four aldermen, the remaining seven being elected, as aldermen at large by the whole city. The people elect three city officers, besides the board of aldermen—the mayor, who is the real as well as the nominal head of the city, the comptroller, who is practically the book-keeper of the city, and the auditor, whose audit is necessary for the payment of every bill against the city, whether large or small. The mayor appoints absolutely, without confirmation by the common council, all the executive heads of departments. He appoints, for example, the police commissioner, the commissioner of city works, the corporation counsel or counsellor at law, the city treasurer, the tax collector, and, in general, all the officials who are charged with executive duties. These officials, in turn, appoint their own subordinates, so that the principle of defined responsibility permeates the city government from top to bottom. The mayor also appoints the board of assessors, the board of education, and the board of elections. The executive officers appointed by the mayor are appointed for a term of two years—that is to say, for a term similar to his own.—Bryce's " American Commonwealth," vol. i.

This Charter first came into effect in January, 1882, and Brooklyn has been governed by Tsar-Mayors ever since. Mr. Seth Low, who was the first Tsar-Mayor in America, and who subsequently served a second time, claims for it the virtues and vices of all despotisms. When you have a good Tsar, nothing can be better. When you have a bad Tsar, nothing can be worse. As he says, the Brooklyn system " made clear to the simplest citizen that the entire character of the city government depends upon the man chosen for the office of Mayor." It is, of course, playing double or quits. If you get a good man, his immense power enables him to be potent for good, but if you get a bad one, Heaven help the city !·

The Brooklyn system was adopted with modification in several towns, notably in Cleveland, in Cincinnati, and to a certain extent in Philadelphia. The same system was carried out to its ultimate extreme in the Charter of the City of Quincy, in Massachusetts. Mr. Gamaliel Bradford, of Boston, in the May number of the *Annals of the American Academy of Political and Social Science* for 1893, thus explained the evolution of the Tsar-Mayor as it could be seen in the Quincy Charter :—

> It was provided that the mayor should be the only executive official elected at all, and he by general vote of the city, so that he might be the embodiment of the whole administration and responsible for it. That he might be this, he was given the full power of appointment and removal of all subordinates except the school committee, as to whom even the radical framers of the charter shrank from encountering the popular prejudice. It was held that the separate election of officials, whether by popular vote or that of the council, is destructive of all subordination, of all firm or efficient administration, and of all personal responsibility. But the Quincy charter ran counter to another prejudice much more deeply rooted : the requirement of confirmation of the mayor's appointments by the council or aldermen.
>
> The New York charter of 1884 gave to the mayor the full power of appointment, though that of removal, which seems to be necessary to make the other effective, was still jealously withheld. The Quincy charter gives both powers in full measure. Another object aimed at, though with some compromises, was to get rid of boards or commissions, as overriding the mayor and destroying that personal responsibility which was regarded as so important to public opinion. One man in every place, that man directly responsible to the mayor alone, and the mayor himself to the people, at short intervals; this was the guiding theory. To obviate the almost morbid dread of one man power, it was provided that the mayor might be removed from office by a three-fourths vote of the council, and a new election ordered. The theory was developed by another provision wholly new in the practice of the country: that the heads of departments, as well as the mayor, should be required to be present at the sessions of the council, to explain the wants of administration, and to give a public account of their stewardship in response to the questions of individual members. It was expected that in this way the strength or weakness of the mayor would be made clear to the popular apprehension, and that a better and improving class of men would be chosen with a corresponding effect upon city affairs.

Unfortunately, Mr. Bradford was compelled to admit, what Mr. Charles Francis Adams had previously pointed out, that the experiment of the Tsar-Mayor was, in Quincy, by no means justified by its results. Mr. Bradford says :—

> It must be admitted, upon the evidence of leading citizens of Quincy, that the charter has thus far failed to accomplish its purpose ; that extravagance of expenditure, local jobbing and caucus politics are as rampant as in other cities in the State.

Nevertheless and notwithstanding the disappointment in Quincy, when the Charter of Greater New York came to be discussed, the advocates of what may be called the English or normal system of vesting the government of the town in the hands of an elective council were in a hopeless minority, and the Charter of New York was drawn up upon the Tsar-Mayor basis. The advocates of the Tsar-Mayor used all the familiar arguments which are employed by apologists for autocracy all over the world. Their great keynote was the need for the concentration of responsibility.

"It is necessary," said Mr. Godkin, "to reduce to its lowest possible point the number of executive officers whom the community has to watch." Mr. De Witt, Chairman of the Committee, who drafted the Charter for Greater New York, put the matter succinctly when he wrote:—"I am for a Tsar-Mayor, with a short term, and a free right to go again to the people"; and then he added, recurring to the curious vein of fatalism which in Napoleon found expression in a belief in his destiny, "I believe that the Supreme Ruler of the universe moves through the mind of the multitude, and in this age of free schools and ubiquitous journalism, no mayor with plenary power and full responsibility would dare to permit corruption or inefficiency to exist in any department. If he did, the people would have only one head to hit, and one party to demolish."

This change, to which we may take it American reformers are now definitely committed, may be, as Mr. E. M. Shephard declared, "the most important gain in municipal reform in our time," or it may be the first step down the inclined plane which leads to despotism. My duty is not to dogmatise, but merely to describe. All that I would venture to observe by way of comment is that the new reform seems to be at variance, not only with the universally accepted English idea, which may, of course, be ignored, but equally with the Jeffersonian theory of the fundamental principle of Local Government. It may be necessary to fight fire with fire, and to cast out the Boss by the Tsar-Mayor, but old-fashioned Liberals may be pardoned if they feel that it is a very dangerous game to cast out the Devil by the aid of Beelzebub, the Prince of Devils.

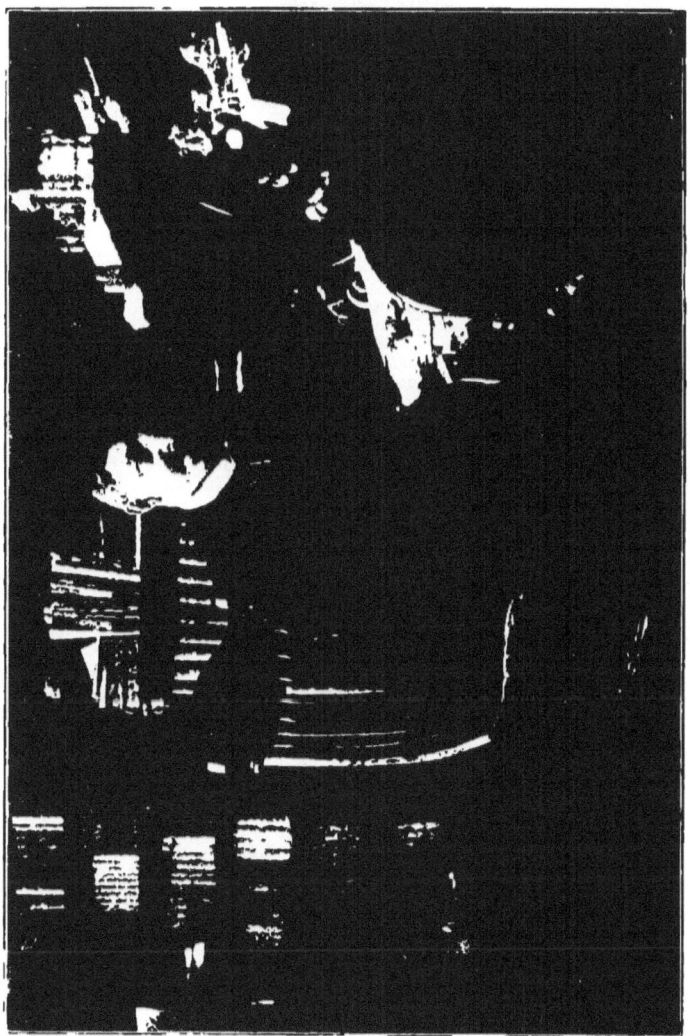

DR. ALBERT SHAW.

CHAPTER III.

THE Charter of Greater New York is the last, or rather the latest, of a long series of Charters granted by the State Legislature of New York for the government of the city. There were eleven distinct Charters granted between 1846 and 1890, so that the average life of a Charter is only four years. The Charter preceding this was regarded by Mr. Godkin as the best because it reduced the elective element almost to vanishing point :—

No community as heterogeneous as ours can manage its affairs successfully through democratic forms without reducing to its lowest possible point the number of executive officers whom it has to watch, and call to account when things go wrong. As soon as responsibility is widely diffused in such a community, "deals" or bargains between politicians for the division of the offices at once begin.

In no community, homogeneous or heterogeneous, can public affairs be managed successfully when the supreme Legislature always stands ready to remodel the Charter whenever the minority in the City can command the support of the majority in the State. It is bad enough in London when the minority in the County Council can appeal to the majority in the House of Commons. But the House of Commons only interferes by way of obstructing legislation desired by the Progressive majority. It never attempts to revolutionise the constitution of the Council, because the majority at Westminster does not agree with the majority at Spring Gardens.

It would not be a very great exaggeration to say that in the past the only effective government of the City of New York has consisted of Tammany Hall Executive as a Lower House, and the Legislature at Albany as an Upper Chamber. These two bodies were not shadows. They were both governing realities. When Tammany did not control the State Legislature, Albany was the only hope of the despairing Republicans. How constant was the interference of the State Legislature may be inferred from the fact, vouched for by a return presented to a State Commission on the Government of Cities, that in the ten years between 1880-9 no fewer than 399 different amending laws were passed at Albany affecting the Charter of New York City. A State Legislature which passes nearly forty laws every year changing or amending the City Charter is a factor to be reckoned with.

The demand for Home Rule for the city, often repeated, does not seem to be supported in earnest by either party. Both admit the need for it. But neither seem willing to risk anything to obtain it. The Charter of the Greater New York sprang from the Commission appointed in 1896 to consider and report upon the proposed consolidation and unification of the government of the great urban area now known as Greater New York. The subject had long been under discussion, but when the Charter came to be drafted many drew back. Mr. Croker asserted that if the citizens had been permitted to vote yea or nay upon the adoption it would never have come into force. The Referendum was not permitted, and the Charter came into force this year without the preliminary of a popular mass vote.

General Tracy, the Republican candidate at the recent election, was President of the Charter Commission, with Mr. De Witt as Chairman of the Committee. Among the other members were Mr. Strong, the Mayor of New York; Mr. Seth Low, the first Tsar-Mayor of Brooklyn; Mr. Gilroy, Tammany comptroller of the City of New York, and several other influential men. They unanimously agreed to recommend the Charter as it stands at present, although Mr. Seth Low and Mayor Strong dissented from one or two of its provisions.

The Commissioners set to work in the belief that they were framing a constitution for a city which in the lifetime of those now living would have 6,000,000 citizens. Mr. De Witt, the Chairman of the Committee, who tells us that "his embattled energies laboured at the Charter for eight long consecrated months," contemplated with pride the result of his handiwork. Speaking of the Charter, he declares :—

It is adequate to all the emergencies of the vast future. It is constructed not merely for the present, but for many centuries to come. It has in it all the virtues of existing charters and the vices of none. It will adapt itself to any extent of domain, and to any multiple of population. As well with a population of ten millions as with a population of three millions, it will give to each neighbourhood the utmost care and attention, and to the imperial metropolis, as a whole, the utmost dignity and power. The form of government for Greater New York, it will be the model upon which Greater London will be constructed.

Without making quite such a lofty claim for the Charter as this, there is no doubt that it is an important document, and one which will well repay a careful study. It is somewhat voluminous, filling with its annexes no less than one thousand pages.

It has, however, been made the subject of a very painstaking and lucid analysis by Dr. Albert Shaw, whose "Studies of Municipal Administration in the Old World and the New" entitle him to speak with some authority on the matters dealt with by the Charter. His analysis of the Charter was published in the *Atlantic Monthly* for June, 1897, under the title of "The Municipal Programme of Greater New York." Mr. De Witt published his clear and concise

idea of the Greater New York in *Munsey's Magazine*, under the title
of "Moulding the Metropolis." The Charter itself, with its 1,620
sections, has been published in popular form at 10 cents by the
Brooklyn *Daily Eagle*. The text of the Charter, with the aid of Dr.
Shaw's and Mr. De Witt's analyses, enables any one to form a
tolerably clear idea as to what the Charter does and what the
Charter means.

Mr. Croker repeatedly assured me, before the recent Mayoral
contest began, that the Charter was a monstrosity and an absurdity,
that the system of government which it established must inevitably
break down, and that not even an archangel could make it work
satisfactorily. Mr. Croker can hardly be said to be an impartial
judge, but his verdict is sufficiently in accord with that of Dr. Shaw
to justify very grave misgivings as to the prospect before the second
city of the world.

During my stay in New York I was simply besieged by inter-
viewers, begging me to tell them what I thought of the Charter. I
turned a deaf ear to their solicitations, preferring to make a more
careful study of the Charter itself with the advantage of the analysis
of Dr. Shaw. Even now I rather shrink from expressing an opinion,
lest it should be misconstrued as implying any claim on my part to
sit in judgment on those who are saddled with the responsibility of
governing New York. But when doctors differ, the people decide,
and when local experts are at hopeless variance as to the merits or
demerits of the Charter, it may perhaps be permitted to a British
onlooker, even at a distance of 3,000 miles, to put on record the
way in which the Charter strikes him. If this should not be
denied me, I may say at once that the Charter seems to have
written on its face thoroughgoing distrust of the people. The
aspect of the Charter is black with despair. It is far worse as an
expression of democratic despair than the Brooklyn Charter, for
the Brooklyn Charter at least trusted the Tsar-Mayor, whereas the
New York Charter shrinks even from doing that.

In explaining the provisions of the Charter, I prefer to quote
from Dr. Shaw's analysis. He says:—

First comes the mayor, who is entitled the chief executive. He is to be elected
for four years and is not eligible for an immediate re-election, and his salary is to be
15,000 dols. a year. The business of city administration is divided into eighteen
executive departments. These are the departments of finance, of law, of police,
of water supply, of highways, of street-cleaning, of sewers, of public buildings,
lighting and supplies, of bridges, of parks, of building, of public charities, of
correction, of fire, of docks and ferries, of taxes and assessments, of education,
and of health.

The members of all these boards, with one exception, are
appointed by the Mayor, not elected by the people. The one
exception is the City Comptroller, who is at the head of the
Finance Department. He is elected at the same time as the

Mayor. The Mayor also appoints all the members of the five school boards, which look after education in the five boroughs of Greater New York:—

> The system provided for in the new charter puts the executive government wholly into the hands of the eighteen departments, which are practically supreme in their respective eighteen spheres, except as they are limited by two important groups, or boards—namely, the board of estimate and apportionment and the board of public improvements. One discovers with some surprise that the ordinance-making power, which would nominally belong exclusively to the municipal assembly, is, in the Greater New York charter, conferred upon all the executive departments.

Where then, it will be asked, does the Municipal Assembly come in, for there is a Municipal Assembly which is divided into two chambers? To which the answer is that the Municipal Assembly is practically reduced to the function of a debating society; for, says Dr. Shaw:—

> The eighteen executive departments take away from the municipal assembly the larger part of the ordinance-making power; the board of public improvements in practice controls municipal plans and policies as regards the construction of works, and the board of estimate and apportionment intervenes to prepare the budget, both on the side of income and on that of disbursement.

It is true that the budget must be voted by the Municipal Assembly, which on that occasion sits as one body. But its control is practically nil. The real financial control is vested in the Board of Estimate and Apportionment. Mr. F. V. Green, writing in *Scribner* for October, 1896, points out that the framers of this board carefully avoided the principle of direct election. He says:—

> Probably in no other part of the globe, however autocratic its government, is such power of taxation and appropriation committed to so unrepresentative a body as in this foremost city of the land of liberty, whose Government originated in a protest against taxation without representation. And it is a still more curious anomaly that this system, which was established as one of the results of the overthrow of the Tweed *régime*, and has been in operation for twenty-three years, is the most successful feature of the present form of city government—the only one of which criticism is seldom heard.

After this non-elective board has approved of the estimates, they are then sent down to the Municipal Assembly to be voted. But, says Dr. Shaw, the Municipal Assembly

> must complete its action within a certain number of days. It may not add a penny to the estimates at any point whatsoever. It is permitted to throw out items or to make reductions, but it must not offset these by voting increased sums for any object. When it has completed its consideration, the budget goes to the mayor for his final action. The mayor has authority to veto any amendments that the municipal assembly may have made. That is to say, he may restore any amounts that have been subtracted.

But, it will be said, the Mayor's veto may be overridden. It may, but only if there is a majority of five-sixths of the Municipal Assembly against him. Such unanimity is practically unattainable.

It would, indeed, seem as if the chief purpose of the Municipal Assembly was to give its members practical lessons in the working of simple sums of vulgar fractions. Again, to quote Dr. Shaw :—

No man will ever become intimate enough with the provisions of this charter—no matter how many years he may sit in the municipal assembly—to know for a certainty, without careful reference to the document, by what kind of a majority a particular piece of business must be carried to have validity. Some actions in the municipal assembly may be taken by a majority of those present and voting, provided there is a quorum. Other things may be done by a simple majority of all those elected ; still others require a two-thirds majority of all those elected, others a three-fourths majority, others a four-fifths majority, others a five-sixths majority, and others absolute unanimity. I suspect that there may be still other percentages or proportions requisite for certain actions ; but the seven that I have mentioned have caught my attention, as I have endeavoured to run through the document.

In the report of the Commission presenting the Charter, the Commissioners point out that the Charter introduces, " in accordance with established American polity, a variety of checks and safeguards against the abuse of the powers conferred upon the Municipal Assembly." There is no doubt on that head. The distrust of the popular elected assembly appears at every turn. The popular assembly is emasculated from the very first moment of its existence. It is carefully deprived of the right of initiative in matters of the first moment, and elaborate provisions are made for depriving it of the exercise of the authority which in England we should regard as absolutely indispensable. To begin with, the Municipal Assembly is forbidden to grant any franchise or right to use the public streets except upon the approval of the Board of Estimate and Apportionment, and then only for limited periods, with due provision for periodical re-valuations. The Municipal Assembly is not allowed to sanction any work involving the expenditure of any large sum of money, or to create any debt, to dispose of any franchise, or to levy any tax, without the concurrence of the Board of Estimate and Apportionment. Even then its decision is subject to the veto of the Mayor. In cases of public improvements of great magnitude and cost; the Municipal Assembly cannot vote by a simple majority. Unless it can muster a majority of three-quarters of its whole membership it can do nothing. It is possible, therefore, for one quarter of the Assembly, plus one, to paralyse that body at will. In fact, it is impossible adequately to explain the impotence of the Assembly which, according to ordinary English ideas, ought to be the source, seat and centre of all powers. No doubt clauses exist conferring upon the Assembly certain powers, but at the end of the clauses you will always find that they have not to be exercised excepting on the initiative of some Department which is not elective, or with the concurrence of some Board which is equally free from the taint of a popular elective origin.

All that, however, is consistent enough with the Napoleonic conception of the true method of democratic government. Napoleon, with his ministers of state, never claimed to exercise such control over the *Corps Législatif* as the Mayor of Greater New York will exercise over his elective assembly. He is allowed a free hand to appoint his own executive, and he can pass his own budget, so long as he can find one-sixth, plus one, of the Assembly to support him. The creation of the Tsar-Mayor, however interesting as indicative of the rooted distrust of elective assemblies which is supreme at present in the American mind, is not the feature of the Charter which reveals most deeply how far the distrust of popular government has gone in the United States. For, after giving the Mayor supreme responsibility, and electing him for a term of four years, these astonishing charter-makers carefully provide that he shall only have a right to remove the commissioners, whom he has been allowed to appoint, during the first six months of his term of office. It is this limitation which shows how thoroughly the modern American distrusts his governing men. Faith in an elective council has perished utterly; but faith in a Tsar-Mayor might have shown the survival of some faith in the elective principle. But the stipulation carefully made in the Charter that the Mayor's right to remove the heads of departments whom he has nominated shall cease six months after his election, is the most astounding illustration yet afforded of the deep-rooted distrust which the American of to-day has in all elected men.

Ex-Mayor Grace, writing after much experience of the working of city governments, declared :—

The absolute power of removal as well as of appointment of all commissioners and heads of departments should be vested in the mayor, the power of removal to be subject to no check beyond that of filing the reasons for such removals—expressed in writing.

Mr. Seth Low, the first Tsar-Mayor of Brooklyn, and Mr. Strong, the Mayor of the Reform Administration in New York, both declared, in a supplementary report, their conviction that the authority given to the Mayor to make appointments without confirmation ought to carry with it, as a matter of course, the authority to make removals in the public interest without charges at any time. Their protests, however, were overruled. The majority dare not trust the Mayor with such powers. The result is that "for three years and six months the government of the City of New York will be carried on by eighteen separate departments, not one of which is directly responsible or accountable to anybody. They do not derive authority directly from the people, and they certainly owe nothing to the Municipal Assembly. On the other hand, there is no power in the Mayor to hold them accountable." Says Dr. Shaw :—

It is bureaucracy pure and simple. I am not ready to assert it positively, but I am of the impression, from some knowledge of the subject, that the very shadowy municipal assemblies provided some years ago for St. Petersburg and Moscow had a greater legislative and financial authority than the new municipal assembly of the

Greater New York; and I am inclined to believe that neither in the administration of those Russian cities nor in the administration of the Russian provincial governments will one find a bureaucratic system so complete and so indirect in its responsibilities to the public as the bureaucracy which the Greater New York charter creates.

There is no necessity to go further. I have quoted enough to justify the title of "Despairing Democracy"; for here we have a democracy in such depths of despair that it first emasculates its elective assembly, and then hamstrings its Cæsar.

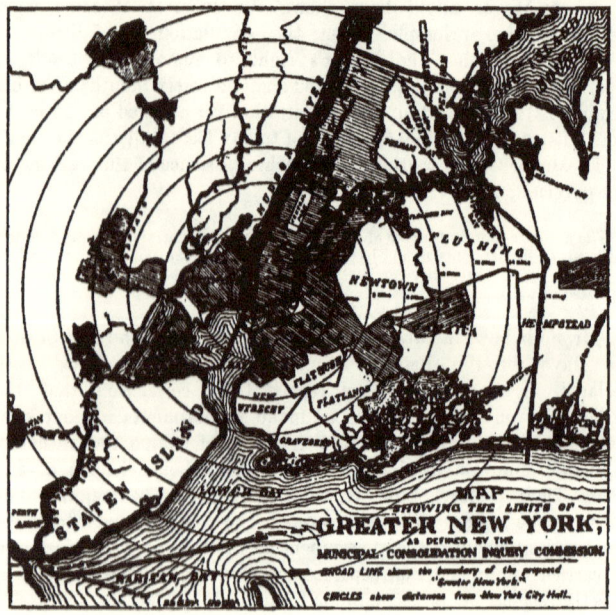

MR. W. R. HEARST,
Editor and Proprietor of the *New York Journal.*

TWELVE years ago I employed part of the leisure I enjoyed in the safe retreat of Holloway Gaol in writing an essay on "Government by Journalism." In that essay, which was published after my release in the *Contemporary Review*, and subsequently republished under the title "A Journalist on Journalism," I expounded a theory as to the natural and inevitable emergence of the journalist as the ultimate depository of power in modern democracy. One passage I may be permitted to quote, as it bears directly upon the subject of the present chapter:—

The future of journalism depends almost entirely upon the journalist, and at present the outlook is not very hopeful. The very conception of journalism as an instrument of government is foreign to the mind of most journalists. Yet, if they could but think of it, the editorial pen is a sceptre of power, compared with which the sceptre of many a monarch is but a gilded lath. In a democratic age, in the midst of a population which is able to read, no position is comparable for permanent influence and far-reaching power to that of an editor who understands his vocation. In him are vested almost all the attributes of real sovereignty. He has almost exclusive rights of initiative; he retains a permanent right of direction; and, above all, he better than any man is able to generate that steam, known as public opinion, which is the greatest force of politics.

To rule—the very idea begets derision from those whose one idea of their high office is to grind out so much copy, to be only paid for according to quantity, like sausages or rope-yarn. Bunyan's man with the muck-rake has many a prototype on the press. To dress contemporary controversy day by day in the jacket of party, to serve up with fresh sauce of current events the hackneyed commonplaces of politics—that in their eyes is journalism; but to rule! Yet an editor is the uncrowned king of an educated democracy. The range of his power is limited only by the extent of his knowledge, the quality rather than the quantity of his circulation, and the faculty and force which he can bring to the work of government.

An extraordinary idea seems to prevail with the eunuchs of the craft that leadership, guidance, governance, are alien to the calling of a journalist. Those conceptions of what is a journalist's duty, if indeed they recognise that imperious word as having any bearing upon their profession, is hid in mystery. If it may be inferred from their practice, their ideal is to grind out a column of more or less well-balanced sentences, capable of grammatical construction, conflicting with no social conventionality or party prejudice, which fills so much space in the paper, and then utterly, swiftly, and for ever vanishes from mortal mind. How can they help to make up other people's minds when they have never made up their own?

Even as it now is, with all its disabilities and all its limitations, the press is almost the most effective instrument for discharging many of the functions of government now left us. It has been, as Mr. Gladstone remarked, and still is, the most potent engine for the reform of abuses that we possess, and it has succeeded to many of the functions formerly monopolised by the House of Commons. But all

M 2

that it has been is but a shadow going before of the substance which it may yet possess, when all our people have learned to read, and the press is directed by men with the instinct and capacity of government.

Now it so happened by a curious coincidence that just about the time I was penning these sentences in happy Holloway, a youth fresh from Harvard, the heir to one of the greatest fortunes in the United States, was deciding to devote his life to the journalistic profession. Mr. W. R. Hearst was the son of Senator Hearst, one of the lucky handful of men who came out from the development of the silver mines of the Far West with many solid millions of sterling gold in his possession. As heir to the Hearst millions, nothing would have been more in accordance with the ways of the millionaire class than for the young graduate to have given himself up to a life of self-indulgent ease. Young Hearst, however, had no inclination for sloth. Journalism attracted him, and he set himself to learn the business of the craft. Money, of course, was available to secure him ample opportunity to indulge his whim, and before long he began to try his prentice hand as editor and proprietor of the *San Francisco Examiner.* He soon proved that he possessed the editorial instinct as well as the capitalist's purse, and the *Examiner* began to be heard of far beyond the Pacific Coast as one of the smartest specimens of American journalism.

But the Pacific Coast is a long way off. To reign in San Francisco is less than to serve in New York, and Mr. Hearst soon began to turn a longing eye to the Eastern capital. The same loadstone that drew Mr. Pulitzer from St. Louis to make the *New York World* the latest and greatest of American newspapers, compelled Mr. Hearst to come to the same city to found a newspaper which would be even later and greater than the *World*. It was with Mr. Hearst as it was with Themistocles when the laurels of Miltiades would not allow him to sleep. The laurels of Mr. Pulitzer were equally productive of insomnia in the *Examiner* office. At last, when Senator Hearst died, and the young editor of thirty found himself in undisputed control of a million or two—pounds, not dollars—with a reversionary right, on the death of his mother, to several millions more, he was in a position to realise his ambition. Crossing the continent, he purchased the *New York Morning Journal* from Mr. Pulitzer's brother Albert, and began the siege of New York. The *World* was then in the height of its prosperity. In ten years it had built up a circulation without a rival in the Western hemisphere. The Paris *Petit Journal* alone distanced the *World* in Europe. The great gilded dome of the *World* office, which every night, radiant with electric light, sits as a crown of flame upon the city's brow, did not rise more conspicuously above the other buildings in its vicinity than the *World* towered aloft above its contemporaries. When Mr. Hearst sat down in New York he had one ambition, and—

MR. JOSEPH PULITZER,

Editor and Proprietor of the *New York World*.

so far as he allowed any one to see his secret thoughts—one ambition only. He would publish a newspaper which would beat the *World*.

He began operations by annexing the pick of the staff of the *World*. Journalists in the United States sit by no means so tightly in their chairs as they do in this country. The Americans are a restless race. Whether it is that the nomad Redskin left a migratory contagion in the air, or whether the force of gravitation has been suspended on their behalf, or whatever else the cause may be, the fact is indisputable. Whether in politics, in the press, or elsewhere, they shift about with a readiness that seems strangely unnatural to the more stolid Englishman, who is apt to root himself like his native oak. Hence it was possible for Mr. Hearst to begin his campaign in New York by taking away from Mr. Pulitzer several of the brightest and brainiest members of his staff. They left the *World* to form the staff of the *Journal*, with regrets no doubt, but without hesitation. For the terms of Mr. Hearst were better than those of Mr. Pulitzer, and they went. Mr. Pulitzer, alarmed by the secession, induced some of them to return by the offer of still better terms than Mr. Hearst, but the young man with the inherited millions outbid the older journalist who had made his own pile, and the *Journal* started with the cream of the *World's* staff. If there be something of Dugald Dalgetty about this sudden transfer of allegiance in English eyes, it was entirely in accordance with the habits and customs of American journalism. A change in proprietors or in editors will be followed by a filing out of all the staff, the members of which no more lament over their fate than gipsies deplore the fall of their tent-poles.

To the men recruited from the *Journal*, Mr. Hearst added some of the best of his Californian staff, and as he paid the highest salaries going, he had the pick of the pressmen of the continent. He picked as a rule wisely and well. But his first choice and the most valuable member of his staff was himself. No one did more to give the newspaper character and success than the young millionaire, who was to be seen in his shirt-sleeves through the hottest nights in the sultry summer toiling away at proofs and formes until the early hours when he saw his paper to press. Members of his staff who were worked like niggers could not complain when they saw their chief working harder than any of his salaried employees. "A millionaire," they said, "in his shirt-sleeves! He could not work harder if he were working on space for his daily bread!"

After having formed his staff, Mr. Hearst launched his paper, publishing it at a cent. The *New York Herald* is published at three cents. The *World* was published at two cents. Mr. Hearst published morning after morning an eight and a twelve page paper at a price below the cost of production. Mr. Pulitzer, recognising that at last he had found a real rival, reduced the price of the *World* to a cent. From that day to this the two rivals have wrestled together without ceasing. They both publish morning and afternoon and Sunday editions. They both are profusely illustrated. They both cater directly and avowedly for the million, and the million responds. The weaker of the old-fashioned papers went down beneath the feet of the contending giants as the forests went down under the trampling of St. Tammany and the Devil. But the circulation of the *Journal* went up steadily, until in two years Mr. Hearst had a Sunday circulation of 400,000 at five cents, while the average daily sales of the morning and evening journals reached 350,000. The circulation of the *World* was not seriously impaired. The *Journal* grew not at the expense of its rival so much as at the expense of the other papers which were less up-to-date.

·Of course this result was not achieved without prodigious expenditure. Never before were such salaries paid on any newspaper. The secrets of the counting-house are not revealed to the outside world, but Mr. Hearst is said to have half-a-dozen editors and artists, each of whom draws the salary of a Cabinet Minister. Money flowed like water. Nothing was too much to pay for a first-class, exclusive piece of intelligence. Journalists of the old school stood aghast at the *Journal's* prices. And, what made the expenditure appear still more outrageous, for a long time there were practically no receipts. Advertisers, even in the United States, are a conservative race. A newspaper appealed in vain for their support. They would come in, but only at low prices. Mr. Hearst said they might stay out; they must come in at his prices or not at all. They took him at his word and stayed out—for a time. But now they are coming in shoals, and the advertisement columns day by day attest the capitulation of the advertiser to the newspaper. The direct cash loss on the first year's editing of the *Journal* could hardly be less than £200,000, if, indeed, it did not largely exceed that sum.

People began to wonder what Mr. Hearst was after. He could not be after the dollars—he had more dollars than he could count. He was not known to have any distinctive political aspirations. He was spoken of sometimes as the Socialist millionaire, but he never professed any belief in Socialism as a dogma of his creed. Was it only to beat the *World?* Who could say. The *Journal* plunged heavily and got hit badly by its advocacy of Bryanism and Free Silver, but Mr. Hearst was no fanatic of silver. He was not a fanatic at all. He was a man as modest in private life as his paper was blatant in print. His editorials were searched in vain to discover any consistent or inconsistent creed. The *Journal* was like Broadway in print. Broadway at high noon, with cars swinging backwards and forwards along the tracks, and the myriad multitudes streaming this

way and that—life everywhere, but one common governing purpose
or direction nowhere.

But after a time there was gradually evolved from this feverish
chaos of sensationalism some trace of a great conception. Mr. Croker,
who, although not glib of tongue, is shrewd of wit and keen of eye,
discerned its drift, and set himself to ridicule and belittle what he
called "government by newspaper." Then the *Journal* itself, taking
heart of grace from a series of successes, boldly printed at the head
of its editorial columns :—

THE "JOURNAL'S" MOTTO:

"WHILE OTHERS TALK, THE 'JOURNAL' ACTS."

This appeared immediately after the announcement of the release
of the fair heroine Evangelina Cisneros from her Cuban gaol by the
enterprise of a *Journal* reporter. It was followed by an editorial
entitled "The Journalism that Does Things." This article expresses
so succinctly the aims and objects of a paper which has played so
conspicuous a part in the recent history of New York that I have no
hesitation in quoting it here :—

The instant recognition accorded throughout the world, outside of Weyler's
palace and offices of most New York newspapers, to the work of the heroes who, in
the service of the *Journal* and of humanity, rescued Evangelina Cisneros from the
prison of the Recojidas is broader and deeper than a mere compliment to a single
newspaper. It is epochal. It signifies that by a supreme achievement the journalism
of action, which is called by its detractors the "new journalism," and proudly
accepts the title, has broken down the barriers of prejudice and vindicated its
animating principle.

Action—that is the distinguishing mark of the new journalism. It represents
the final stage in the evolution of the modern newspaper of a century ago—the
"new journals" of their day—told the news, and some of them made great efforts to
get it first. The new journal of to-day prints the news too, but it does more. It
does not wait for things to turn up. It turns them up.

It has taken some time for the understanding and appreciation of these novel
methods to become general, but from the very first the *Journal* has found an
immense constituency eager to welcome them. It has provided for this sympathetic
body of readers a continuous succession of notable deeds. We may recall a few
examples.

The *Journal* has always been an energetic ally of the Cuban patriots. It has
rendered them a variety of important services, of which the rescue of Miss Cisneros
is merely the latest. Another of a similar, through less dramatic sort, was its
action in forcing the Spanish authorities to issue passports to the widow and
children of Dr. Ricardo Ruiz, the American dentist who was murdered by his
gaolers in Havana.

When the *Casper Whitney* put to sea with water oozing in through every joint,
the *Journal* secured an investigation which resulted in the removal of Captain
Fairchild, of the inspection service.

The *Journal* proved by experiments with chartered vessels off Sandy Hook that
the ordinary flags of the international signal code could be easily read at night from
a great distance under flashlight illumination. This discovery, whose value in
saving life and property at sea is incalculable, it dedicated freely to the maritime
world.

From the beginning the *Journal* has taken a practical as well as a theoretical
interest in the relief of suffering and the elevation of the classes that have lacked a
fair chance in life. Last winter it undertook to mitigate the awful distress that
prevailed so widely at that time by opening a depôt in Grand Street, at which hot
food was distributed daily to those in need. Thousands of starving people were

RIVERSIDE DRIVE AND GRANT'S TOMB.

relieved by this enterprise. On another occasion, when a fire in East Thirty-fifth Street rendered many families homeless, the *Journal* invited them all to a Christmas dinner, and then, with the co-operation of its readers, established them in newly-furnished homes. But the greatest work of the *Journal* in the direction of the improvement of social conditions has been the establishment and maintenance of the *Journal* Junior Republic, which has saved about two hundred boys from the slums, and turned them into good citizens, and which contains the promise of unlimited future development and expansion.

Last winter, when the aldermen had undertaken to grant a perpetual franchise for the use of the streets to a light, fuel and power company, the *Journal* served injunctions upon the board and prevented the outrage. At the same time it fought at Albany for dollar gas with such success that even Mr. Platt's Legislature was compelled to yield to public opinion to the extent of passing a bill providing for a general reduction. The practice of invoking the law against unfaithful public servants has been repeated recently with signal success in the case of Commissioner of Public Works Collis and his pet contractors, who have been compelled to raise the siege of Fifth Avenue.

When the East River murder seemed an insoluble mystery to the police, the *Journal* organised a detective force of its own, and in two or three days identified the victim, Guldensuppe, and his assassins. And when the Long Island Railroad attempted to excuse its wholesale manslaughter at Valley Stream by alleging that an engine could be seen for a distance of one thousand five hundred feet, the *Journal* took a counterpart of the wrecked tally-ho outfit to the scene, and proved by actual measurement that the driver could not have seen the approaching train until his leaders were on the track, with the engine eighty-four feet away.

These are a few of the public services by which the *Journal* has illustrated its theory that a newspaper's duty is not confined to exhortation, but that when things are going wrong it should itself set them right if possible. The brilliant exemplification of this theory in the rescue of Miss Cisneros has finally commended it to the approval of almost the entire reading world.

These things, all of them, or almost all, are good. Some of them are very good. But all of them together do not prove that in Mr. Hearst we have the man of whom Mr. Lowell spoke when he said :—

> Methinks the editor who should understand his calling and be equal thereto, would truly deserve that title of ποιμὴν λαῶν, which Homer bestows upon princes. He would be the Moses of our nineteenth century . . . . the Captain of our Exodus into the Canaan of a truer social order.

Nevertheless, Mr. Hearst is far and away the most promising journalist whom I have yet come across. He has education, youth, energy, aptitude, wealth, and that instinctive journalistic sense which is akin to genius. If in addition to these great qualifications he were to realise the possibilities of his vocation, and to become inspired by a supreme enthusiasm—say to redeem New York, and make the second city in the world in size the first city of the world as a place of human habitation—there is no knowing what incalculable good might lie within his grasp. Certainly no man in all New York has such a chance of combining all the elements that make for righteousness and progress in the city as the young Californian millionaire-editor who founded the *Journal*.

There is, however, no greater delusion than to imagine that a newspaper in America has any influence merely because it is a news-paper. The habit of running newspapers as if they were mere commercial dividend-earning undertakings has so largely discounted the influence of the press as to lead many shrewd observers to declare that they would just as soon have the newspapers against them as in their favour. Carter Harrison had every newspaper in Chicago against him—but his own—and he was elected to the mayoralty by an overwhelming majority. Mr. Croker declared over and over again that if he had stood for the mayoralty of New York he would wish for nothing better than that every newspaper in the city should be against him, in which case he regarded his success as a certainty. Tammany at one time corrupted the newspapers. At another time it bullied them. Now it disregards them. "Mere newspaper talk"—nothing can be more contemptuous than that.

If New York is to be raised to the position of being the ideal city of the New World it will not have to be by mere newspaper talk, but by the man behind the newspaper who can make his newspaper the organising, vivifying, rallying centre for all the best forces and influences of the city. If Mr. Hearst has soul enough and heart enough he may do it. I do not know any one else who has got his chance.

TAMMANY HALL OF TO-DAY.

THOMAS C. PLATT.
Chief of the Republican Party in New York.

CHAPTER V.

"NEVER prescribe until you are called in," is an excellent maxim, which like that other more pithy saying, "Mind your own business," has one somewhat serious drawback. If they were construed literally and obeyed in spirit as well as in letter, what would become of the journalist's business? For the chief business of the journalist is to look after other people's business. To chronicle it in the first place; to comment upon it in the second. It is the privilege of the profession.

There is no cause for resenting the innocent liberty of criticism and suggestion which is exercised by the press. It can only too easily be ignored; nor has the journalist any means beyond the opportunity of representation and of persuasion for giving effect to his proposals. He has no authority except that which belongs to every man who sees things as they are, and the authority pertains to his ability to make others see them with his eyes rather than to his personal position. Hence those who object to the "damned impudence of the newspaper man" have only to shut their eyes and close their ears, to remove themselves effectively from the area of his jurisdiction.

The journalist who in the course of his public duty ventures to pry into "the secrets of the prison-house" is always met by its keepers with an outcry of indignation and resentment. "Why are you poking your nose in our affairs?" they cry in aggrieved chorus; "you stay at home and attend to your own business!" How often have we not heard that plausible demand put forward by the thieves and scoundrels and oppressors of the world, when first the adventurous newspaper man ventures to expose their misdeeds and suggest ways and means for curtailing their evil power. Tammany Bosses have often angrily denounced the meddling of the newspapers in their pickings and stealings. Nor is it only journalists who are met by this protest. We have seen how Police Commissioner McClave was distressed at the wickedness of the hayseed Senators up at Albany who sent the Lexow Committee to trouble the "honest men" of the Police Department. The evildoer who is waxing fat upon his misdeeds, always objects to any one interfering with his plunder.

And as the accusation of officious meddling in " what is no concern of yours " is the first brick that lies handy for hurling at the head of the intruder, it is thrown accordingly.

The difficulty is immeasurably increased when the journalist is commenting on the affairs of another city or country than his own. For then the crooks can invoke the sentiment of offended patriotism, and shelter their picking and stealing behind the sacred folds of the national flag.   When I was in Chicago five years ago I was seriously told by a distinguished American author that it was insufferable impertinence on my part to publish any opinion on current American affairs until I foreswore allegiance to the Queen and naturalised myself as an American citizen!   I venture humbly and with all deference to suggest that if a cat may look at a king, it may be permitted to an English-speaking journalist to describe what he sees and to say what he thinks even concerning the affairs of those other English-speaking communities which prefer the Stars and Stripes to the Union Jack.   This curious recrudescence of perverted nationalism which would deny the right of comment on American affairs to everyone not born or naturalised in the American Republic, is after all nothing more than a partial reversion to the savage's jealousy of the stranger who was not a member of the tribe.   Let us be thankful that the reversion is not complete, otherwise I should have cause for thankfulness that I escaped with my life.

We may, however, brush on one side these absurdities born of the morbid sensitiveness of the Half-grown, who are always suspecting that every word of criticism conceals an assumption of superiority, and a denial of the rights, which the Full-grown regard as too self-evident to be questioned.   Rational adults do not in these days require a certificate of origin before listening to the ideas of those who are interested in their affairs.   The stranger, no doubt, will often make mistakes, which any tyro to the manner born would have avoided. He is like a Frenchman attempting to make a speech in English. But, despite his blunders in details, he looks at things from a different standpoint, he brings to their consideration the experience gained in other communities, and although he may make himself a fool now and then—which Lowell reminded us is one of the inalienable rights of man—he will often strike out new ideas which perhaps by their very absurdity may bear good fruit by rousing attention and provoking discussion.

At the close of this cursory survey of one of the gravest problems which can occupy the attention of mankind, the reader may fairly expect me to say whether I see any way out.   Must we despair of democracy, then, after all, and abandon all hope of governing great cities by the time-honoured machinery of elective assemblies ?   Is the Dictator indispensable for the salvation of the Republic ?   And if we cannot get along without his authority, dare we not trust him to remove his ministers after the first eighth of his term of office ?

If to these questions I venture to suggest any replies, I hope that I may not be accused of attempting arrogantly to dogmatise upon the solution of local problems the conditions of which it has been obviously impossible for me to master at first hand. I make no pretence to be free from bias or partiality. If my critics complain that my suggestions are based upon my inherited ingrained prejudices, strengthened by a professional instinct, rather than upon a scientific and judicial examination of all the facts, I make no demur. For in dealing with all these complex questions it is extremely difficult to eliminate the habit of mind that dates back to the cradle and beyond the cradle.

Hence, for instance, if I scout the notion that there is any reason for despairing of democracy even in New York City, this adoption of the watchword of "Never despair!" is due primarily to two antecedent convictions, neither of which has anything to do with the local circumstances of New York. One is a fundamental faith in the Providential government of the universe, the other a belief that in the evolution of human society, Democracy has arrived, and has come to stay. " Time brings not back the mastodon "; and, despite the present reversion to the tyrant of the old Greek city, in the shape of the Tsar-Mayor, I cannot believe that the great stream of progress is about to change its channel. I cannot believe that the American democracy is permanently forsaking what Jefferson regarded as the fundamental principle of democratic institutions. Jefferson's familiar and weighty words—". As Cato concluded every speech with the words, *Delenda est Carthago*, so do I every opinion with the injunction, ' Divide the counties into wards' "—embody advice that is in accord with all the traditions of the English-speaking race. I may be pardoned for believing that it expresses the sound principle of local self-government, rather than the new-fangled innovation of the vesting of all power in a Dictator elected by a mass vote of so huge a unit as a city of three millions.

If this be so, then it follows that it would be well to endeavour, as speedily as it could be done with safety, to regain the ancient ways, and return to fundamental principles by dividing the city into wards, and making the elected representatives of these wards the governing authority of New York. Until the Common Council—composed of representatives each directly elected by ward or district, and held personally responsible by the citizens in that ward for the efficient and honest discharge of his municipal duties—is restored to its natural position as the source and seat and centre of civic authority, it seems to me that we shall continue wandering in the wilderness. The elective assembly is the mainspring of the machine, and although you may turn the pointers round with the watchkey of a Tsar-Mayor, the watch will never keep right time till the mainspring is restored to its right place.

This, however, may only be an English prejudice. However frankly I may express my fear that the Tsar-Mayor will not prove a permanent source of security to the law-abiding, honest citizens, I shall be delighted if my forebodings are falsified by the event. For good or for ill the great experiment is to be tried, and the whole human race is interested in its success.

I come to safer ground when I say that, whether the centre of authority be the Tsar-Mayor or the Common Council, there is no security for the good government of the city except the public spirit and loyal co-operation of all good citizens. I know nothing more admirable than many of the recent efforts made by the Citizens' Union and the Patriotic League of New York to arouse an intelligent interest in the community at large in the government of the city. The campaign of Education which has been going on for these last three years is a much more solid security for good government than any tinkering of the civic administrative machine. What seems to be most needed is, that the admirable work done in certain districts should be universalised and made equally effective in all quarters of Greater New York. The need for making general or universal the best work done in certain localities, points to the need of some central body, like the Civic Federation or Citizens' Union, or Civic Centre, which would cover the same area as the civic administration, and within which it would seek to secure for all voluntary effort the same system and regularity and universality that is attained in the municipal service. Such a Civic Centre or nucleus for the co-operation of all societies and agencies, social, moral, intellectual and religious, would stand to the civic authorities much as the spiritual power stands to the State. A federation so constituted would be the Civic Church of the city; and the State without the Church, is the body without the soul.

These are broad general propositions, which seem to me to lie at the root of the whole matter. But I would not like to close this chapter without making one suggestion which, although it will be scouted at first and treated with ridicule and contempt, may nevertheless contain within it the germ of an institution which may remedy some of the more flagrant evils which afflict the body politic. The creation of the Tsar-Mayor shows that the American citizen is not hidebound by prejudice. In presence of the hideous abuses glanced at in the former chapters he has sacrificed his ancient prejudices against Despotism and the One Man power, in order to re-establish the Greek Tyrant as the autocrat of the American City. What I wish, with all deference, to suggest, is that having enthroned the Tyrannus, they should hasten to establish the Inquisition.

The proposition is made in all seriousness. As a palliative and corrective for the existing evils I see no suggested solution that holds out more promise.

I need not, I hope, explain that I do not suggest the resurrection of the old dread ecclesiastical tribunal, with its familiars and its *auto da fe.* Neither do I suggest that heretics should be burned alive in Madison Square. What I am after is much more serious business. The suggestion is the offspring of two facts, both unmistakably conspicuous in the contemporary history of New York. One is the emergence of a great journalistic ambition, not merely to chronicle, but to do. The other is the record of the Lexow Committee. The success of the latter in its work of investigation, together with the existence of the new ideal of journalistic duty, seem to suggest that the best immediate remedy for the malady of the body politic would be the establishment on a permanent footing of a Tribunal of Investigation and Inquisition, armed with all necessary powers, to administer oaths, to compel the attendance of witnesses, to commit for contempt, and to punish summarily for perjury. And I would further venture to suggest that in the Journalism that Acts there is here a field even more legitimate for the enterprise of the new journalists than breaking into a Spanish prison or dredging the river for the head of a murdered man.

To put it briefly, I would respectfully ask those who are in despair over the corruption that eats like a canker into the hearts of American cities, why not give statutory authority to American journalism to create, maintain and carry on a Lexow Committee *en permanence*, with extended powers for the purpose of discovering and handing over for punishment all those who are preying upon the public?

There is no remedy like the light of day. These evils exist in the midst of our communities because they can be done in secret. The crook in office relies upon the cloak of darkness. Tear away that cloak, proclaim the things done in secret upon the housetop, and the crook will walk in the straight path. The enterprise of the American newspaper is great. But although it can discover Livingstone and rescue Miss Cisneros, it cannot locate the boodler and prove who paid him the boodle. It may suspect. It may know, and it may accuse. But without its Lexow Committee it can neither prove nor convict.

It may be objected that to institute such a tribunal would be to create a frightful engine of tyranny, and that the remedy might be worse than the disease. The experience of the Star Chamber is not exactly reassuring.

But to this there are several answers. In the first place, beyond arming the proposed Inquisition with adequate powers to enforce attendance by subpœna, to punish contempt of court, and to impose

N

summary penalties for perjury, it would not be vested with any power of inflicting punishment. Having ascertained the facts, it would hand over the guilty person to the ordinary civil and criminal tribunals, binding over all witnesses to appear when the case came on for trial. Its functions would be those of investigation, for the purpose of providing a case for the ordinary tribunals, so that there would be no interference with the safeguards provided by the law and the constitution for the liberty of the subject and the impartial administration of justice.

Secondly, the proceedings of the Inquisition would be from the first conducted under the full glare of publicity. Even if it were within its powers to hold a secret session, no action could be taken at such session until it had been confirmed in the light of day. Both at the inception and at the close of a case the Inquisition would be a public tribunal, liable to public criticism and amenable to public opinion. Its chief duty would be the obtaining of material in the shape of authentic information capable of being proved in court, for the protection of the public. It would, therefore, be unreasonable to fear that such a Court, whose *raison d'être* is to bring evil out of the darkness into light, could be capable of the abuse which sprang up in the Star Chamber or the Inquisition, where secrecy made power irresponsible.

If it be admitted that such a tribunal might with advantage be created, the question would then arise how it should be constituted. The paralysis of faith in the integrity of the elected man which prevails in American citizens would seem to preclude any hope of securing a competent and inflexible Inquisitor-General by an appeal to the principle of popular election—direct or indirect. If, however, the Journalism that Acts is to be allowed to follow the natural path of evolution, it might perhaps be recognised as a power in the State, to whose initiative might be left by statute the task of appointing the Inquisitor and of bringing cases before the Inquisition. If the choice of Inquisitor-General were left to the journalists, each of whom is an inquisitor himself in his own way, you would at least have a small expert constituency, each member of which would have a direct interest in making a good selection. And if the duty of bringing cases before the Court were limited in the first instance to the journalists, the door would be closed against the irresponsible calumnies of miscellaneous scandal-mongers, for the only persons who could then set the tribunal in motion would be the newspaper, which would lose in prestige and in authority should it bring forward a case which on investigation proved to be baseless.

I am well aware that the suggestion will be ridiculed, and by no one so much as the journalist in whom the consciousness of his responsibility has not yet been evolved. But if the Journalism that Acts is to do its share in the cleansing of the Augean stable of municipal corruption, it could hardly find a more legitimate field for development than in providing a simple but effective tribunal for the purpose of dragging out of the darkness and secrecy in which they flourish those evils which can never be dealt with until they are accurately located, and brought within the range of public opinion by the searchlight of the Inquisition.

ONE OF THE ELEVATED RAILWAYS IN GREATER NEW YORK.

GENERAL TRACY.

CHAPTER VI.

THE PLÉBISCITE FOR A CÆSAR.

THE contest for the mayoralty of Greater New York, which was fought out at the polls on the 2nd of November, has been one of the most famous elections ever fought. To begin with, never before have half a million electors voted in the same day for the election of a chief magistrate. Greater New York contains more that 3,000,000 inhabitants, and 567,000 registered electors. The constituency is not more vast than the powers of the mayor are unlimited. As no chief magistrate before received the suffrages of so many electors, so no chief magistrate was ever invested with such absolute authority. Mr. Van Wyck, the new Mayor of Greater New York, for six months at least is almost as much master of New York as Napoleon III. was master of France after the *plébiscite* which installed him at the Tuileries. The two-chambered elective council of the city has even less control over his municipal appointments than the senate and *Corps Législatif* of the Second Empire. For so great a stake it was natural that all parties should enter their best men, and that the contest should be fought witl. as much energy as a Presidential Election.

The first to enter the field was Mr. Seth Low, the President of Columbian University, and the candidate of the Citizens' Union. Mr. Low —or Seth Low as he is usually called—was the first Reform Mayor of the City of Brooklyn, where he was re-elected and served a second term. Although he belongs to the Republican party, he stood as the candidate of those who object to the subordination of municipal to national issues. The one great curse which has plagued New York in the past has been that its citizens never had a chance of voting upon a straight civic issue, but were always pulled hither and thither by the conflicting interest of the Republican or Democratic parties, compared with whose real or imaginary interests the welfare of the city was regarded as dust in the balance. Mr. Low was one of the leading members of the Commission which framed the Charter of Greater New York. He is a man of education, of leisure, of experience, and of the highest character. The Citizens' Union was formed last winter in the old City of [New York, with the object of electing what is called a non-partisan mayor. The Citizens' Union, although nominally non-partisan, was really recruited in a great

THE HIGHEST BUILDING IN NEW YORK.

American Surety Company.

measure by the Republicans. Hence it was regarded by the leaders of the Republican machine as virtually a revolt against the Republican Caucus, and the Chairman of the County Republican Committee publicly declared that the Republican party would much rather see a Tammany man installed as the first Mayor of Greater New York than a mayor who was not the nominee of the Republican organisation. And the Republican Party men have had their wish.

It was this declaration that led Mr. Seth Low to join the Citizens' Union, which he had not previously done. About the middle of the year, the ticket which had long been current as to the advisability of nominating Seth Low for the Mayoralty began to crystallise into action. The Citizens' Union had increased its membership from 6,000 to 25,000, and it had secured nearly 100,000 signatures to a memorial requesting Mr. Low to be put in nomination as a candidate for the Mayoralty. Earlier in the year he had contemplated standing only as a unifying force among the friends of good government, but when the memorial was presented, and the Citizens' Union insisted upon taking independent action without conferring with the other organisations, he accepted the nomination, and in the beginning of September issued his address.

His appeal to the constituency was based, according to his own statements, upon the following principles. First, he stood for the idea of having a free man in the Mayor's chair, a man who would be responsible to the people who put him there, and not to any party machine. The Reform Mayor of New York, he said, in a passage which stung General Tracy into unwonted fury, must be in the City Hall of New York, and not on a racecourse in England, or in the Senate Chamber of Washington. The suggestion, of course, being that if the Tammany candidate were elected, its master would be Richard Croker, who was supposed to spend his time on English race tracks, while if General Tracy were elected, he would take his orders from Senator Platt, the Republican Boss. Secondly, Mr. Low stood for the idea of Home Rule — Home Rule for New York. A community of three million and a quarter of people ought to be entitled to shape their own destinies in matters that are purely local. Further, he stood as the advocate of good city civic administration, which he defined as a civic government so well administered that no interest in the great metropolis shall be so small as to be beneath its care, and no interest so great that it shall timidly shrink from attempting to deal with it. In Mr. Seth Low's address, accepting the nomination, he frankly avowed that he was a Republican, and expected to remain one; but he would pledge himself that, in making appointments, he would fill every place with an eye single to the public good. "The patronage of the city shall not be used, so far as it is in the mayor's power to prevent it, for purposes of either strengthening or weakening one party or another, or any fraction of another

party." On the subject of public franchises, by which the streets of
New York have been practically handed over to irresponsible corporations, he made the significant suggestion that the city should be able
to deal with every application for a change of the power by which the
street railways were worked, as being equivalent to a demand for a
new franchise. There is more in this than is discernible at first sight
by an English reader. The tramways of New York are largely
operated at present by cables and horses. These are being super-
seded as rapidly as possible by electricity. If no street railway
were to be allowed to adopt electricity as a mode of traction,
unless it surrendered what we should call its local Act of Parliament,
empowering it to use the streets, and had to make terms *de novo* for that
privilege, the relation between the public and the companies would
be immediately transformed. At present the companies have got all
they want, and pay the city next to nothing. It may not be possible
to adopt Mr. Seth Low's suggestion, but the idea is well worth
consideration.

In his reference to the Labour Laws of the City, he maintained
that they should be administered in the letter and in the spirit.
The vexed question of the saloon was dealt with in a lengthy paragraph, in which he balanced himself as best he could between the two
schools of restriction and of freedom. The Raines Liquor Law, which
was imposed upon the City of New York by the State Legislature,
has created an immense amount of irritation by its attempt to secure
Sunday closing, and to enforce stricter discipline on the saloons. Mr.
Low condemned the Raines law for not taking into account the
public sentiment of so cosmopolitan a city as New York. This being
interpreted, means that the German citizens object to be deprived
of their Sunday beer, and that, to adopt the local vernacular, you
cannot swing a great world-city on principles of the hayseed legislators up at Albany. What Mr. Low would do in relation to the
licensing does not precisely appear, beyond desiring to adopt some
system of local option :—

> In my opinion, an excise law, so far as it affects the daily life and the habits of
> the people, should reflect the public opinion of the city. On such points, in case of
> radical differences of opinion, I should take the appeal to the people themselves.

The keynote, therefore, of his address lay in the sentence that he
desired to secure for "this Imperial City" the opportunity to start
upon its new career under an administration pledged to make the
interests of the city its supreme care. Mr. Low had the great advantage
of not being a mere theorist, but one who had had four years'
experience in the application of the principles upon which he would
propose to act as Mayor of Greater New York. The city government, he maintained, should be organised on business principles.
Quite recently he contributed a chapter to Mr. Bryce's "American
Commonwealth" on City Government in the United States, in

which he embodied the result of his experience and observation as Mayor of Brooklyn. His dominant idea is that the government of a city should be conducted upon very much the same principles as the management of any corporation, railroad, or joint stock company. The Mayor should be general manager, and the head of every department should hold office at his supreme discretion. Another principle upon which he insists is that wherever executive work is to be done, it must be put in the hands of one man, but that wherever it is not an affair for action, but for discretion, in the multitude of councillors there is wisdom. Where the work is discretionary have a board, where it is executive have one man.

The second candidate to enter the field was one as well known in this country as he is in his native land. Henry George, whose sudden death on the eve of the poll gave so tragic a note to the contest, was nominated by the Bryanite section of the Democratic party. He commanded, and deserved to command, a great deal of public support, and still more of popular sympathy. Henry George stood as candidate for Mayor some years since, and was defeated by Tammany Hall joining hands with the Republicans, in order to elect Mr. Hewitt. Mr. Croker talked over that ancient history with me on the steamer, and then expressed a confident conviction that the Labour Unions would never again support Henry George. They were all in line, he said, with Tammany. Henry George, whose book, "Progress and Poverty," was practically discovered in Great Britain after it had fallen very flat in the United States, was an honest man, full of all generous enthusiasms, and his candidature deserved and obtained general sympathy, because it was the most emphatic, picturesque, and sensational method of expressing dissatisfaction with things as they are. Mr. George was a strong Free Trader, but he was not an advocate of Free Silver.

His followers, however, tolerated all differences of opinion in return for the value of his support. They even left him to nominate his own ticket. He was selected as candidate for a party calling itself the United Democracy, which adopted the Liberty Bell as its emblem. The speaker who moved the nomination of Mr. George in the Convention, spoke of him as "the great, the immortal Henry George, the man who had shown the working people the way out of their difficulties. When George is mayor, the problems which vexed the municipality will cease. Corruption and bribery will keep away from the City Hall if George is there. They fear him as the inhabitants of the lower regions do the angels of heaven." When he accepted the nomination, he declared that he stood not as a Silver Democrat or a Gold Democrat, but as one who believed in the cardinal principles of Jeffersonian Democracy. The defeat of Bryan, he declared, was "the defeat of everything for which our fathers had stood, and it looked to him as though the

United States were fast verging into a virtual aristocracy and despotism." He stood, therefore, upon the doctrine of the equality of men, and in the conviction that in the democracy that believed that all men were created equal lay the power that would vivify not merely New York, but the world.

The platform of the United Democracy, after denouncing unscrupulous corporations and corrupt combinations, whose influence is felt alike in local and national courts, proceeds to define the aims and aspirations of its supporters in a manifesto, of which the following is a summary :—

> It reaffirms the Chicago platform, demands home rule in municipal affairs, denounces the Excise laws, demands not only municipal ownership of franchises but their operation by the municipal government, three cent (or less) car fares on surface and " L " roads, dollar gas, the abolition of contract work for the city, enforcement of the eight-hour law on city work, the representation of labour in the Administration, increase of school accommodation and the introduction into the schools of industrial training : the designation of public places for free exercise of the right of free speech, the opening of court houses and schools for the free use of the people in the evening : it denounces the abuse of injunctions by the courts, and demands the abolition of property qualifications for grand and petit jurors.

The clause in the plank of the Tammany platform which refers to the Raines Liquor Law ran as follows :—

> We condemn the so-called " Raines " Liquor Law as iniquitous and intolerant. It was passed at the instigation of the Republican State machine against the protest of the majority of the people of New York, irrespective of party. It has injured owners of real estate. It has closed avenues of legitimate employment. It has deprived thousands of our citizens of rational enjoyment. It has given rise to a system of spying and official intermeddling abhorrent to a free people. It extorts exorbitant revenues from this city to aggrandise other portions of the State. It sought to deprive the citizen of a trial by jury, and, in the collection of penalties, compels the licensee, at the caprice of the State Commissioner of Excise, to defend himself in remote localities. It protects and masks the dive-keeper, while it harasses and impoverishes the reputable dealer. It promotes intemperance, furnishes a legalised refuge for vice, imperils the innocence of children, and destroys the sanctity of home. We therefore demand its prompt repeal and the enactment of an Excise law, conservative of the public morals and liberal in its provisions, that shall place its administration and revenue, so far as shall apply to this city, within the control of this municipality, thus insuring strict enforcement of law by the consent of the governed.

Tammany is almost as pronounced as Henry George was as to the municipal ownership. The following is the paragraph referring to this subject in their manifesto :—

> All proper municipal functions should be exercised by the municipality itself, and not delegated to others. We favour municipal ownership and municipal control of all municipal franchises. We oppose the granting of any public franchise in perpetuity. We oppose the granting or extending of any such franchise, or the bestowal of any new privilege upon a corporation holding such franchise, without adequate compensation.
>
> We, therefore, approve, as a step in the right direction, the provisions of the new Charter, which require adequate compensation to the city for all franchises hereafter to be granted, and which limit the terms of all such franchises, with reversion to the city on their expiration. We denounce the Republican party for its wasteful and reckless grant of valuable public franchises to private individuals by special legislation, with no provision for compensation to the municipality, whereby this city has already lost some of the most valuable franchises on its most important streets.

THE LATE HENRY GEORGE.

The most significant plank in the platform is that demanding municipal ownership of monopolies of service as essential to the purification of politics and the protection of the citizen against taxation :—

We declare that the functions of street railway transportation, the lighting of the streets and homes of the people, whether by gas or electricity, the carriage of the people by ferries about the waterways of Greater New York, the facilitation of the interchange of speech by telephones or telegraphs, are all purely municipal functions, things which can better be done by organised society than by individuals ; we insist that the present system of delegating these functions to corporations has resulted in a heavy sacrifice of public wealth and convenience, the practice of extortion upon citizens compelled to enlist the services of these corporations, and the creation of powerful moneyed interests which, enjoying rich · public grants, systematically employ every art of corruption in politics to control the city government for their own profit.

Mr. George declared he was a poor man as the candidate of poor men. Mr. George simply stood where he did in 1886. Hence, he simply had to fall back upon his old thunder, and to reproduce the fierce denunciations which he hurled against the existing state of things by which the control of the modern American city was given over to the · worst classes of the community. Here, for instance, is a passage in which he lashed the corrupt influences that dominate American politics :—

The influences which have degraded the rich and debased the poor, and, under the forms of Democracy, given over the metropolis of our country to the rule of a class more unscrupulous and more arrogant than that of the hereditary aristocracy from which it is our boast that we of the new world have emancipated ourselves ?

The type of modern growth is the great city. Here are to be found the greatest wealth and the deepest poverty. And it is here that popular government has most clearly broken down. In all the great American cities there is to-day as clearly defined a ruling class as in the most aristocratic countries of the world. Its members carry wards in their pockets, make up slates for nominating conventions, distribute offices as they bargain together, and—though they toil not, neither do they spin—wear the best of raiment and spend money lavishly. They are men of power, whose favour the ambitious must court, and whose vengeance he must avoid.

Who are these men? The wise, the good, the learned—men who have earned the confidence of their fellow citizens by the purity of their lives, the splendour of their talents, their nobility in public trusts, their deep study of the problems of government ? No; they are gamblers, saloon keepers, pugilists, or worse, who have made a trade of controlling votes, and of buying and selling offices and official acts.

It is through these men that rich corporations and powerful pecuniary interests can pack the Senate and the Bench with their creatures. It is these men who make school directors, supervisors, assessors, members of the Legislature, Congressmen.

Mr. George was a magnetic man—a man of intense enthusiasm and tireless energy. He spoke night after night, and as the contest waxed hotter and hotter his discourses rose in temperature, until, before the contest came to a close, he pledged himself to send Richard Croker to the Penitentiary as a thief; and he left his hearers in very little doubt that if he could have had his way, the Republican boss would occupy the adjacent cell. To Mr. Seth Low, Mr. George was a great speculative writer and a dreamer. To General Tracy, he was a man who went in for Free License and

Free Everything excepting Free Silver. To Tammany he was a most dangerous foe.

The following extract from a speech delivered by Charles Frederick Adams is a fair illustration of the kind of ferment that is working under the surface of American politics :—

Everywhere that man is oppressed by man the people are straining their ears to hear of Henry George's election. He is a man of men, one who does not confine his attention to the great individuals and the more fortunate classes, but one who lends his head and heart to the cause of man. He is the Moses to whom we all look to be led out of the wilderness. He is the lodestar of suffering humanity.

This is no single tax movement. It is a movement to benefit down-trodden man, a movement to throw off the chains of serfdom in order that we may once again breathe God's pure air with freedom. Henry George has the respect of every intelligent man and woman in this country. His name is the keynote to truth and freedom. And yet there are men who claim to be his friend who went to him and asked him not to accept a nomination for first Mayor of the Greater New York. They appeal to his modesty, telling him that he is only wanted by a handful of mere agitators. They know they lied when they tried to turn him aside, and yet they call themselves his friend, but their friendship is like a celebrated kiss in a celebrated garden.

It is not a question of silver, the tariff, or anything of that kind ; it is the more vital question of trying to rescue a great city from a lot of organised robbers. As a guarantee of our sincerity we ask Henry George to be our candidate and raise us from the contemptible tyranny of little men. If we were held in thraldom by a Cæsar or a Napoleon we might stand it, but, my God! a Croker, a Croker, gentlemen ; a Croker or a Platt !

The time has come when the common man, that great crucified of eternity, shall say like the crucified divinity : " Choose ye now which ye will serve; he that is not with me is against me," and with these words I ask you to take off your coats and work for the election of Henry George.

The Tammany candidate, who was elected by a majority of 85,000 votes, was Mr. Justice Van Wyck. Henry George stood 5 ft. 6 ins. in his shoes. Mr. Van Wyck stands 5 ft. 7 ins. Mr. Van Wyck is not yet fifty years of age. In 1880 he distinguished himself by publicly denouncing Boss Kelly in Tammany Hall for betraying John Hancock, the Democratic nominee for the Presidency. He was howled down, but he bided his time, and when Mr. Croker and Mr. Sheehan, the past and present Bosses of Tammany, put their heads together to find a man who is best calculated to carry the election, they decided that there was none so good as Mr. Van Wyck. He is a clear speaker, but he refused at this election to follow his opponents on to the platform.

Tammany's victories are not won by oratory. Tammany's platform had many planks, but three were prominent :—(1) The denunciation of Reform administration, for raising the rates, and increasing the expenditure of the city. (2) An attack upon the Streets Department, with Mr. Colles at its head. The ground for this attack was the irritation that was produced in Fifth Avenue and elsewhere by the Works Department permitting the drainage and other works to be carried on so slowly as to practically render the traffic in the thoroughfares impossible for twelve months at a time. (3) An attack on the Raines Law as in every way an intolerant measure, which protected the evil, and persecuted the reputable. In this respect Mr. Van Wyck was at one with Henry George. The two candidates also agreed in demanding Dollar Gas, a phrase which needs a moment's explanation. The gas companies which supply New York charge 5s. per thousand feet. It was proved before a Committee of the Legislature that gas can be sold at a profit at 4s. per thousand feet, but the influence of the wealthy corporations was too great to permit such a heavy cut in their charges. The price of gas, therefore, has to come down 2½d. a year for five years, a postponement of the interests of the consumer to the greed of the gas companies which is bitterly resented in New York.

Like Mr. Low and Mr. Henry George, Mr. Van Wyck was in favour of building fresh schools for the children, who are at present without school accommodation, and also in favour of more rapid transit and more bridges. On municipal ownership he spoke with an uncertain sound, merely remarking that the corporations now in the control of their streets have gone to such lengths as to require legislation and municipal oversight. By way of appealing to the labour party, he declared that the eight hour law on the Statute Book on the State was a righteous one, and must be maintained, and he denounced government by injunction as a violation of the rights of man, striking at time-honoured principles which are the foundation of the laws. Everything, he declared, was possible for an administration which would have as its guiding thought the future rather than the present, prosperity rather than patronage, progress rather than politics. To be the first Mayor of Greater New York seemed to him to be an opportunity of a generation. If he were elected, he declared that before the end of four years there would be such progress as this hitherto divided city had never before enjoyed. Mr. Van Wyck is the Chief Justice of the City Court. His father was a lawyer of Dutch extraction. It remains to be seen whether his confident prognostication will be fulfilled.

General Tracy, the nominee of the Republican Convention, was too good a man to be sacrificed in such a fight. He has served the nation as Secretary for the Navy, and if common rumour be not a common liar, he did a good deal of the work of Secretary of State in the last years of Mr. Blaine. England owes him a special meed of gratitude, because it was he who, when he was in supreme control of the American Navy, insisted upon breaking through all rules and precedents in order to allow Captain Mahan to continue at a post on land, where he had leisure to finish his great work on "Sea Power in History." General Tracy is also too old a man to be intrusted with the onerous task of governing this great heterogeneous conglomerate of cities which is known as Greater New York. He is nearly sixty-eight years of age, and, although he is hale and hearty, he will be over three score and ten by the time the first Mayor of the Greater New York has to retire from office. His nomination was due to the fixed determination of his partner's father, Mr. Senator Platt, the Republican machine man, to assert himself at this election. In his eyes the Citizens' Union is an arrogant upstart, a mutinous offshoot, which has the audacity to deny to the regular Republican machine its legitimate voice in the control of affairs in New York. Mr. Platt and Mr. Croker agree in believing that it is impossible to govern New York without a regular party machine. The Citizens' Union, of course, would in time become a party machine, but as it starts on non-partisan lines, the process of evolving a Boss from the Citizens' Union would be slower than would be the case of other organisations based upon regular party lines. In order to secure a platform for General Tracy, the Republican Party men had to repudiate the programme for which they had repeatedly committed themselves in times past. The separation of municipal from national issues had been repeatedly affirmed in the strongest terms by previous Republican conventions; but on this occasion, in order to justify General Tracy's candidature, the Republican platform was throughout an attempt to introduce the national issues into the city contest. The one great issue before the people, it declared, was the Chicago platform, an admission of which Mr. Bryan after the victory has naturally made the most.

Bryanism was confounded with Tammany Hall, and it was asserted in the strongest possible terms that "the code of good government, meaning thereby honest and intelligent administration, can never be divorced from the Republican party." "We are the people, and wisdom will die with us," and not wisdom only, but honesty, ability, righteousness and all manner of virtue will only perish from the land unless the regular Republican candidate is put into office and kept there. That is always the burden of their song. General Tracy appealed to the citizens as the candidate of sound money, which has absolutely nothing to do with any municipal issue—the candidate of social order, and the endorser of the patriotic and successful administration of William McKinley. Forgetful of the fact that they had declared they would prefer to see a Tammany mayor elected than the candidate of the Citizens' Union, the Republicans denounced Tammany in no measured terms. "The crimes of the Tammany democracy should never be forgotten or forgiven." The platform then commends the Raines law on the ground that by removing power from the excise or local license board, and conceding the right to sell intoxicating liquors to any citizen who paid the tax and obeyed the law, it had taken the saloon out of politics, and had liberated the saloon-keeper from the politician. It had also been financially advantageous. But having endorsed the Raines Law up to this point, they hedged in the final paragraph, in which, after referring to the cosmopolitan character of the city, they said that "provisions of the law relating to the times and conditions at and under which liquor may be sold, and the provisions of the law enforced, are wisely to be left to the will of the people of the city rather than to the judgment of their duly constituted authorities."

Finally, the platform pledged the party to a strict enforcement of the labour laws, which were defined as follows:—"The Factory Inspection Law, the Mechanics Lien Law, the Law Regulating the Employment of Minors in Mercantile Establishments, the Anti-Sweating Law, the Law Guaranteeing Union Wages on all Public Works, and the Law Preventing the Subletting of Contracts." General Tracy in accepting the nomination declared that it was not enough for the Mayor to be negatively honest. "He must be affirmatively and aggressively honest." But he also harped upon the spectre of Bryanism, which would not down, and invoked for the exorcising of that spectre "the Republican Party, which in the Providence of God, for more than forty years, has been the great bulwark of national honour and prosperity." Any attempt to disintegrate, weaken or destroy that organisation seemed to him a grievous mistake, fraught with calamity and disaster.

On September 27th the *Journal* sent out an army of reporters, with instructions to interview all the citizens whom they met in the course of the day in certain well-defined districts, in order to ascertain their preference as between General Tracy and Seth Low. The voters were approached indiscriminately, and represented all sorts and conditions of men, from hod-carriers to bankers. The result was that 9,102 citizens were interviewed, 4,835 of whom preferred Seth Low, and 4,267 voted for Tracy. This poll suggested the holding of a much more comprehensive census of opinion. An attempt was made to interrogate a whole vast constituency. Three hundred reporters were sent out with the following ticket:—

NEW YORK JOURNAL.

VAN WYCK.	TRACY.
GEORGE.	LOW.

As between B. F. Tracy, the Republican candidate; Seth Low, the Citizens' Union candidate; R. A. Van Wyck, the regular Democratic candidate; and Henry George, the Independent Democratic candidate, whom do you prefer for Mayor of the Greater New York?

NAME OF CANDIDATE..

YOUR SIGNATURE..

YOUR ADDRESS...

BOROUGH OF ....

Sign this Ballot and send it to the Journal.

The town was marked out into districts, and the canvassers proceeded systematically from house to house. Never before had there been so extended a canvass introduced of what they call a straw ballot in any constituency. It was, of course, not a ballot in the sense of secret voting at all, for all the citizens signed their papers, which were then taken to the central office and carefully examined. The census began on the 4th of October and was continued for a week. It was closed with the following result :—

Each elector was required to sign his name and address upon a voting card supplied by the canvasser. When the poll was closed the *Journal* had obtained signed declarations from no fewer than 277,871. The voting was divided as follows :—

	Total *Journal* Poll.
Van Wyck	89,056
George	85,050
Low	59,764
Tracy	44,001
Total	277,871

These figures show that Mr. Van Wyck had 32 per cent. of the constituency, Henry George 30½, Low 21½, and Tracy nearly 16. If on the 2nd of November the whole 550,000 electors had gone to the poll, and those who have not been reached by the canvassers had voted in the same proportion as those who have, the result would have worked out as follows :—

	Position in Greater New York.	Actual Vote.
Van Wyck	176,269	235,181
George	168,345	20,727
Low	118,288	149,873
Tracy	87,098	101,823
Total	550,000	507,604

All calculations, however, were vitiated by the death of Henry George. His son, whose name was substituted for his father's at the eleventh hour, naturally could not command the same amount of support.

POLITICAL WATERS

GREATER NEW YORK : AN OPTIMISTIC VIEW OF THE FUTURE.

CHAPTER VII

THE FIRST MAYOR OF GREATER NEW YORK.

Edgar A. Whitney, examined by Chairman Lexow: I was in the gaming-house when the door opened, and Mr. Glennon, the police wardman, gave the word and said, "Is Mr. Pease in?" I said, "No, sir; I am taking care of the game while he is at his supper." He said, "Come to one side:" he said, "That captain wants this game closed up until after election time; that if the Tammany Hall ticket is elected," he says, "we will protect you for anything from a poker game to a whorehouse."—Report of Lexow Commission, vol. ii., p. 1603.

THE above extract from the evidence taken before the Lexow, Committee at the end of 1894, immediately after the election which overturned Tammany rule in New York City, condenses into one coarse but expressive sentence the moral issue usually raised by elections in New York. Whether the latest victory of Tammany will have the same result remains to be seen.

The election of Mr. Van Wyck, the Tammany candidate, as the first Mayor of Greater New York, which has taken place as these pages were passing through the press, is a curious and suggestive comment upon "Satan's Invisible World Displayed."

"Ephraim is joined to his idols, let him alone!" has been the reflection of many a reformer on hearing of the immense majority by which the second city in the world elected to place itself under the governance of the elect of Tammany Hall. But the worst of such an attitude is that Ephraim does not leave other people alone, for in his worship of the false gods he brings down disasters upon other heads than his own. The welfare and good government of the first city in America can never be a matter of indifference to the rest of the world.

Tammany Hall seated its candidate by a majority of votes sufficiently decisive. But although Mr. Van Wyck was 85,000 votes ahead of his nearest competitor, he did not poll a majority of the citizens. If the principle of a second ballot which is established on the Continent of Europe had been the law in New York, the issue would have had to be fought out again in a single-handed fight between Mr. Van Wyck and Mr. Seth Low. In default of such a provision, all that can be said is that at the first election of Greater New York Tammany polled 235,000 and the three anti-Tammany candidates 272,000 votes, making a majority against Tammany of 37,000.

If Tammany be as black as it is painted, the worst thing about the election is not the return of Mr. Van Wyck, but the divisions of his opponents. That Tammany should be beloved of her own progeny is nothing. What is serious is that those children of light who see the evil of Tammany rule should treat it as a matter of trivial importance compared with the passion and prejudice of personalities and parties. If good men do not combine when bad men conspire, the inference is very obvious. Either the conspiracy of the bad men is not very bad, or the good men hardly deserve their name.

The familiar saying of Burke that he refused to draw an indictment against a whole nation may be applied to cities as well as to nations. What is clear enough is that Tammany in the past has discredited democracy. It has done so twice in the most conspicuous and unmistakable fashion.

Under Tweed it became a synonym for Thieving. Under Croker's government the Lexow Report proved it became an organised system of Blackmail.

What is it to be under Mr. Van Wyck?

That is the question which it is for Tammany to decide.

Mr. Croker professed admirable sentiments as to his resolution to make New York the ideal city of the world. Nothing could have been worthy of the man to whom the citizens have entrusted their destiny. We should, however, have had more right to face the future with confidence had Mr. Croker's contemplation of the past—and such a past—not been quite so complacent.

Nevertheless it is a good rule that which Cardinal Manning laid down for dealing with those who protest that they have been cruelly misjudged by their contemporaries.

"When a man tells me that he is an honest man," said the great Cardinal, " I never enter into a controversy with him as to the past. The past is past. And although I may have in my hand conclusive proofs of his guilt, I never refer to the subject. I always say, 'My friend, you say that you are an honest man. I am delighted to hear it. We will not discuss the past. We might be unable to agree on that subject. But the future is before us. Act as an honest man from henceforth, and I shall treat you as an honest man.'"

The Cardinal's rule may be invoked in favour of extending the same act of oblivion to Tammany and its Chief.

The account of past misrule placed on record in the Report of the Lexow Committee cannot be effaced from the page of history.

It is a useful and timely service to Tammany itself to popularise the findings of that Committee, if only to remind the men, who are now summoned to make New York the ideal city of the world, of the hole from which they were digged. A vivid remembrance of the horrible pit and the miry clay has ever been regarded as salutary for the pilgrim to the Celestial City.

Nothing is more likely to help Mr. Croker and his men to try to obey the Apostolic maxim to forget the things that are behind in order to press forward to those which are before, than the knowledge that every one can give chapter and verse in support of their belief that New York under Tammany rule in the past really deserved the title of " Satan's Invisible World."

On that point there is no longer any room for difference of opinion. To question it is to justify disbelief in the honesty of the sceptic or the sincerity of his professions as a Reformer. But we may well be content to let the dead past bury its dead if, rising upon the wreck and ruin of these evil days, Tammany should now attain to nobler things.

There is at least one great historical precedent justifying a hope that this may be so.

When Madcap Hal succeeded to the English throne, there was the same jubilant exultation among Falstaff, Bardolph and all the roystering crew when Pistol rushed in helter-skelter, crying :—

> And tidings do I bring, and lucky joys,
> And golden times, and happy news of price.

But the story of their disappointment is one of the most familiar and dramatic scenes in the history of the English-speaking race. The question now is whether Mr. Croker will dare to address his old companions of misrule in the words of Henry the Fifth :—

> Presume not that I am the thing I was:
> For Heaven doth know, so shall the world perceive,
> That I have turn'd away my former self;
> So will I those that kept me company.

If so we may hope that it may be in New York even as it was in olden time in England, and that it may be said of the era that opened when Tammany elected the first Mayor of Greater New York by 85,000 majority :—

> Yea, at that very moment,
> Consideration like an angel came,
> And whipp'd the offending Adam out of him.
> . . . . . .
> Never came reformation in a flood,
> With such a heady current scouring faults ;
> Nor never Hydra-headed wilfulness
> So soon did lose his seat, and all at once,
> As in this King.

THE END.

APPENDIX.

MAYOR VAN WYCK'S PROGRAMME.

MAYOR VAN WYCK's Letter of Acceptance in reply to the Democratic City Convention, which invited him to stand as candidate for the Mayoralty, was published a fortnight before the polling day. In the *New York Journal* of October 24th, Mr. Van Wyck, in the course of an interview with Alfred Henry Lewis, a representative of the paper, said:—"There need be no doubt or mistiness concerning my attitude on all questions now craving reply. I wish most heartily that every citizen of New York would read my letter of acceptance. It was not carelessly prepared; it was in no sort the suggestion or work of other men; it presents my exact position on every subject it suggests, and I meant every phrase of it, and I mean it now."

The text of the Letter of Acceptance is as follows:—

Hon. Almet F. Jenks, chairman; John C. Sheehan, Bernard J. York, Dr. John L. Feeney, James McCartney and John H. Sutphen, committee.

Gentlemen: In response to your official notification of the action of the Democratic City Convention in selecting me as its candidate for the office of Mayor of Greater New York, I now formally accept the nomination.

The duty before the first Mayor of the City of New York, as it is to be the beginning of the coming year, is of a magnitude too vast to be undertaken without misgivings by any man of mind enough to comprehend the problems it involves. While it is to be the second city in the world in population, it is to be, at the very outset, the first—by far the first—in point of the strictly municipal powers to be exercised by its local government.

To approach the task in any other spirit than that of American liberty, coupled with a realising sense of the cosmopolitan character of the population to be served, would, in my judgment, be to err fundamentally.

The temper of mind which benefits the villager or the inhabitant of towns in which there is but one type of citizenship to deal with is little fitted for the work before us.

At all events, should the people repose their confidence in me, I will endeavour to act with that largeness of view which considers the rights of every man, regardless of race, creed or colour.

A successful administration of the affairs of this municipality must depend, in great measure, upon the honesty and the efficiency of the officials appointed by the Mayor. In this regard I shall, if elected, exercise the greatest care to provide, in all the departments, for such intelligent and honest supervision and direction as will secure to the public not only a wise and efficient service, but as well the return to them of a dollar's worth for every dollar expended.

To make of the several boroughs a homogeneous city requires that, in the control of the administration of affairs, there should be a government responsible and responsive to the people. It should be honest, efficient and liberal. It should be guided by sound political principles, securing a more perfect discharge of public duty than is possible under such conditions as have imposed upon us the factious, discordant and demoralising administration from the misdeeds and negligences of which all elements of our citizenship have suffered.

What is here said of the present city of New York applies, I am persuaded, in considerable measure, to Brooklyn. There, also, the taxpayer has had reason for serious complaint. Within the past four years taxes have been heavily increased, the cost of most of the departments has been largely augmented, and the debt has not only been carried up to the Constitutional limit, but has been positively swollen to the extent of over ten millions of dollars.

To permit a continuance of the disregard thus shown for the ability of property to contribute to the support of the government would obviously be to give to confiscation a practical sanction. The metropolis is not to be made prosperous by any policy which involves the ruin of the investors in its real estate.

The results here exhibited furnish one of the most costly object lessons ever taught a community as to the wasteful character of a Government permitted to whirl incoherently with the whims of its several officials, as contrasted with the economy enforced by the organised vigilance and definite policy of responsible Government controlling all the expenditures of its subordinate departments.

Coupled with the extravagance and waste against which our citizens have protested, there has been an utter disregard of the rights and convenience of the people; the most scandalous example of which is to be found in the present shocking condition of our streets and thoroughfares.

There can be no justification for such a complete surrender of our road-beds to corporations and contractors. Undoubtedly the prosecution of necessary and useful improvements requires an occasional disturbance of some part of the pavements of our streets, and sometimes a partial interference with the movements of traffic. It needs, however, but ordinary care and supervision in the consideration of demands made in this direction to so arrange that no single locality may be unduly disturbed, and that all the discomforts and inconveniences of the situation shall not fall upon the citizen to the profit and advantage of the contractor.

While a proper opportunity must always be given for the prosecution of public work, and while no unnecessary delays should be permitted in its completion, this does not mean that entire streets and avenues are to be delivered over to the exclusive use of public and private contractors; that for miles the stores and shops in the most prominent of our thoroughfares are to be practically shut out from business; that our citizens are to be denied any but the most difficult access to their homes; that in some cases traffic between the various points of our city be made impossible, and in all cases difficult and dangerous, and that the health of the entire community should be imperilled and injuriously affected by open trenches, wherever the people may turn.

Such a condition of the streets as we are now compelled to endure may result from gross inefficiency. It can be attributed to only one other cause, and that is, gross corruption. It should be treated as a criminal disregard of the public comfort and safety, and any administration responsible therefor must stand discredited before the community.

The flagrant violations of the principles of Home Rule by the Republican majorities in recent Legislatures have challenged the attention and excited the indignation of our citizens. The usurpation of the rights of our municipality and its people has become such an intolerable wrong that it cannot be too strongly rebuked. A cosmopolitan constituency, exceeding the population of the United States at the time of the adoption of the federal Constitution, should not be required to protest against such interference with its purely domestic concerns as attempts to dictate even its harmless customs, habits and pursuits.

And yet, again and again we have been subject to legislation conceived either in ignorance of, or contempt for, the wishes and sentiments of our people, and enacted as a revenge upon our politics or an assault upon our revenues.

In the Raines Liquor Law we have an example of a class of legislation utterly without public sanction. It was imposed upon our citizens against their vigorous and united protest. It has failed to secure a single one of the advantages urged in justification of its enactment. It has only succeeded, by dispensing with local supervision and control, in removing the salutary restraints which heretofore protected the reputable dealer from the open rivalry of the divekeeper. It employs the spy, and necessitates methods which can never be approved by men who believe in the Democratic theory of government. I favour its prompt repeal.

I join in the demand of your platform for "the enactment of an excise law conservative of the public morals and liberal in its provisions, that shall place its administration and revenues, so far as shall apply to this city, within the control of this municipality."

With you, I believe that one of the chief duties of the incoming administration will be to provide adequate school accommodation. I recognise the obstacles in the way. It is difficult to keep pace with the changes which affect the residence or business character of localities. It is not with the intention of reproaching any one for the condition of affairs in this direction in the past, but simply to emphasise a determination for the future, that I express my full indorsement of your demand that every child desirous of education in our schools shall be afforded full opportunity, whatever labour or expense may thereby be involved.

In common with all citizens, I recognise that, to make effectual the advantages which all expect to flow from the consolidation of the various boroughs, there must at once be devised and put in execution a system of rapid transit which will afford quick and comfortable travel between the homes and places of business of our people in the boroughs of Manhattan and of the Bronx; bridges facilitating communication between the boroughs of Brooklyn and Queens with Manhattan Island, and the expansion of the ferry system, at reduced fares, between the borough of Richmond and the rest of the city.

In your platform there is, I am pleased to see, a comprehensive appreciation shown of the directions in which the general well being, not less than the material interests, of the people ought to be promoted by the administration. It is there felicitously said :—"Subject to the limitations of reasonable, but not parsimonious expenditure, the municipality should provide all needed facilities for the open-air recreation of the people. Good roads, bicycle paths, improved pavements, open-air playgrounds, small parks and pier gardens are improvements in this direction." I deem it proper to make special mention in this relation of the pressing necessity for proper bicycle paths, and to add that, if elected, I shall make it my duty to have them constructed.

The demand made in the platform for dollar gas, used both as fuel and light, also commends itself to my judgment.

The proper limits of a letter of acceptance will not permit an adequate presentation of the importance to the commercial supremacy of the city of having its water front improved to the uttermost. The endeavour of other cities to wrest from us the position to which we are entitled by reason of the natural advantages which we enjoy, and the enterprise of our merchants, should awaken a vigilance which will furnish us with dock accommodations sufficient for our largest commercial needs.

I heartily approve and indorse every pledge of the platform of principles adopted at the Convention. The great essential for municipal progress is home rule in the management of local concerns. Almost as a necessary consequence will we then enjoy that measure of personal liberty which imposes and permits only such restraint of the citizen as is necessary for the peace and protection of all.

All lawful combinations which deny to any or all of our citizens a free field of competition must be suppressed. The municipality itself should both own and control its franchises, and where now such franchises are operated under grants to corporations, a fair charge, and that only, for the service rendered or convenience furnished should be permitted.

In the prosecution of public improvements a liberal, but not extravagant, policy, as already remarked, should be adopted. The needs and claims of the various boroughs should be carefully considered and fairly determined.

The eight hour law should be enforced, and, where practicable, resident labour should be directly employed. In all cases the prevailing rate of wages should be paid. As I understand the declaration of your platform upon this point, it means that every contractor doing work for the city should be required to pay as high a rate of wages as the city itself is required to pay for similar work. To this I give my unqualified assent.

Let me add, in conclusion, that, should the people intrust me with the grave responsibility of the Mayoralty, I shall make the promotion of their welfare, to the exclusion of all antagonistic ends, the object to be striven for with every power of my mind and body.—Yours respectfully, ROBERT A. VAN WYCK.

INDEX.

www.ingramcontent.com/pod-product-compliance
Lightning Source LLC
Chambersburg PA
CBHW030125030726
47498CB00007B/2555